Shakespeare's Ghost Writers

Shakespeare's Ghost Writers

Literature as uncanny causality

MARJORIE GARBER

New York and London

First published in 1987 by
Methuen, Inc.
29 West 35th Street, New York
NY 10001

Published in Great Britain by
Methuen & Co. Ltd.
11 New Fetter Lane, London
EC4P 4EE

British Library Cataloguing in
Publication Data
Garber, Marjorie
    Shakespeare's ghost writers:
    literature as uncanny causality.
    1. Shakespeare, William –
    Criticism and interpretation
    I. Title
    822.3'3   PR2976

ISBN 0 416 07432 5
ISBN 0 416 09122 9 Pbk

Library of Congress Cataloging
in Publication Data
Garber, Marjorie B.
    Shakespeare's ghost writers.
    Bibliography: p.
    Includes index.
    1. Shakespeare, William, 1564–
    1616—Criticism and interpretation.
    I. Title.
    PR2976.G37 1987   822.3'3
    87–18595
ISBN 0 416 07432 5
ISBN 0 416 09122 9 (pbk.)
ISBN 978-0-415-91869-5

For Rhoda and for Barbara

Who is the third who walks always beside you?
When I count, there are only you and I together
But when I look ahead up the white road
There is always another one walking beside you
Gliding wrapt in a brown mantle, hooded
I do not know whether a man or a woman
– But who is that on the other side of you?

T. S. Eliot, "The Waste Land"

Nearly every man who loses a limb carries about with him a
constant or inconstant phantom of the missing member, a
sensory ghost of that much of himself, and sometimes a most
inconvenient presence, faintly felt at times, but ready to be called
up to his perception by a blow, a touch, or a change of wind.

S. Weir Mitchell, *Injuries of Nerves*

. . . the phantom is meant to objectify, even if under the guise of
individual or collective hallucinations, the gap that the conceal-
ment of some part of a loved one's life produced in us. The
phantom is, therefore, also a metapsychological fact. Consequently, what haunts are not the dead, but the gaps left within us
by the secrets of others.

Nicolas Abraham, "Notes on the Phantom"

Contents

Acknowledgments

An earlier and briefer version of the chapter entitled "Shakespeare's ghost writers" appeared in *Cannibals, Witches and Divorce: Estranging the Renaissance*, ed. Marjorie Garber, Selected Papers from the English Institute 1985 (Baltimore and London: Johns Hopkins University Press, 1987). I am grateful to the publisher for permission to reprint. I would also like to express my gratitude to the various audiences – at the English Institute, the Modern Language Association, the Conference on Feminism and Psychoanalysis at Illinois State University, Dartmouth College, Haverford College, Mount Holyoke College, the University of Massachusetts, Yale University, Harvard University – who have listened with care and patience to early versions of the arguments put forward in these pages. Their suggestions and criticisms have been invaluable.

My particular and heartfelt thanks go to Rebecca Monroe, who has worked tirelessly in preparing the manuscript copy, and whose perceptive comments and generous encouragement were not only welcome but, indeed, essential to the completion of this book. Janice Price and Bill Germano at Methuen have been immensely supportive and helpful. I owe thanks as well to Leonard Barkan, Deborah Carlin, Heather Dubrow, Margaret Ferguson, G. Evelyn Hutchinson, Rachel Jacoff, David Kastan, Arthur Kinney, Barbara Packer, Peter Stallybrass, Richard Strier, Nancy Vickers, and Carolyn Williams. To Shoshana Felman I am indebted for a whole way of reading. My most profound debt is to Barbara Johnson.

Preface:
Ghostlier demarcations

Another book on Shakespeare? That is, indeed, one of the questions
this book is about. In the essays collected here I will explore the
ways in which Shakespeare has come to haunt our culture, the ways
in which the plays are central not only to English Studies but also to
recent, more subversive, theoretical approaches to literature – new
historicism, deconstruction, feminism, and psychoanalysis.

Readers will note the recurrence in these pages of many familiar
ghosts of poststructuralism – Freud, Lacan, Derrida, Marx, de Man,
and Nietzsche – alongside Thomas More, Samuel Johnson, A.C.
Bradley, and Superman comic books. Why the emphasis upon the
canonical figures of postmodernism and poststructuralism? Because,
once again, what interests me is the uncanny extent to which
these writers are *themselves* haunted by Shakespeare, the way in
which Shakespearean texts – and especially the most canonical texts
of Shakespearean tragedy – have mined themselves into the
theoretical speculations that have dominated our present discourses,
whether in literature, history, psychoanalysis, philosophy, or
politics.

The ghostly traces I have followed have led me on the kind of
journey that Freud describes in his essay on "The Uncanny" (1919),
when, in trying to hasten away from the red light district of a small
provincial town in Italy, he found himself, again and again, "back in
the same street, where my presence was now beginning to excite
attention. I hurried away once more, but only to arrive yet a third
time by devious paths in the same place."[1] This sense of the
uncanny, which Freud himself says "recalls that sense of helplessness
sometimes experienced in dreams," is very much part of the aura
that surrounds the Shakespearean ghost, a figure that is always
already somewhere else, always already gone, and yet, at the same
time, always just around the corner. "Maeterlinck says: *If Socrates
leave his house today he will find the sage seated on his doorstep. If
Judas go forth tonight it is to Judas his steps will tend.* Every life is
many days, day after day. We walk through ourselves, meeting

robbers, ghosts, giants, old men, young men, wives, widows, brothers-in-love, but always meeting ourselves."

The essay on "The Uncanny" plays a major part in my approaches to these plays, and it is an uncanny fact that the Shakespeare plays Freud singles out – precisely to demonstrate that their ghosts are *not* uncanny – are the plays that appear in my text: *Hamlet, Macbeth, Julius Caesar*. The other specters to appear in these pages include Richard III, King Lear, Shylock (present to mind because *un*mentioned in another essay by Freud), a host of silenced women from Cordelia to Sycorax, and Shakespeare himself.

There is, however, yet another way in which Freud inflects my argument, and that is through the concept – and the mechanism – of transference. The transferential relationship Freud describes as existing between the analyst and the patient is, I will argue, precisely the kind of relation that exists between "Shakespeare" and western culture. The overdetermined presence of Shakespeare – as text, as authority, as moral arbiter and theoretical template – in the critical discourse of our own and earlier times is testimony to (or, to use Freud's term for the acknowledgement of transference, confession of) that fact. "Shakespeare" is the transferential love-object of literary studies.

Freud says of the transference-love between patient and analyst that once it is acknowledged and brought out into the open it cannot be suppressed or denied. To do so "would be the same thing as to conjure up a spirit from the underworld by means of a crafty spell and then to dispatch him back without a question".[3] The "spirit from the underworld" that has to be interrogated *is* that overdetermined transference-relation, whether we call it bardolatry, canonicity, or post-structuralist discourse. And the "question" – the question raised in the course of the analysis, the question it would be folly to repress and *not* to ask the conjured spirit – that question is the question with which this book begins: Another book on Shakespeare – why? and why now?

These essays are about ghosts, and about writing. One of the things those topics have in common is that they stand in the place of something that – perhaps – was once present, and is now gone. Or do they? *Was* there a Caesar or an old Hamlet, before their ghosts appeared? Yes – but are the ghosts ghosts *of* those persons, those names – or are they new originals? Are they, in fact, not originals at all, but signs of the lostness and unrecoverability of origins, figures *instead*, loosed to power and authority *because* of their belatedness? Again and again in Shakespeare's plays ghosts and writing occur together, are twisted together in the same skein: the letter read by

Lady Macbeth, or the "letter G" that Richard makes stand for both
George and Gloucester; Hamlet's "tables" and his "new commission" commanding the deaths of Rosencrantz and Guildenstern;
the letters thrown in at Brutus's casement, urging the assassination
of Caesar. Who writes – or what writes, these fateful messages?

Keats' poem "This Living Hand," with its closing *trompe-l'oeil*
gesture across the boundaries of life and death, writing and reading,
makes a move very similar to that figured by Shakespeare's ghosts:

> This living hand, now warm and capable
> Of earnest grasping, would, if it were cold
> And in the icy silence of the tomb,
> So haunt thy days and chill thy dreaming nights
> That thou wouldst wish thy own heart dry of blood
> So in my veins red life might stream again,
> And thou be conscience-calmed – see here it is –
> I hold it toward you.[4]

The act of writing is a sleight of hand through which the dead
hand of the past reaches over to *our* side of the border. "See – here it
is – I hold it toward you." "Dismembered limbs, a severed head, a
hand cut off at the wrist, feet which dance by themselves – all these
have something peculiarly uncanny about them," writes Freud,
"especially when . . . they prove able to move of themselves".[5]
What is uncanny is not that the moving finger writes but that the
writing finger moves. What this book attempts to explore, then, is
the uncanny connection between Shakespeare's propensity to write
ghosts and his continuing capacity to write *us*.

1

Shakespeare's ghost writers

– Shakespeare? he said. I seem to know the name.

James Joyce, *Ulysses*

I

Who is the author of Shakespeare's plays? To many scholars and admirers of Shakespeare, this question has the rhetorical status of the question "Who is buried in Grant's tomb?" It is greeted by orthodox Stratfordians with umbrage, derision, and contemptuous dismissal of so intense an order as to inevitably raise another question: what is at stake here? Why, in other words, has the doubt about Shakespeare's authorship persisted so tenaciously, and why has it been so equally tenaciously dismissed?

The issue, as participants in the controversy see it, is whether the author of the plays is in fact the man who lived in Stratford, received with his father a grant of arms making him a propertied gentleman, prospered and bought New Place, one of the finest houses in Stratford, married Anne Hathaway, and bequeathed her his second best bed. No one denies that a man named William Shakespeare lived in Stratford; what is vigorously objected to in some quarters is that it was this same man who wrote the plays. It is argued that the very paucity of literary biographical material suggests that the authorship is in doubt, or, indeed, is itself a fiction, designed to obscure the "real" author, who by virtue of rank, gender, or other disabling characteristics could not with safety have claimed the plays for his (or her) own. Here, very briefly, is the case against Shakespeare as Shakespeare:

1. We know relatively little about the life, despite a significant collection of legal or business documents. Surely the greatest poet of his time would have left a more vivid record, including the comments of his contemporaries. No one in his home town seems to have thought of him as a celebrated author. Most of the encomia for "Shakespeare" were written after the death of the Stratford man, and some, like Jonson's famous poem affixed to the Folio, praise "Shakespeare" but may not identify him with the prosperous citizen of rural Warwickshire.

2. The plays show a significant knowledge of the law, more than could have been acquired in a casual way. Francis Bacon was a lawyer; Bacon wrote the plays.

3. The plays are clearly written by someone at home with the court and the aristocracy, and could not have been written by a plebeian. Edward de Vere, seventeenth Earl of Oxford, was a nobleman; Oxford wrote the plays. (If this belief held general sway, Stanley Wells would now be presiding over the publication of "*The Oxford Oxford.*")

4. The plays show a significant degree of classical learning, and also a certain witty detachment about university education. The Shakespeare of Stratford may have picked up his small Latin and less Greek at the Stratford grammar school, but we have no records proving that Shakespeare attended the school, and several rival claimants (Marlowe, Bacon, Oxford, the Countess of Pembroke, Queen Elizabeth) had demonstrably more rigorous training in both language and the classics.

5. Finally, it is pointed out that there are extant only six signatures of Shakespeare, all of which are so crabbed and illegible as to suggest illiteracy or illness. Three of the signatures appear on his will and three others on business documents, none of them in a literary connection. One scene from *Sir Thomas More*, a play in six distinct manuscript hands, is said to be by Shakespeare: these 147 lines, ascribed to "Hand D," have been subjected to much scrutiny, and have given rise to elaborate conjecture about Shakespeare's process of composition. Yet even G. Blakemore Evans, who goes so far as to include the lines in *The Riverside Shakespeare*, and who describes them as "affording us a unique view of what Shakespeare's 'foul papers' may have looked like,"[1] admits that the evidence for the attribution, which was in fact not suggested until 1871, is inconclusive.

Against these latter two arguments, orthodox Stratfordians respond in a number of ways: first, by touting the excellence of the Stratford grammar school (according to James G. McManaway in the official Folger library pamphlet on the controversy, its headmaster made as much money as his counterpart at Eton, and a person with equivalent training today would, in his words, be "a Ph.D. at Harvard"[2]); second, by insisting that Shakespeare's father would "never deny his first-born son the privileges of schooling to which his . . . position entitled him";[3] and third, by asserting that the nonsurvival of Shakespeare's literary hand "has no bearing on the subject of authorship."[4] Manuscripts that went to the print shop prior to 1700 were universally discarded once the plays were set in type, and other English Renaissance authors (e.g. Spenser,

Ralegh, and Webster) left similarly scanty paper trails. Yet no one quarrels about Spenser's authorship, or Ralegh's, or Webster's, or Milton's.

This, of course, is precisely the point. Why is it different for Shakespeare? Why is so much apparently invested in finding the "real" ghost writer, or in resisting and marginalizing all attempts to prove any authorship other than that of "the poacher from Stratford" (to cite the title of a recent book on the Shakespeare authorship)? "Without possibility of question," maintains the Folger ghost-buster, "the actor at the Globe and the gentleman from Stratford were the same man."[5] Then why does the question persist? *That* is the question, or at least it is the question that I would like to address. I would like, in other words, to take the authorship controversy seriously, not, as is usually done, in order to round up and choose among the usual suspects, but rather in order to explore the significance of the debate itself, to consider the ongoing existence of the polemic between pro-Stratford-lifers and pro-choice advocates as an exemplary literary event in its own right.

One of the difficulties involved in taking the authorship question seriously has been that proponents of rival claims seem to have an uncanny propensity to appear a bit loony – literally. One of the most articulate defenders of the Earl of Oxford authorship is one John Thomas *Looney*. (An "unfortunate name," commented *Life* magazine in an article on the authorship question – but, his defenders say, "an honorable one on the Isle of Man, where it is pronounced "Loney."[6] It was Looney, appropriately enough, who won Freud to the Oxford camp.) Nor is Mr Looney the only contender for unfortunateness of name: a zealous Shakespearean cryptographer, who proves by numerological analysis that the real author could be either Bacon or Daniel Defoe, is George M. *Battey* ("no more fortunately named than Mr. Looney," comments an orthodox chronicler of the controversy, and, "quite properly, no more deterred by it"[7]). Batty or loony, the ghost seekers' name is legion, and they have left an impressive legacy of monuments to human interpretative ingenuity.

It was not until the mid-nineteenth century that the full energies of the authorship controversy declared themselves, on both sides of the Atlantic, with the 1857 publication of Delia Bacon's 675-page *The Philosophy of the Plays of Shakespeare Unfolded*, arguing the case for Francis Bacon (no relation) and of William Henry Smith's *Bacon and Shakespeare*, shortly followed by the first impassioned defense, *William Shakespeare Not an Impostor*, by George Henry Townsend.[8]

Out of these diverse beginnings has grown a thriving industry, which to this day shows no signs of abating. Some sense of its magnitude can be gleaned from the fact that when, in 1947, Professor Joseph Galland compiled his bibliography of the controversy, entitled *Digesta Anti-Shakespeareana*, no one could afford to publish the 1500–page manuscript.[9] And that was forty years ago. The flood of publications has continued, culminating in the recent and highly acclaimed version of the Oxford case, *The Mysterious William Shakespeare: The Myth and the Reality*, by Charlton Ogburn, Jr.

What, then, can be said about this strange and massive fact of literary history? It is significant that the Shakespeare authorship controversy presents itself at exactly the moment Michel Foucault describes as appropriate for appropriation: the moment when the "author-function" becomes, in the late eighteenth and early nineteenth centuries, an item of property, part of a "system of ownership" in which strict copyright rules define the relation between text and author in a new way. It is not until there is such a thing as property that violations of property can occur; it is not surprising that the claims for rival authorship arise at the moment at which, in Foucault's words, "the transgressive properties always intrinsic to the act of writing became the forceful imperative of literature."[10] It may well be, therefore, that an analysis of the Shakespeare case will shed light on the general question raised by Foucault: "What is an author?"

Instances of the appropriative, even mercantile nature of the controversy abound. Described by one observer as a kind of "middle-class affair,"[11] the debate has largely been waged by lawyers and medical men, followed by members of the clergy and retired army officers. Not surprisingly, it became a popular forensic topic and inevitably the subject of litigation. In 1892–3, the Boston monthly magazine *The Arena* sponsored a symposium which took testimony for fifteen months. Among the pro-Baconian plaintiffs was Ignatius Donnelly, a Minnesota Congressman who had written a book called *The Great Cryptogram*, in which he attempted at great length to apply a cipher invented by Bacon. Donnelly had come across the cipher in his son's copy of a children's magazine entitled *Every Boy's Book*. By means of Bacon's "Bi-literal cipher," a secret "infolded" message could be placed within an innocent "infolding" text. The twenty-five-member jury in the case, which included prominent Shakespearean scholars and actors, found for the man from Stratford. A different verdict, however, was forthcoming in the 1916 courtroom battle on the tercentenary of Shakespeare's death. Two convinced Baconians, the cryptographer Elizabeth

Wells Gallup and her financial backer Colonel Fabyan, were sued by a motion picture manufacturer, William N. Selig, who hoped to profit from the tercentenary by filming some of the plays, and felt that the slur on the Stratfordian authorship would lessen the value of his product. In this case the judge, finding that "Francis Bacon is the author," awarded Colonel Fabyan $5000 in damages. Although the verdict was later vacated, the case made legal history.

Since both of these cases involved claims for a secret cipher, this may be the moment to say something about the role of codes and ciphers in the anti-Stratfordian cause. The purported discovery of a latent message encrypted in the manifest text provides the grounds for a startling number of cases for alternative authorship. The proliferation of ciphers can be seen as another transgressive correlative to the conception of literature as property. Here, the property violation happens not *to* the text but *within* the text. While copyright laws attempt to demarcate the bounds of literary property, cryptographers set out to uncover ghostlier demarcations, to show that the text itself is haunted by signs of rival ownership. Such codes, ciphers, anagrams, and acrostics can be as fanciful as Mrs C. F. Ashmead Windle's assertion that proof of the existence of a cipher was to be found in *Othello*: the island of Cyprus clearly was meant to be read by those in the know as "cipher us."[12] Or they can be as complex as Dr Orville Ward Owen's wheel, a remarkable contraption the size of two large movie reels, across which some 1000 pages of Renaissance literary texts could be wound and stretched for the better application of the cipher. Strictly speaking, Owen was not the inventor of the wheel – he credits that achievement to Bacon himself, in Bacon's "Letter to the Decipherer," which Owen found "infolded" in the text of the so-called Shakespeare plays. The letter to the decipherer, which is in code, contains instructions for cracking the code – useful, of course, only to one who has already done so. Owen's commitment to the truth of his method ultimately compelled him to believe that Bacon was the author not only of the works of Shakespeare, Greene, Marlowe, and so on, but also of a posthumous translation of one of his own Latin works, heretofore credited to his literary secretary and executor, Dr Rawley. During the writing of his book on *Sir Francis Bacon's Cipher Story*, Dr Owen received periodic visitations from Bacon's ghost, thus becoming perhaps the first to pursue his research under the aegis of the ghost of a ghost writer. Convinced that tangible proof of Baconian authorship was to be found in a set of iron boxes, he obtained financial backing from the ever-optimistic Colonel Fabyan, and began excavations for them in the bed of the River Wye.

The search for buried treasure indeed often accompanies the unearthing of encrypted messages here, just as it does in Poe's *Gold Bug*. Delia Bacon is notorious for having waited, shovel in hand, in Shakespeare's tomb, suddenly assailed by doubts about what she was digging for. On that occasion, the ghost of Shakespeare (whoever he was) declined to unfold himself.

But if, on the one hand, the isolated Looneys and Batteys always seem to be out there with their shovels, on the other hand examination reveals a significant degree of institutional as well as financial investment in the question. As recently as 1974, the most articulate contemporary spokesman for the Oxford case, Charlton Ogburn, Jr., created a scandal by publishing an article urging his views in *Harvard Magazine*, the alumni bulletin of his alma mater. The outcry was intense and prolonged. Harvard Professors Gwynne Evans and Harry Levin published a scathing reply in a subsequent number of the magazine, and letters deploring the threat to *veritas* continued to pour in for months. ("I'm amazed, shocked, and disgusted that THE magazine of the world's greatest university should actually publish more of the stale old spinach on the Oxford lunacy"; "I am certain that Professor Kittredge is turning over in his grave"; "Charlton Ogburn is a fool and a snob," and much more in the same vein.[13]) Reviving the notion of legal recourse to proof, Ogburn called for a trial to settle the issue. Philip S. Weld, a prominent newspaperman and former president and publisher of *Harvard Magazine*, offered to defray the costs of litigation, including "box lunches and sherry for the opposing players," and proposed that "If no one at Harvard wishes to argue the case for the Stratfordian, perhaps you could engage someone from the Yale English Department."[14]

In fact, a survey of the available literature on the "Shakespeare question" produces an uncanny number of references, often seemingly superfluous, to Harvard as an institution. The rhetorical role assigned to Harvard in the authorship controversy is not adventitious. The University itself becomes in effect a Ghost Underwriter, guaranteeing the legitimacy of whatever side invokes its name as a sign of power and authority. This is one reason why the outcry over Ogburn's article in *Harvard Magazine* became so heated, moving one letter writer to characterize the published defense of the Stratford man by the Harvard professors as "paranoid, shrill, and even hysterical."[15] Something else is being defended – or attacked – here. What is the ghost that walks?

At this point it might be useful to hazard a few conjectures about the kinds of investment that motivate the controversy on both sides:

1. *Institutional investments.* Anti-Stratfordians accuse the

"orthodox" of economic and egocentric commitment to such establishments as the Shakespeare Birthplace and the thriving tourist industry in Stratford, England; the Folger Shakespeare Library in Washington, with its handsome building, theater, and gift shop; and publishing projects like *The Riverside Shakespeare*, from which considerable financial benefit – as well as professional advancement – can be reaped. But there is institutionalization on the other side as well. Both Baconians and Oxfordians have established organizations to further their causes. The Bacon Society was founded in England in 1885; the Bacon Society of America in 1922; the Shakespeare Fellowship, later the Shakespeare Authorship Society, promoting the claims for Oxford, was formed in London in 1922; and its American counterpart, the Shakespeare Fellowship, in 1939. The *Shakespeare-Oxford Society Newsletter* and the *Shakespeare Authorship Review* are going concerns.

2. *Professional investments.* Related to such institutions is what might be called the guild mentality of the academic community. Professors who regularly lecture and publish on the plays of Shakespeare do not as a rule write books extolling rival claimants for authorship. A Shakespearean's identity seems to hinge on the identity of Shakespeare. This produces a schism that can be read in a number of ways: either as representatives of sanity protecting scholarly seriousness against the Looneys and Batteys, or as guardians of the ivy tower protecting their jobs and reputations against true intellectual openness and the subversive ideas of outsiders.

3. *"Psychological" investments.* For some combatants, "Shakespeare" represents a juggernaut, a monument to be toppled. Thus he is fragmented, marginalized into a committee (the group authorship theory) or even a conspiracy. As the author of *An Impartial Study of the Shakespeare Title* puts it, "No one man in the Sixteenth Century, or in any century before or since, leaving out the God-man, our Savior, could use as many words as are found in the plays."[16] A related phenomenon follows the pattern of Freud's family romance, which involves the desire to subvert the father, or to replace a known parent figure with an unknown, greater one, in this case a member of the nobility instead of a country fellow from Stratford. S. Schoenbaum persuasively suggests this as one reason for Freud's own belief in the Oxford candidacy.[17]

4. *"Territorial" investments.* By far the greatest number of contributions, on both sides of the question, have come from Americans; in an 1884 bibliography containing 255 titles, almost two-thirds were written by Americans. In 1895 the Danish critic Georg Brandes fulminated against the "troop of half-educated

people" who believed that Shakespeare did not write the plays, and bemoaned the fate of the profession. "Literary criticism," which "must be handled carefully and only by those who have a vocation for it," had clearly fallen into the hands of "raw Americans and fanatical women."[18] Delia Bacon, often credited with beginning the whole controversy, was, of course, both. But while she was ultimately confined to a mental hospital, she had succeeded in attracting to her defense – though not necessarily to her point of view – such distinguished allies as Hawthorne and Emerson. Nor can we ignore the redoubtable Maria Bauer, who in the late 1930s received permission to excavate in Williamsburg, Virginia, for the proof of Bacon's authorship, and who, in her book *Foundations Unearthed*, exhorted her fellow Americans: "Cast your vote for [Bacon as] the great Founder, the empire-builder of your Nation and your Culture" by digging up the treasure trove in the "Bruton Vault."[19] This was the democratization of authorship with a vengeance.

Writers as different as John Greenleaf Whittier and Mark Twain, too, professed doubts about the Stratford man. Twain, who himself wrote under a pseudonym, and who had felt impelled to correct exaggerated reports of his own death, wrote an essay entitled "Is Shakespeare Dead?" in which he faults the Stratfordians for conjecturing a life story out of little or no evidence. Twain then goes on to declare himself a "Brontosaurian," theorizing an immense body from a few ambiguous bones. "The Brontosaurian doesn't really know which of them did it, but is quite composedly and contentedly sure that Shakespeare *didn't*, and strongly suspects that Bacon *did*."[20] As Emerson wrote to his brother about the forthcoming publication of *Representative Men*: "Who dare print, being unlearned, an account of Plato . . . or, being uninspired, of Shakespeare? Yet there is no telling what we rowdy Americans, whose name is Dare, may do!"[21]

"We rowdy Americans" have had a variety of motivations for interest in the authorship question. First, there is what might be called an impulse to reverse colonization, a desire to recapture "Shakespeare" and make him new (and in some odd way "American") by discovering his true identity, something at which the British had failed. Second, and in some sense moving in the opposite direction, there is an ambivalent fascination with aristocracy, as something both admired and despised. Thus the great democrat, Walt Whitman, declares himself "firm against Shakespeare – I mean the Avon man, the actor."[22] Those "amazing works," the English history plays, could, he asserted, have only had for their "true author" "one of the 'wolfish earls' so plentiful in the plays themselves, or some born descendant and knower."[23] Charlie Chaplin, born in England but achieving success in America as the common man's hero, declared in his autobiography: "I'm not concerned with who wrote the works of Shakespeare . . . but I hardly think it was the Stratford boy. Whoever wrote them had an aristocratic attitude." Authorship of the autobiography is on the title page attributed to *Sir* Charles Spencer Chaplin.[24]

A third American motivation might loosely be described as mythic or "Unitarian" – the desire to believe in Shakespeare as a kind of God, transcending ordinary biography and fact. Thus, taking a gently ironic view of the efforts of "the Shakespeare Society" to find salient facts about the poet, Emerson asserts, "Shakspeare is the only biographer of Shakspeare; and even he can tell nothing, except to the Shakspeare in us."[25] "He was," writes Emerson, "the farthest reach of subtlety compatible with an individual self – the subtlest of authors, and only just within the possibility of authorship."

But attachments to Shakespeare have not always remained on this side idolatry, as the pious reference to the vocabulary of the God-man (a Holy Ghost-writer?) attests. Another American, Henry James, confessing himself to be "sort of 'haunted' by the conviction that the divine William is the biggest and most successful fraud ever practiced on a patient world,"[26] fictionalized the skepticism as well as the fascination provoked by such bardolatry in a late short story entitled "The Birthplace." The story is often described as being about the tourist industry at Shakespeare's birthplace in Stratford. But the proper names never, in fact, appear. The poet is referred to throughout as "Him" with a capital "H," and his writings, similarly capitalized, as a "Set" of the "Works." Far from casting doubt on the story's referent, however, James's typical indirection is here the perfect vehicle for his subject: no direct naming could have represented as well the paradoxes of the authorship controversy.

As the story opens, Mr and Mrs Morris Gedge have just been hired as docents of the Birthplace. The Birthplace Trust appears in the story as the "Body," the indwelling poet as the "Spirit," the process of exhibition is known as the "Show," and the "Show" includes the telling of certain "Facts" about which Gedge becomes increasingly dubious. He suggests to his wife a modification of discourse which amounts to an imposition of Jamesian style:

"Couldn't you adopt . . . a slightly more discreet method? What we can say is that things have been *said*; that's all *we* have to do with. 'And is this really' – when they jam their umbrellas into the

floor – 'the very *spot* where He was born?' 'So it has, from a long
time back, been described as being.' Couldn't one meet Them, to
be decent a little, in some such way as that?"[27]

In search of enlightenment, Gedge haunts the "Holy of Holies of
the Birthplace," the "Chamber of Birth," scene of the Primal Scene,
which should contain the Fact of Facts – the fact that He was born
there – or indeed, born at all. "He *had* to take it as the place where
the spirit would most walk and where He would therefore be most
to be met, with possibilities of recognition and reciprocity.[28] But
the ghost never appears. Like Gertrude in *Hamlet*, Gedge sees
nothing at all. In a proto-New-Critical or proto-Foucauldian move,
he finally confides to a pair of visiting Americans that the author
does not exist. "Practically, . . . there *is* no author; that is for us to
deal with. There are all the immortal people – *in* the work; but
there's nobody else."[29]

The rest of Gedge's career is instructive for academics, for he first
makes the mistake of openly displaying his doubts – "giving the
Show away," as the representative of the Body says when he arrives
to reprove him. But once reminded of his jeopardy, Gedge turns
completely around, and, freed of the burden of an indwelling
author, himself becomes one, gaining such fame as a raconteur that
the Body doubles his stipend.

The crucial point here is the independence – both in terms of
entrepreneurship and of artistic freedom – conferred upon the
Morris Gedges of the world by the absence of the author – by the
hole at the center of things. In a similar spirit Mark Twain alleged
rather gleefully about Shakespeare that "*he hadn't any history to
record*. There is no way of getting around that deadly fact."[30]
Emerson, we can recall, likewise rejoiced in the picture of a
Shakespeare "only just within the possibility of authorship," and in
his *Journals* he raises the question once more: "Is it not strange," he
asks, "that the transcendent men, Homer, Plato, Shakespeare,
confessedly unrivalled, should have questions of identity and of
genuineness raised respecting their writings?"[31] This is in part what
makes them transcendent.

In fact, poets and writers who address the "Shakespeare
Question" in the nineteenth and twentieth centuries tend to
embrace the question *as* a question, preferring its openness to the
closure mandated by any answer. This is as true in England as it is in
America. Dickens remarks – in a letter much cited by anti-
Stratfordians – that "It is a great comfort, to my way of thinking,
that so little is known concerning the poet. The life of Shakespeare
is a fine mystery and I tremble every day lest something should turn

up."[32] With this splendid reversal of Mr Micawber, Dickens aligns himself with the Gedge camp.

Moreover, the most famous statements about Shakespeare as a creative artist – the ones we all grew up on – make very similar kinds of assertions. Coleridge characterizes him as "our myriad-minded Shakespeare."[33] Keats evolved his celebrated concept of "Negative Capability" to describe the quality "which Shakespeare possessed so enormously ... that is, when a man is capable of being in uncertainties, mysteries, doubts, without any irritable reaching after fact and reason,"[34] and wrote that "Shakespeare led a life of Allegory; his works are the comments on it."[35] Dryden, in a phrase equally familiar, calls Shakespeare "the man who of all modern, and perhaps ancient, poets had the largest and most comprehensive soul."[36] The suggestion in all of these cases is of a kind of transcendent ventriloquism. It is as though Shakespeare *is* beyond authorship, beyond even the "plurality of egos" that Foucault locates in all discourse that supports the "author-function."[37] Matthew Arnold's sonnet on Shakespeare marks out the issue clearly:

> Others abide our question. Thou art free.
> We ask and ask – Thou smilest and art still,
> Out-topping knowledge.[38]

The "foiled searching of mortality" fails to disclose the answer: "Thou, who didst the stars and sunbeams know,/Self-schooled, self-scanned, self-honored, self-secure,/Didst tread on earth unguessed at – Better so!" (8–11) Better so indeed. We have described the investment in various answers, but a great deal seems invested in *not* finding the answer. It begins to become obvious that Shakespeare is the towering figure he is for us not despite but rather *because of* the authorship controversy. He is *defined* by that controversy, as, equally, he defines *it*, making Foucault's use of him as an example almost tautologous. "Shakespeare" is present as an absence – which is to say, as a ghost. Shakespeare as an author is the person who, were he more completely known, would not be the Shakespeare we know.

Formulations like "What is an author?" and "the death of the author," which have engaged the imagination of contemporary theorists, draw much of their power and fascination from "the kinship between writing and death"[39] – a little less than kin and more than kind. Freed from the trammels of a knowable "authorial intention," the author paradoxically gains power rather than losing it, assuming a different kind of authority that renders him in effect his own ghost. It begins to become clear that to speak about "ghost writing" is not merely to play upon words. As Foucault writes,

> we find the link between writing and death manifested in the total effacement of the individual characteristics of the writer . . . If we wish to know the writer in our day, it will be through the singularity of his absence and in his link to death, which has transformed him into a victim of his own writing."[40]

If you want to know the author – *in* the text, as well as *of* or *behind* the text – look to see who's dead.

Consider, for example, the tradition that has grown up about Shakespeare as an actor in his own plays. Nicholas Rowe, in the *Life* printed with his 1709 edition of the *Works*, writes that "tho' I have inquir'ed I could never meet with any further account of him this way, than that the top of his performance was the ghost in his own *Hamlet*."[41] Rowe's edition was published ninety-three years after Shakespeare's death – his information is hearsay, rumor, or better, but it is not an eyewitness account. It therefore belongs properly with the affect of the Shakespeare story rather than with its irreduceable facts. A less reliable account reports that Will Shakespeare's younger brother, having been asked about the parts played by his celebrated sibling, described seeing him "act a part in one of his own comedies, wherein being to personate a decrepit old man, he wore a long beard, and appeared so weak and drooping and unable to walk, that he was forced to be supported and carried by another person to a table, at which he was seated among some company, who were eating, and one of them sung a song."[42] This part has been identified as that of Old Adam in *As You Like It*, who enters the scene in question (2.7.) borne on Orlando's shoulders, like Anchises borne on the shoulders of his son Aeneas.

Both of these traditional accounts are suggestive. Each casts Shakespeare as a father figure advising his son, and placed at a disadvantage by age (or death) so that he requires the son to enact his will. Old Adam, in whom appears "the constant service of the antique world" (2.3.57) personates the dead Sir Rowland and his lost ways of civility. It is he who warns Orlando about treachery in the Duke's court, and encourages him to seek safety in Arden. We may see this as appropriate to a playwright's role, giving his protagonist motive for action, so that the casting acts as a kind of metadramatic shadow or reflection of the relationship between author, actor, and plot. But the role of ghost writer here is doubled. Each of these figures achieves his own erasure, first presenting or representing the imperative of the father, then disappearing from the play.

II

> We would search the "public" in vain for the first reader: i.e., the first author of a work. And the "sociology of literature" is blind to the war and the ruses perpetuated by the author who reads and by the first reader who dictates, for at stake here is the origin of the work itself. The *sociality* of writing as *drama* requires an entirely different discipline.
>
> Jacques Derrida, "Freud and the Scene of Writing"

Let us return, then, to our original question. Who is the author of Shakespeare's plays? Is it possible that, in this already over-determined controversy, there is at least one more determining factor? Is there something in the nature of these plays that somehow provokes, as it responds to, the authorship controversy? Are there, in other words, explicit scenes of ghost writing in the plays themselves? It has long been noted that Shakespeare's plays are full of questions of authority, legitimacy, usurpation, authorship and interpretation. Indeed, drama as a genre not only permits but also encodes the dissemination of authority. This is in part what authorizes such formulations as "negative capability" and "myriad-mindedness". But can the more *particular* details of the authorship controversy as we have just documented it somehow be seen to be anticipated and overdetermined by the plays? Can the "Shakespeare Question" be situated within the text itself? Is the authorship controversy in part a textual effect?

There are in fact an uncanny number of ways in which the plays can be seen to stage the controversy. Such scenes of encoded authorship encompass everything from ghosts that write and writers who function as ghosts, to handwriting analyses, signature controversies, the deciphering of codes, the digging of graves, the silencing of madwomen, the staging of plays that get away from their authors, and the thematizing of myriad other forms of doubt and discontinuity within authorial identity and control. Before I come to mention some specific instances in which ghost writing takes place in Shakespeare's plays, however, it may be useful to set these remarks into a theoretical framework, and to give some idea of how I will be using the concept of a *ghost* here and in the chapters that follow.

In *Beyond the Pleasure Principle* (1920), Freud discusses the ways in which the compulsion to repeat results from "the power of the repressed" – the ways, that is, in which that which has been repressed, because of its repression, keeps breaking through. Transference neurosis, the repetition of repressed memory as present experience, results from the retention of unconscious ideas, their refusal to become conscious and accessible to the patient and the analyst. The patient "is obliged to *repeat* the repressed material as a contemporary experience instead of . . . *remembering* it as something belonging to the past."[43] We might make use of a theoretical metaphor here, and describe such repetition as restaging or replaying. Freud himself explicitly refers to the unconscious as "another theater," and compares the reenactment involved in repetition, with its apparently paradoxical yield of pleasure even in unpleasurable experience, to the experience of drama – and, specifically, tragedy:

> the artistic play and artistic imagination carried out by adults, which, unlike children's, are aimed at an audience, do not spare the spectators (for instance, in tragedy) the most painful experiences and can yet be felt by them as highly enjoyable. This is convincing proof that, even under the dominance of the pleasure principle, there are ways and means enough of making what is in itself unpleasurable into a subject to be recollected and worked over in the mind.[44]

A tragedy is like an unpleasurable memory – or, rather, it is like the displacement of that repressed memory into the "working through" that is "artistic imagination" but also theatrical performance. This compulsion to repeat, this "perpetual recurrence of the same thing"[45] that strikes us as uncanniness in life and as structure in art, is one of the functions performed in Shakespeare's plays by the figure of the ghost.

Another useful analogue for the concept of a *ghost* as I am using it here can be found in what Jacques Derrida has called the "logic of the supplement."[46] The word "supplément," in French, means both a *substitute* and an *addition*. These terms, normally thought of as mutually exclusive, come together in the supplement in such a way that the binary logic of identity and noncontradiction is replaced by a different kind of logic. Barbara Johnson glosses that other logic as follows. In this chart, all statements are to be taken as equivalent to the statement, "A is a supplement to B."

1. A is added to B.
2. A substitutes for B.
3. A is a superfluous addition to B.
4. A makes up for the absence of B.
5. A usurps the place of B.
6. A makes up for B's deficiencies.
7. A corrupts the purity of B.
8. A is necessary so that B can be restored.

9. A is an accident alienating B from itself.
10. A is that without which B would be lost.
11. A is that through which B is lost.
12. A is a danger to B.
13. A is a remedy to B.
14. A's fallacious charm seduces one away from B.
15. A can never satisfy the desire for B.
16. A protects against direct encounter with B.[47]

The ghosts in Shakespeare's plays function as supplements in many, perhaps all, of these ways. The reader can test this out by selecting a ghost (or a character performing a ghost-function) and filling in the blanks. But if A stands for the ghost, who or what is B? If A is the Ghost of Old Hamlet, for example, is B the living Old Hamlet, Hamlet, Claudius, Ophelia, Horatio, Denmark, *Hamlet*, Shakespeare, the England – or the court – of Queen Elizabeth, a modern theatrical audience? Yes. Such is the promiscuous supplementarity of ghosts. Such, too, is the source of their power, and their danger.

A ghost is an embodiment of the disembodied, a re-membering of the dismembered, an articulation of the disarticulated and inarticulate. "Were I the ghost that walked," says Paulina to Leontes in *The Winter's Tale*, discussing his "dead" wife Hermione,

> I'ld bid you mark
> Her eye, and tell me for what dull part in't
> You chose her; then I'ld shriek, that even your ears
> Should rift to hear me, and the words that follow'd
> Should be, "Remember mine." (5.1.63–7)

We might notice the similarity of this scenario to *Hamlet*, where the ghost of the dead spouse does walk and cries "Remember me," the import of his words entering like daggers into his wife's ears when Hamlet, like Paulina, transmits the message.[48] In both of these dramatic cases, the appearance of the ghost comes at the time when the living spouse has effected, or is about to effect, a repetition and a substitution, through remarriage.

The effect of uncanniness produced by the appearance of a ghost is related simultaneously to its manifestation as a sign of potential proliferation or plurality and to its acknowledgement of the loss of the original – indeed, to the loss of the certainty of the concept of origin. The representation of the fear of loss through multiplication is familiar from the interpretation of dreams and myths, as for example in Freud's essay on "Medusa's Head" (1922), where the proliferation of swarming snakes compensates for and covers over the fear of castration, or in the "The Uncanny" (1919), where he writes that "this invention of doubling as a preservation against extinction has its counterpart in the language of dreams, which is fond of representing castration by a doubling or multiplication of the genital symbol."[49] The dual question – of plurality and the lost original – is directly relevant to the phenomenology of ghosts. And it is equally relevant to the phenomenology of the work of art. It is here, in the overlapping status of the ghost and the art object, or the ghost and the text, that the further significance of Shakespeare as a ghost writer – as a writer of ghosts, and as their ghostly written – manifests itself.

This peculiar characteristic of ghostliness – that the ghost is a copy, somehow both nominally identical to and numinously different from a vanished or unavailable original – has special ramifications for art forms which, like Elizabethan and Jacobean drama, are regarded by their contemporary cultures as marginal, popular, or contestatory. Consider the status of such analogous art forms as translation, photography, and film, forms that depend upon the production of "original copies." In two important essays, "The Task of the Translator" and "The Work of Art in the Age of Mechanical Reproduction," the cultural critic Walter Benjamin returns again and again to these two themes: multiplication and "the original."[50] For translation and mechanical reproduction are, precisely, means by which the original and its primacy are put in question. And thus they are ways of making – of calling up – ghosts. The two essays are uncannily concerned with the same issues, and the language in which Benjamin conducts his argument is itself suggestively ghostly – e.g., "A translation issues from the original – not so much from its life as from its afterlife,"[51] or "Even the most perfect reproduction of a work of art is lacking in one element: its presence in time and space, its unique existence at the place where it happens to be."[52] "The technique of reproduction," writes Benjamin, "detaches the reproduced object from the domain of tradition. By making many reproductions it substitutes a plurality of copies for a unique existence. And in permitting the reproduction to meet the beholder or listener in his own particular situation, it reactivates the object produced."[53] In fact, if we substitute the word *ghost* for *translation* or *reproduction* in any of these statements ("in permitting the *ghost* to meet the beholder or listener in his own particular situation . . .") we can see how cognate the conditions of ghostliness and reproduction or nonoriginality really are. It may be objected that in the last passage quoted above, Benjamin refers to "a plurality of copies," where in Shakespeare's plays the ghosts of Hamlet's father and Banquo and Julius Ceasar are not multiply replicated, but are themselves possessed of "a unique existence." This is certainly the case; but the "unique existence" each possesses is, I would contend, importantly different from the nonghostly existence of those characters as we encounter them (Banquo, Caesar) or hear about them (Old Hamlet) in the plays. I will have more to say about this gap between the ghost and its living "original" in the chapters that follow. For the present, though, I want to suggest that the idea of a "plurality of copies" does play an important role in the ghostly uncanniness of Shakespeare's plays, as for example in the phenomenon of many men marching in the king's coats (*1 Henry IV* 5.3.25; also *Richard III* 5.4.11–12: "I think there be six Richmonds in the field;/Five I have slain today instead of him"); in the disturbing capacity of ghosts to move about (*Hamlet* 1.5.156: "*Hic et ubique?* Then we'll shift our ground"); and in the profoundly uncanny sensation of doubleness experienced in and produced by the "twin" plays, *The Comedy of Errors* and *Twelfth Night*. In *The Comedy of Errors* the mechanism of textual effect is at work, as the concept of a ghostly double is transferred from that of the twin sons to their father:

Adriana.	I see two husbands, or mine eyes deceive me.
Duke.	One of these men is genius to the other:
	And so of these, which is the natural man,
	And which the spirit? Who deciphers them?
S. Dromio.	I sir, am Dromio, command him away.
E. Dromio.	I sir, am Dromio, pray let me stay.
S. Antipholus.	Egeon art thou not? or else his ghost? (5.1.332–8)

Perhaps the most instructive parallel suggested by Benjamin's essay on mechanical reproduction is that of photography, and of the photographic negative, which is described as a shadow or reverse of a work that has no "original":

> To an ever greater degree the work of art reproduced becomes the work of art designed for reproducibility. From a photographic negative, for example, one can make any number of prints; to ask for the "authentic" print makes no sense.[54]

In this connection it is interesting to recall that one of the familiar terms used in modern parlance to describe a faint, false, sometimes secondary photographic image is *ghost* – and that a *ghost* is also, in printing, a variation or unevenness in color intensity on a surface intended to be solidly tinted, a phenomenon often observed in the printing of newspapers. The photographic negative is in fact very like a ghost; it reifies the concept of an absent presence, existing positively as a negative image. In a negative we see light as dark and dark as light; we see, in effect, what is not there.

Hamlet.   Do you see nothing there?
Queen.   Nothing at all, yet all that is I see.
Hamlet.   Nor did you nothing hear?
Queen.   No, nothing but ourselves.
Hamlet.   Why, look you there, look how it steals away!
          My father, in his habit as he lived!
          Look where he goes, even now, out at the portal!
                              Exit Ghost. (3.4.132–6)

The analogy between a ghost and a photograph is made by
Robert Lowell in a poem suggestively titled "Epilogue":

> We are poor passing facts,
> warned by that to give
> each figure in the photograph
> his living name.[55]

Without the label of the "living name," inscribed on the back of the
photograph or beneath it in the album, such figures will become
anonymous, dislocated from the context in which they are
identifiable and identified. So writing fixes, pins down. This is ghost
writing too, writing that calls up ghosts from the past, from the
passing.

In 1927 Abel Gance, who made the great film, *Napoléon*,
predicted that "Shakespeare, Rembrandt, Beethoven will make
films."[56] The study of films made of, or from, Shakespeare's plays
has by this time, of course, become a recognized subspeciality of
Shakespeare studies, so that in that sense we can say Gance's
prediction has come true. "Shakespeare" – Shakespeare's works –
has made films. But in another sense, his words describe what
Shakespeare had already achieved, in furnishing his plays with ghost
writers, with writing ghosts and ghosts who demand to be written.
Gance's exultant claim for some Shakespeare of the future writes
history backward, and describes not "Shakespeare" but Shakespeare,
whoever he was.

The appearance of ghosts within the plays is almost always
juxtaposed to a scene of writing. Hamlet takes dictation from the
Ghost of his father: "My tables, meet it is I set it down/That one
may smile, and smile, and be a villain!" (1.5.107–8) Old Hamlet's
script is a revenge tragedy, perhaps the Ur-*Hamlet*. Hamlet will alter
the script, will himself sign and seal what he will describe as a
"play" on the voyage to England. But in this first encounter with
the Ghost we see a further rewriting of authority as well.

> I'll wipe away all trivial fond records,
> All saws of books, all forms, all pressures past

> ˙ That youth and observation copied there,
> And thy commandment all alone shall live
> Within the book and volume of my brain. (99–103)

"Thy commandment" (to revenge) replaces all the saws and pressures, or seals, of the past. In this post-Mosaic transmission of the law from father to son one kind of erasure (or "wiping away") is already taking place. The Ghost himself is under erasure – " 'tis here, 'tis here, 'tis gone" – visible and invisible, potent and impotent. But *all* ghosts are under erasure; that is their status.[57] What Hamlet writes down in *his* tables is the doubled plot of the Mousetrap play, for to smile and smile and be a villain is not only a description of Claudius, but also of Hamlet, just as Hamlet glosses the figure of "one Lucianus, nephew to the King" in the Mousetrap as both a sign of his knowledge of Claudius' guilt in the past, and a threat of his own revenge in the future. The integration of the Ghost into the composite figure of "Hamlet the Dane" begins with this scene of writing, as Hamlet writes himself into the story and writes the Ghost out, revising the revenge imperative (and the imperative of the revenge play).

The ghost of Julius Caesar is appropriated as a ghost writer by Mark Antony in the funeral oration. It is clear from the moment of the assassination that the conspirators have killed the wrong Caesar, the man of flesh and blood and not the feared and admired monarch. They have, so to speak, killed the wrong author-function, the one associated with the proper name and not with the works. Brutus's despairing cry, "O Julius Caesar, thou art mighty yet!/Thy spirit walks abroad and turns our swords/In our own proper entrails" (5.3.94–6) records his sense of Caesar as uncanny omnipresence, and conflates his two sightings of the Ghost with the self-destructive actions of the conspirators. Antony will himself become a "seizer" of opportunity, in the public reading of Caesar's *will*, "under Caesar's seal" (3.2.240), that leaves his money and pleasure-grounds to the people. In effect he makes Caesar, the dead and living Caesar of the author-function, his own ghost writer, the more effaced, the more powerful.

Brutus, who actually sees great Caesar's ghost, participates in a crucial scene of writing and authorial appropriation, an appropriation that occurs, significantly, *before* the assassination itself, as Brutus walks at night in his orchard. A letter is thrown in at his window, and, as he reads it, he writes it:

> "Brutus, thou sleep'st; awake, and see thyself!
> Shall Rome, etc. Speak, strike, redress!"
> "Brutus, thou sleep'st; awake!"

> Such instigations have been often dropp'd
> Where I have took them up.
> "Shall Rome, etc." Thus must I piece it out:
> Shall Rome stand under one man's awe? What, Rome?
> My ancestors did from the streets of Rome
> The Tarquin drive when he was call'd a king.
> "Speak, strike, redress!" Am I entreated
> To speak and strike? O Rome, I make thee promise,
> If the redress will follow, thou receivest
> Thy full petition at the hand of Brutus! (2.1.46–58)

Brutus supplies this anonymous document with what is in fact a dead (i.e. inanimate) author – "Rome." "Rome" enjoins him to join the conspiracy. "Shall Rome, etc." – like many of the Shakespeare ciphers – gives the interpreter considerable latitude to inscribe his own message ("thy full petition at the *hand* of Brutus"). The hand that rewrites here is of course also the hand that kills. The anonymity of the communication itself encodes authority – the importunings of a mere individual, like Cassius, are suspect because they are tied to a flawed human persona, and to personal motives. Receiving the letter, Brutus elects to ignore the possibility of a merely human agent, and to regard it instead as an uncanny answer to his own latent thought, about himself and his love-relationship to Rome. Here Brutus becomes his own ghost writer, and gives to the author he creates the pseudonym of "Rome."

Another kind of ghostly self-erasure can be seen in the famous "deposition scene" in *Richard II* (4.1.). There Richard, denying any possibility of a split between persona and role, the king's two bodies (or the proper name of the author and his works, to use Foucault's partition), sees himself as erased, tranformed into a shadow or ghost of himself, when he is deposed by Bullingbrook:

> I have no name, no title,
> No, not that name was given me at the font,
> But 'tis usurp'd . . .
> O that I were a mockery king of snow,
> Standing before the sun of Bullingbrook,
> To melt myself away in water drops! (4.1.255–62)

A "deposition" is both a forced removal from office and a piece of testimony taken down for use in the witness's absence (as well as the term describing the lowering of Christ's body from the cross – Richard's view of the event). Richard here deposes at his own deposition, figuring himself as a snowman whose whiteness and impermanence is tragically vulnerable to the kingly sun. He is already a voice from the past, and the disembodied voice, the ghost of Richard II, will haunt the rest of the tetralogy with increasing power.

Bullingbrook had faulted the "skipping king" Richard for his availability to the people. He himself, by being seldom seen, will be more wondered at, more the stuff of legend, reverence, and fantasy. Like Arnold's vision of a Shakespeare "unguessed-at. – Better so!" – this strategy locates power in absence: absence of personality, absence of fact, absence of peculiarity. But the question is also one of suitability, of fitting the role. Richard is the lineal king, the king by Divine Write, by Holy Writ. But Bullingbrook, like Bacon, fits the part, with his winning manners and his "fair discourse" (2.3.6). It is striking that one of his complaints against Richard is that the king has erased his name and coat of arms from the windows of the family estate, "leaving me no sign,/Save men's opinion and my living blood,/To show the world I am a gentleman" (3.1.25–7).

As with a "deposition," so with a "will" – the dead hand is a living voice replacing the original author, and open to interpretation. Thus, in *The Merchant of Venice*, Portia complains that in the mandatory casket choice "the will of a living daughter [is] curb'd by the will of a dead father" (1.2.24–5). Shakespeare – if it is he – puns on his own name as an absent presence enforcing desire and authority (or failing to enforce them) throughout the *Sonnets*, and, as we have seen, Mark Antony makes of the "will" of the murdered Caesar read aloud to the plebeians a document that encodes his own "will," his own authority over the original conspirators.

But if ghosts are often writers, so too are writers often ghosts. The question of Shakespeare's signature, especially as it appears (three times) on his *will*, can also be situated within the text. A signature, as Derrida has shown, is a sign that must be iterated to be recognizable, a sign of the simultaneous presence and absence of a "living hand," which stands for its signator in that person's absence. "By definition, a written signature implies the actual or empirical nonpresence of the signer."[58] A signature, then, is very like a ghost, as will become explicitly the case when Hamlet on shipboard takes his father's signet, providentially carried in his purse, and signs the name of "Hamlet" to the letter he has forged in the careful calligraphy of a professional scribe. ("I once did hold it, as our statists do, a baseness to write fair . . . but, sir, now/It did me yeman's service" (5.2.33–6). The "changeling" letter that sends Rosencrantz and Guildenstern to their deaths is signed by Hamlet – but by which Hamlet? It is the underwritten script of the Ghost's imperative superscribed by the son's educated hand.

III

> As the current affected the brachial plexus of the nerves, he
> suddenly cried aloud, "Oh! The hand, the hand!" and attempted
> to seize the missing member. The phantom I had conjured up
> swiftly disappeared, but no spirit could have more amazed the
> man, so real did it seem.
>
> S. Weir Mitchell, *Injuries of Nerves*

Again the plays are thematizing the authorship controversy: the
question of the identification of signatures and handwriting (could
Shakespeare write? could his parents? could his daughters? why
have we no literary remains in his hand, or – if any – just the
Thomas More fragment?) is a question configured in the plays not
only in Hamlet and Old Hamlet, but in Edmund's forged letter
purporting to come from his brother Edgar. "You know the
character to be your brother's?" asks Gloucester, using the
Renaissance term for handwriting, for letter of the alphabet, and
also for cipher or code. "It is his hand, my lord; but I hope his heart
is not in the contents" (*King Lear* 1.2.62; 67–8). The character, of
course, is Edmund's, the letter a forgery of *his* jealousy and not of
Edgar's. Likewise, Maria's forged letter to Malvolio in *Twelfth
Night* is made possible by an uncanny resemblance between her
handwriting and Olivia's. Indeed, the phenomenon of life imitating
art has never been more amply demonstrated than in the proliferation
of questers after the Shakespeare cipher. Their great model and
predecessor, the most ingenious cryptographer of them all, is
Malvolio, who opens Maria's forged letter to discover not only
ciphers and codes but an anagram as well: "Why, this is evident to
any formal capacity, there is no obstruction in this. And the end –
what should that alphabetical position portend? If I could make that
resemble something in me! Softly! M.O.A.I. – . . . M. – Malvolio;
M – why, that begins my name . . . M – but then there is no
consonancy in the sequel that suffers under probation. A should
follow, but O does . . . M.O.A.I. This simulation is not as the
former; and yet, to crush this a little, it would bow to me, for every
one of these letters are in my name" (2.5.116.41). Mrs Windle, Dr
Owen, and Ignatius Donnelly are pale shadows of this strong
precursor.

In these forgeries the text itself becomes a ghost writer: the
scriptwriting capacity takes on a power of its own, supplementing
the plot and radically altering it. And once more, as in the plays, so
in the authorized biography. Critics search in vain for the "speech
of some dozen lines, or sixteen lines" (2.2.541–2) that Hamlet

inserts in "The Murder of Gonzago" as an indicator of his secret knowledge. In just the same way, editors have scrutinized the manuscript of *Sir Thomas More* for undoubted proof of Shakespeare's authorship, and have fixed at last on the 147 lines written by "Hand D."

The spectral presence of the "hand" haunts the editorial tradition in another way as well, in connection with a particularly compelling example of authorial fragmentation. In *Titus Andronicus* Lavinia, who enters the stage with "*her hands cut off, and her tongue cut out, and ravish'd*" (2.4. stage direction) is assigned the task of writing *without* hands. Urged by his brother Marcus to moderate his language of grief and despair, "teach her not to lay/Such violent hands upon her tender life," Titus (who has himself been tricked into cutting off one of his own hands) retorts angrily: "What violent hands can she lay upon her life?":

> Ah, wherefore dost thou urge the name of hands . . .
> O handle not the theme, to talk of hands,
> Lest we remember still that we have none.
> Fie, fie, how franticly I square my talk,
> As if we should forget we have no hands,
> If Marcus did not name the word of hands! (3.2.25–33)

In the next scene (4.1.) Lavinia begins to rifle through her nephew Lucius's books with her stumps, turning the leaves of Ovid's *Metamorphoses*, to point to the "tragic tale of Philomel . . . of Tereus' treason and his rape" (47) as the narrative of her own experience. But her audience is puzzled. "Give signs, sweet girl," implores Titus (61), and Marcus devises a better plan. As so often in this play, the stage direction says it all: "*He writes his name with his staff, and guides it with feet and mouth*:

> This sandy plot is plain; guide, if thou canst,
> This after me. I have writ my name,
> Without the help of any hand at all. (69–71)

Lavinia's inscription on the "sandy plot" indicates the truth of her condition, identifying her rapists as the sons of Tamora. "There is enough written upon this earth/To . . . arm the minds of infants to exclaims" (84–6). *In-fans*, unable to speak, disarmed by her mutilation, Lavinia signs her deposition with a missing hand, a hand that is both "bloody and invisible."

Given this no-holds-barred approach to the act of writing in the play, it is unsettling to notice how often phrases like "on the one hand . . . and on the other" appear in criticism of the play. T. S. Eliot calls it "a play in which it is incredible that Shakespeare had any hand at all," M. C. Bradbrook observes that in the play "Shakespeare was trying his hand at the high style," and E. M. W. Tillyard points out admiringly that "the author holds everything in his head" – all textual effects of the play's embarrassing power.[59] J. C. Maxwell, the Arden editor of *Titus Andronicus*, writes of the authorship question that "in the palmy days of disintegration of the Shakespeare canon, almost all practising dramatists of 1585–95 were called in to take a hand in *Titus*"[60]; three times he mentions "Peele's hand" (twice on p. xxv, and again on p. xxvi), and he comments about Kyd that "there is nothing in the writing to suggest that he had any hand in it" (xxvii). Twice in the introduction he uses the formulation "on the one hand . . . and on the other" (xxxiv; xxxviii), and in the textual apparatus of the play he is fond of the technical designation "headless line" to denote a line of verse with only nine metrical feet. Thus the footnote to 2.3.115 reads, "best read as a headless line," and 5.2.62 is described as "an effectively solemn headless line" while Titus's multiply overdetermined request, "Speak, Lavinia, what accursed hand/Hath made thee handless in thy father's sight" (3.1.66) is likewise described as "a headless line." Nor is Maxwell wholly unaware of these anatomical excrescences. In a note to Act 5 scene 2, when Tamora comes to Titus's study and finds him writing "in bloody lines," lamenting his loss of eloquence ("how can I grace my talk,/Wanting a hand to give it action?"), the Arden editor cites B. L. Joseph, *Elizabethan Acting*, who quotes in turn from John Bulwer's *Chironomia* (1644):

> "The moving and significant extension of the *Hand* is knowne to be so absolutely pertinent to speech, that we together with a speech expect the due motion of the *Hand* to explaine, direct, enforce, apply, apparrell, & to beautifie the words men utter, which would prove naked, unless the cloathing *Hands* doe neatly move to adorne and hide their nakednesse, with their comely and ministeriall parts of speech."[61]

Here body parts and parts of speech seem inextricably intertwined. Titus asks Tamora on this occasion, "Is not thy coming for my other hand?" (5.2.27), and she later comments to herself, "I'll find some cunning practice out of hand/To scatter and disperse the giddy Goths" (77–8). At the close of the play Marcus urges that "the poor remainder of Andronici . . . hand in hand all headlong hurl ourselves" (5.3.131). It is tempting to add to this proliferating textual effect by pointing out that the style of *Titus Andronicus*, characterized by distortion of scale and perspective, has much in common with the late sixteenth-century expressive style known as Mannerism – a style that traces its etymology to the word "hand"

(ME *menere* from Norman French, from OF *maniere*, from Vulgar Latin *manuaria*, "way of handling," manner, from *manuarius*, of the hand, from *manus*, the hand).

Literal ghosts, portentous Senecan stalkers from the revenge tradition, tend in Shakespeare's plays to be male and paternal. But as the example of Lavinia suggests, there is another whole group of ghost writers in his plays who are similarly under erasure, and these ghost writers are women – women marginalized by their gender, by their putative or real madness, or by their violation. The story of Delia Bacon – overprotected by her brother, misled by a theology student into thinking he would marry her, gaining authority as a seer and prophetess from her rejection, and with it the license to go abroad and speak dangerous things, dying mad – this is the story of Ophelia. "Her speech is nothing," says a Gentleman to Horatio and the Queen,

> Yet the unshaped use of it doth move
> The hearers to collection; they yawn at it,
> And botch the words up fit to their own thoughts,
> Which as her winks and nods and gestures yield them,
> Indeed would make one think there might be thought,
> Though nothing sure, yet much unhappily. (*Hamlet* 4.5.7–13)

To this statement, itself a foreclosure of judgment ("her speech is nothing"), Horatio adds an even more political warning? " 'Twere good she were spoken with, for she may strew/Dangerous conjectures in ill-breeding minds" (14–15). The "unshaped use" of Ophelia's speech – rather like the "questionable shape" in which the Ghost appears to Hamlet (1.4.43) – is an invitation to fill in the blank. Traditionally dressed in white, Ophelia is marked as "virginal and vacant," as Elaine Showalter points out,[62] her white dress in contrast to Hamlet's suits of solemn black. If his costume is explicitly described (indeed, self-described) as an "inky cloak" (1.2.77), she is the blank page, the tabula rasa. But the white dress is also the sign, and the shroud, of a ghost. And just as Horatio's word "strew," in the passage we have just noticed, predicts Ophelia's flower-giving, so Laertes's description of the scene as "a document in madness, thoughts and remembrance fitted" (178–9) identifies the documentary evidence, the displacement of the written and the writable, that Ophelia's subject position compels. The flower-giving scene and its "document" closely resemble Lavinia's tracing on the "sandy plot." Both incidents present women writing as ghosts. Both suggest that women's writing is ghost writing.

Similarly marginalized, similarly erased, moving through the events of her play like a ghost, Cassandra is dismissed by her brothers as "our mad sister" (*Troilus and Cressida* 2.2.98), but the design toward which she moves, the story she tells, is the story of the Trojan War. Cassandra's authority is such that she speaks the truth and is not believed – and this is also the case with Ophelia and indeed with Lady Macbeth. For, as I will discuss in Chapter 4, Lady Macbeth's sleepwalking places her physically in exactly the condition of present absence, marginal stance, and legible erasure we have come to expect of such ghosts. Indeed, perhaps the most threatening female authority of all in the plays is also the most effaced – Sycorax, Caliban's mother, predecessor magician to Prospero, whose name is evoked as the justification for his authority and authorship on the island – and who never appears in the play. Like Claribel, who would be the next heir to Naples but is half a world away in Tunis, Sycorax exists beyond the play's margins, and only Miranda remains as another figure of female self-erasure in the present, eagerly accepting her father's tutelage in the Elizabethan World Picture.

Thus, again and again, the plays themselves can be seen to dramatize questions raised in the authorship controversy: who wrote this? did someone else have a hand in it? is the apparent author the real author? is the official version to be trusted? or are there suppressed stories, hidden messages, other signatures?

As will become clear in the chapters that follow, the plays not only thematize these issues, they also theorize them, offering a critique of the concept of authorship and, in particular, of the possibility of origin. Authorship itself will be seen as a belated and disputable matter. When Troilus cites the fidelity of his love for Cressida as "truth's authentic author" (*Troilus and Cressida* 3.2.181) for lovers "in the real world to come" (173), or when Brutus and Cassius view themselves as heroic regicides in the eyes of "ages hence" (*Julius Caesar* 3.1.111) they are not, as they think, standing at the beginning of the story, but somewhere in the middle. The histories of which they imagine themselves authors are already in process. Neither Troilus nor Cassius is "author of himself," and the texts they so confidently envisage are inflected, ironically, toward tragedy.

If it is a wise father that knows his own child, so it is a wise character who knows he is in search of an author. The undecidability of paternity, articulated again and again in the plays by putative fathers like Lear, Leontes, Leonato, and Prospero, is analogous to, and evocative of, the undecidability of authorship. Thus a play like *Pericles*, long thought to be the product of dual authorship, enacts its own family romance by dwelling insistently on the incest riddle with which it begins:

He's father, son, and husband mild;
I mother, wife – and yet his child.
How they may be, *and yet in two*,
As you will live, resolve it you. (1.1.68–71)

And even this incest riddle, later rearticulated in the mystery of
Marina's parentage (5.1.90ff.) is qualified by Gower's narrative
prologue: "I tell you what mine authors say" (1. Chorus. 20). The
origin is always deferred. The search for an author, like any other
quest for parentage, reveals more about the searcher than about the
sought, for what is demanded is a revisitation of the primal scene.

2

Descanting on deformity: Richard III and the shape of history

And thus having resolued all the doubts, so farre as I can imagine, may be moued against this Treatise; it onely rests to pray thee (charitable Reader) to interprete fauorably this birth of mine, according to the integritie of the author, and not looking for perfection in the worke it selfe. As for my part, I onely glory thereof in this point, that I trust no sort of vertue is condemned, nor any degree of vice allowed in it: and that (though it not be perhaps so gorgeously decked, and richly attired as it ought to be) it is at the least rightly proportioned in all the members, without any monstrous deformitie in any of them.

James I, *Basilikon Doron*

Upon a time when Burbidge played Richard III there was a citizen grew so far in liking with him that, before she went from the play, she appointed him to come that night unto her by the name of Richard the Third. Shakespeare, overhearing their conclusion, went before, was entertained and at his game ere Burbidge came. Then, message being brought that Richard the Third was at the door, Shakespeare caused return to be made that William the Conqueror was before Richard the Third.

John Manningham's *Diary*, 13 March 1601

I

How does the logic of ghostly authorship inform – or deform – not only the writing of literature but also the writing of history? As a way of approaching this question, I begin with a passage from *The Comedy of Errors*:

> O! grief hath chang'd me since you saw me last,
> And careful hours with time's deformed hand
> Have written strange defeatures in my face:
> But tell me yet, dost thou not know my voice?
>
> (5.1.298–301)[1]

A complex interrelationship between time and deformation is clearly outlined in Egeon's plea for recognition. For time's hand is already deformed as well as deforming, and it is, explicitly, a writing hand. Between the "deformed hand" and the still recognizable speaking voice comes, as always, the shadow. Hand/voice; written/ spoken. Here, though, that which is *written* is deformed, twisted out of shape, imbued with "strange defeatures." The wonderful word *defeature* means both "undoing, ruin" and "disfigurement; defacement; marring of features" (*OED*). In *The Comedy of Errors* it is twice used to describe the change of appearance wrought by age upon the face, both in Egeon's speech given above, and in Adriana's lament for her lost beauty, its loss hastened, she thinks, by her husband's neglect: "Then is he the ground/Of my defeatures" (2.1.97–8). It is unfortunate that "defeature" has become, as the *OED* points out, "obsolete," "archaic," "now chiefly an echo of the Shakespearean use" because it offers a superbly concrete picture of the *effects* of ruin, the visible, readable consequences of being – or coming – undone.

I would like to arrive, in this chapter, at a consideration of the way in which "time's deformed hand" writes, and thus defaces, history. The concept of "defeature" is a useful place to start from, since the visible marks of political defeat are often written, or characterized, in what one age will call history-writing and another, propaganda. My subject, the "defeatured" player in this exemplum, will be Richard III, an especially interesting case not only because of the fascination that history has exercised on both admirers and detractors, but also because, like Oxford and Bacon in the Shakespeare authorship controversy, Richard III has been the occasion for more amateur detective work, and for the foundation of both English and American societies to clear his name. The Richard III Society, originally known as the Fellowship of the White Boar, was founded in England in 1924; the Friends of Richard III Incorporated, the Society's American counterpart, included among its founding members the actresses Helen Hayes and Tallulah Bankhead.

The most recent full-length study of Richard, by Charles Ross,[2] while in most ways apparently an extremely careful and balanced account, shows the usual pique at this "amateur" espousal of Richard's cause, which has led in turn to the unwelcome development of amateurs writing history: "an Oxford professor of English law, a headmaster at Eton, several peers of the realm and a number of historical novelists and writers of detective stories," prominent among them women. Ross cites Josephine Tey, Rosemary Hawley Jarman, and "a number of others, nearly all women writers, for whom the rehabilitation of the reputation of a long-dead king holds a strange and unexplained fascination."[3] By implication these women are following the self-deluded path of the Lady Anne, whose "strange and unexplained" capitulation to Richard's suit in Shakespeare's play demonstrates female folly and a slightly sentimental belief that a bad man can be reformed or redeemed by the love of a good woman.

Ross's view of Richard is fact-oriented, balanced but binary. He concludes that Richard "does not appear to have been a complex man," and that "any contrarity of 'character' of Richard III stems not from what we know about him but from what we do not know about him."[4] It is the historian's job to discover the facts, and thus to dispel mystery, fantasy, undecidability. With this decidedly "professional,"[5] male, and hegemonic view of the use and abuse of history-writing, set forth in an introductory chapter that is designed to articulate "The Historical Reputation of Richard III: Fact and Fiction," we may begin our consideration of a dramatic character who is self-described as both deformed and defeatured, himself compact of fact *and* fiction: "Cheated of feature ... Deformed, unfinished ... scarce half made up" (*Richard III* 1.1.19–21).

Shakespeare's use and abuse of history in the *Henry VI* plays, and particularly in *Richard III*, is often viewed as a consequence, deliberate or adventitious, of the move by Tudor historians to classify Richard III as self-evidently a villain, his deformed body a readable text. Shakespeare, in such interpretations, emerges as either an unwitting dupe of More, Hall, and Holinshed, or as a co-conspirator, complicit in their design, seizing the opportunity to present the Plantagenet king defeated by Elizabeth's grandfather as unworthy of the throne, as unhandsome in person as in personality. Either the dramatist was himself shaping the facts for political purposes, or he was taken in by the Tudor revisionist desire to inscribe a Richard "shap'd" and "stamp'd" for villainy.

In either case, the persuasive power of the portrait has endured. As recently as 1984, for example, René Girard could assert confidently that "When Shakespeare wrote the play, the king's identity as a 'villain' was well-established. The dramatist goes along with the popular view, especially at the beginning. Richard's deformed body is a mirror for the self-confessed ugliness in his soul."[6]

It is clear, however, that no account of Shakespeare's literary or political motivations in foregrounding his protagonist's deformity is adequate to explain the power and seductiveness of Richard's presence in the plays. Indeed, the very fascination exerted by the historical Richard III seems to grow in direct proportion to an increase in emphasis on his deformity.

It may be useful here to document briefly the ways in which the vagaries of transmission, like a game of historical telephone, succeeded in instating Richard's deformity as the party line. The story of Richard's prolonged gestation, "held for two years in his mother's womb, emerging with teeth, and with hair down to his shoulders," like the picture of the hunchback, "small of stature, having a short figure, uneven shoulders, the right being higher than the left," is first told in the *Historia Regium Angliae* of Warwickshire antiquary John Rous, who died in 1491.[7] Polydore Vergil, Henry VII's Italian humanist historian, situated Richard in the scheme of providential history as the antagonist of Tudor ascendancy. Thomas More's *History of Richard III* established the enduring popular image of the villainous king as monster, in an account that artfully ascribes some of the more lurid details to rumor while passing them on:

> Richarde the third sonne, of whom we nowe entreate, was in witte and courage egall with either of them, in bodye and prowesse farre vnder them bothe, little of stature, ill fetured of limmes, croke backed, his left shoulder much higher then his right, hard fauoured of visage, and suche as in states called warlye, in other menne other wise. He was malicious, wrathfull, enuious, and from afore his birth, euer frowarde. It is for trouth reported, that the Duches his mother had so muche a doe in her trauaile, that shee coulde not bee deliuered of hym uncutte: and that hee came into the worlde with the feete forwarde, as menne bee borne outwarde, and (as the fame runneth) also not vntothed, whither menne of hatred reporte aboue the trouthe, or elles that nature chaunged her course in hys beginninge, whiche in the course of his lyfe many thinges vnnaturallye committed.[8]

More's account was borrowed by both Hall and Holinshed, and survives substantially unchanged in Shakespeare's *Richard III*. We might note that there is already a disparity between Ross's "history" and More's. Ross describes Richard's right shoulder as being higher than his left. More, with equal particularity, asserts that "his left shoulder [was] much higher than his right." The augmentation *much* puts a spin on the reversal; More grounds his own authority in rhetorical emphasis, and in doing so further distorts the figure of Richard – and the rhetorical figure for which he will come to stand. Both the change of shoulder – toward the sinister – and the emphasis implied by *much* suggest the pattern of amplification and embellishment characteristic of the Richard story throughout its own history.[9]

In the first tetralogy, unusual stress is placed on Richard's physical deformity, which is repeatedly anatomized and catalogued. King Henry calls him "an indigested and deformed lump" (3 Henry VI 5.6.51), Clifford a "foul indigested lump,/As crooked in thy manners as thy shape!" (2 Henry VI 5.1.157–8), and the Lady Anne a "lump of foul deformity" (Richard III 1.2.57). Significantly, he is at once "misshap'd," unshaped, and preshaped. Born in a sense prematurely ("sent before my time"), feet first, and with teeth already in his mouth, to the wonderment of the midwife and waiting women (3 Henry VI 5.6.52; 75–6), he is disproportioned and deformed, but also at the same time unfinished, incomplete, as his own testimony makes plain. Nature, he says in 3 Henry VI, conspired with love

> To shrink mine arm up like a wither'd shrub,
> To make an envious mountain on my back
> Where sits deformity to mock my body;
> To shape my legs of an unequal size,
> To disproportion me in every part,
> Like to a chaos, or an unlick'd bear-whelp
> That carries no impression like the dam.
>
> (3.2.156–62)

In the opening soliloquy of Richard III, he recurs to this description, again placing the blame on nature and love:

> I, that am rudely stamp'd, and want love's majesty
> To strut before a wanton ambling nymph;
> I, that am curtail'd of this fair proportion,
> Cheated of feature by dissembling nature,
> Deformed, unfinished, sent before my time
> Into the breathing world scarce half made up,
> And that so lamely and unfashionable
> That dogs bark at me as I halt by them –
> Why I, in this weak piping time of peace,
> Have no delight to pass away the time,
> Unless to spy my shadow in the sun,
> And descant on mine own deformity.   (1.1.16–27)

Generations of readers have been strongly affected by this relation between the deformity and the moral or psychological character of Richard. One such reader was Sigmund Freud, who turned to the example of Richard's deformity to characterize patients who think of themselves as "exceptions" to normal rules.

Such patients, Freud says, claim that "they have renounced enough
and suffered enough, and have a claim to be spared any further
exactions; they will submit no longer to disagreeable necessity, for
they are *exceptions* and intend to remain so too."[10] This claim seems
apt enough for Richard's opening soliloquy, which Freud goes on
to quote: "that figure in the creative work of the greatest of poets in
whose character the claim to be an exception is closely bound up
with and motivated by the circumstance of congenital injury."[11] But
when Freud comes to discuss the passage, he finds it to signify r t
Richard's desire to deflect his energies from love (for which his
deformity renders him unsuitable) to intrigue and murder, but
rather a more sympathetic message for which the resolution to
"prove a villain" acts as a "screen." The "something much more
serious"[12] that Freud describes behind the screen is, essentially, a
variation on the theme of the family romance. His Richard declares

> Nature has done me a grievous wrong in denying me that beauty
> of form which wins human love ... I have a right to be an
> exception, to overstep those bounds by which others let
> themselves be circumscribed. I may do wrong myself, since
> wrong has been done to me – and now [says Freud] we feel that we
> ourselves could be like Richard, nay, that we are already a little
> like him. Richard is an enormously magnified representation of
> something we can all discover in ourselves. We all think we have
> reason to reproach nature and our destiny for congenital and
> infantile disadvantages; we all demand reparation for early
> wounds to our narcissism, our self-love. ... Why were we born
> in a middle-class dwelling instead of a royal palace?[13]

For Freud, then, Shakespeare's Richard III represents not so
much a particular aberrant personality warped by the accident of
congenital deformation, as (or, but rather) the general psychological
fact of deformation at birth and by birth, the congenital deformation that results "in ourselves," in "all" of us, by the fact that we are
born to certain parents, and in certain circumstances, incurring,
inevitably, certain narcissistic wounds. Thus for Freud the character
of Shakespeare's Richard marks the fact of deformation in the
register of the psychological, just as we shall see the same character
mark the inevitability of deformation in the registers of the political
and the historiographical.

Moreover, in Freud's narrative the political is also explicitly
present, though it is signified by a lacuna, a lapse in the progress of
his exposition:

> For reasons which will be easily understood, I cannot communi-
> cate very much about these ... case-histories. Nor do I propose

to go into the obvious analogy between deformities of character resulting from protracted sickliness in childhood ai he behaviour of whole nations whose past history has been full of suffering. Instead, however, I will take the opportunity of pointing to that figure . . .[14]

and so on to Shakespeare and Richard III. What is the "obvious analogy" he resists? It seems reasonable to associate the "deformities of character resulting from protracted sickliness in childhood," and, indeed, the "behavior of whole nations whose past history has been full of suffering" with some specific rather than merely general referent. And if we consider the year in which this essay was first published, in *Imago* 1915–1916, we may be reminded of the circumstances of Germany in the First World War, and, most directly, of the personal circumstances of Kaiser Wilhelm. For Wilhelm II of Prussia was born with a withered arm, a congenital defect that made him the target of gibes from his childhood playmates, including his cousin, who would become Czar Nicholas of Russia. As a recent historical study describes him, Wilhelm II

> was a complicated man of painful insecurity – his left arm was withered and useless – who sought in pomp and bluster, in vulgar displays of virility, to mask his handicap and to assert what he devoutly believed in: his divine right to rule. But he craved confirmation of that right and yearned to be loved and idolized. Beyond the flawed character was a man of intelligence and vision.[15]

Wilhelm II, then, is also considered – or considered to have considered himself – an "exception" to normal rules. Freud takes exception to mentioning him – or even, perhaps, to consciously identifying him – and instead displaces his analysis onto the safely "literary" character of Shakespeare's Richard. And Richard's opening soliloquy, descanting on deformity, provides a revealing narrative of the ways in which the line between the "psychological" and the "historical" is blurred.

"Unlick'd," "unfinished," "indigested" – "not shaped" for sportive tricks, "scarce half made up." The natal circumstances and intrapsychic discourse of Shakespeare's Richard, who ironically resolves, despite his initial disclaimers, to "court an amorous looking-glass" (1.1.15; 1.2.255; 1.2.262), uncannily anticipate the language of Jacques Lacan's description of the "mirror stage." Lacan writes of

> the view I have formulated as the fact of a real specific prematurity of birth in man . . . This development is experienced

as a temporal dialect that decisively projects the formation of the individual into history. The *mirror stage* is a drama whose internal thrust is precipitated from insufficiency to anticipation – and which manufactures for the subject, caught up in the lure of spatial identification, *the succession of phantasies that extends from a fragmented body-image to a form of its totality that I shall call orthopaedic* – and, lastly, to the assumption of the armour of an alienating identity, which will mark with its rigid stricture the subject's entire mental development.[16]

Characteristically, Richard turns his chaotic physical condition into a rhetorical benefit, suggesting that he can "change shapes with Proteus for advantages" (*3 Henry VI* 3.2.192); be his own parent and his own author, lick himself into shape – whatever shape the occasion requires. Queen Elizabeth tells him that he cannot win her daughter "Unless thou couldst put on some other shape" (*Richard III* 4.4.286). But the shape in which we encounter him is already a deformed one – the natural deformity of historical record.

Peter Saccio gives a highly useful account of the evolution of Richard the monster in his study of Shakespeare's English kings:

> This lurid king, hunchbacked, clad in blood-spattered black velvet, forever gnawing his nether lip or grasping for his dagger, has an enduring place in English mythology. He owes something to the facts about the historical Richard III. He owes far more to rumor and to the political bias, credulity and especially the literary talent of Tudor writers . . .
>
> As myth, the Tudor Richard is indestructible . . . As history, however, the Tudor Richard is unacceptable. Some of the legend is incredible, some is known to be false, and much is uncertain or unproved. The physical deformity, for example, is quite unlikely. No contemporary portrait or document attests to it and the fact that he permitted himself to be stripped to the waist for anointing at his own coronation suggests that his torso could bear public inspection.[17]

In fact, when we come to examine the portrait evidence, we find that it is of considerable interest for evaluating Richard's alleged deformity. A portrait now in the Society of Antiquaries of London, painted about 1505, shows a Richard with straight shoulders. But a second portrait, possibly of earlier date, in the Royal Collection, seems to emblematize the whole controversy, for in it, X-ray examination reveals an original straight shoulder line, which was subsequently painted over to present the raised right shoulder silhouette so often copied by later portraitists.[18]

Richard is not only deformed, his deformity is itself a deformation. His twisted and misshapen body encodes the whole strategy of history as a necessary deforming and *un*forming – with the object of *re*forming – the past. Shakespeare exemplifies this strategy with precision in a remarkable moment in *Much Ado About Nothing*, when the vigilant and well-intentioned Watch overhears a comment by Borachio. "Seest thou not what a deformed thief this fashion is?" "I know that Deformed," remarks the Second Watch wisely to himself, " 'a has been a vile thief this seven year; 'a goes up and down like a gentleman. I remember his name" (3.3.125–7). Like Falstaff's eleven buckram men grown out of two, this personified concretion takes on an uncanny life of its own in the scene. When Borachio and Conrade are confronted with their perfidy, Deformed is identified as a co-conspirator: "And one Deformed is one of them; I know him, 'a wears a lock" (169–70), and again, "You'll be made bring Deformed forth, I warrant you" (172–3). This is precisely what happens to the reinvented historical figure of Richard III.

Created by a similar process of ideological and polemical distortion, Richard's deformity is a figment of rhetoric, a figure of abuse, a catachresis masquerading as a metaphor. In a viciously circular manifestation of neo-Platonic determinism, Richard is made villainous in appearance to match the desired villainy of his reputation, and then is given a personality warped and bent to compensate for his physical shape.

For Shakespeare's play, in fact, encodes what we might call a suppositious presupposition. Richard's deformity is not claimed, but rather presupposed, given as fact in service of the question, "was his villainy the result of his deformity?" – a question not unlike "have you stopped beating your wife?" Jonathan Culler has shown that the presuppositions that govern literary discourse are mistakenly designed as givens, as "moments of authority and points of origin," when in fact they are only "retrospectively designated as origins and . . . therefore, can be shown to derive from the series for which they are constituted as origin." As with literary conventions, so also with historical presuppositions that constitute the ground of a discursive continuum – here the "History" of Richard III. To adapt Culler's argument about speech acts, "None of these [claims of historical veracity] is a point of origin or moment of authority. They are simply the constituents of a discursive space from which one tries to derive conventions."[19]

Richard's deformity, itself transmitted not genetically but generically through both historiography and dramaturgy, becomes the psychological and dramatic focus of the play's dynamic. Shakespeare has written history backward, taking Hall's and More's objective correlative (he looked the way he was; he should have looked this way because he was in fact this way; he should have been this way, so he must have looked this way) and then presupposed it. Richard's own claim that he can "change shapes with Proteus for advantages" is a metahistorical comment on his Lamarckian evolution as villainous prototype, every misshaped part an over-determined text to be interpreted and moralized, descanting on his own deformity. Shakespeare's play brings "Deformed forth" as an embodiment of the historical process that it both charts and epitomizes.

History is indeed shown by the play to be a story that is deformed from the outset, by its very nature. The figure of Hastings, for instance, seems predestined to bring out particularly uncanny modes of deformation through the ghostly doublings of the Scrivener and the Pursuivant. The Pursuivant (an official empowered to serve warrants) who accosts Lord Hastings in *Richard III* Act 3 scene 2 is also named Hastings, and appears by that name not only in the Quarto text but also in Hall's *Union of the Two Illustre Families of Lancaster and York*. The absence of his name from the Folio has caused some editorial speculation, and the Arden editor's long discussion of this absent name emphasizes the strangeness of the figure:

> The entire episode as it appears in F seems pointless: it merely repeats what has already been said by Hastings, adds a super-fluous character, and would probably be cut by an economy-minded producer. The fact that it was not cut in Q suggests that someone felt strongly enough about it to retain it, and that the identity of the pursuivant served to make an ironical point.[20]

According to both Hall and Shakespeare, Hastings receives a number of warnings of the fate that is to befall him. His horse stumbles, Stanley dreams that the boar will rase their helms and sends a cautionary word to Hastings, and still Hastings remains adamantly blind to his danger.

At this point, in a remarkable scene reported by Hall and dramatized by Shakespeare, Hastings encounters the Pursuivant who bears his own name. He greets him warmly, reminiscing about the last time they met, when Hastings was fearful for his life. Now, ironically feeling more secure, he rejoices to note that his former enemies, the Queen's allies, have been put to death, and he himself is "in better state than ere I was" (3.2.104). Hall moralizes with some satisfaction on this latest ironic twist: "O lorde God, the blyndnesse of our mortal nature, when he most feared, he was in moste surety, and when he reconed him selfe most surest, he lost his lyfe, and that within two houres after."[21] Shakespeare makes the same point more subtly and forcefully by prefacing this encounter with Richard's decision to "chop off his head" if Hastings will not agree to their "complots" (3.1.192–3) and then following it with a knowing aside from Buckingham to the audience. The encounter with the Pursuivant (literally, a "follower") named Hastings is an example of the uncanny in one of its most direct forms, recognizable and strange at once. The action itself is doubled, as Hastings meets "Hastings" coming and going, and does not understand what he sees. Hastings's own name functions in a subdued allegorical way throughout this scene, which could be emblematized as *festina lente*, making Hastings slowly.[22]

Another example of doubling and displacement within a historical event is provided by the odd little scene with the Scrivener (3.6). Borrowed by the playwright from his chronicle sources, this scene becomes in its dramatic embodiment a model of history as a kind of ghost writing, since it encodes and "engross[es]" the fashioning of a rival text. The Scrivener complains that he has spent eleven hours copying the indictment of Hastings "in a set hand," or legal script. The first draft, or "precedent" (7), "was full as long a-doing,/And yet within these five hours Hastings liv'd/Untainted, unexamin'd, free, at liberty" (7–9). The Scrivener laments the duplicity of the times – "Who is so gross/That cannot see this palpable device" (10–11) "engross'd" by his own set hand (2) – and yet who dares to say he sees it?

This packed little scene demonstrates at once the play's preoccupation with writing and the preemptive – indeed prescriptive – nature of its political design. The Scrivener's indignation is both moral and professional, for his task of scriptwriting had begun before the incident that was to occasion it, and ended too late to authorize – although it will retrospectively "legitimitize" – the death of Hastings. Since the previous scene has already presented the spectacle of Hastings's decapitated head, displayed by Lovell and Ratcliffe to the London populace and an apparently griefstricken Richard, the existence, belatedly revealed, of a meticulously crafted indictment undercuts the idea of historical accident or spontaneous action. History is not only deformed but also preformed. Hall recounts the story with particular attention to the length of time the drawing of the indictment would take:

> Nowe was thys proclamacion made within two houres after he was beheaded, and it was so curiously endyted and so fayre writen in Parchement in a fayre hande, and therewith of it selfe

so long a processe, that every chyld might perceyve that it was prepared and studyed before (and as some men thought, by Catesby) for all the tyme betwene hys death and the proclamacion proclaimyng, coulde skant have suffyced unto the bare wrytyng alone, albeit that it had bene in paper and scribeled furthe in haste at adventure."[23]

Like the disparity between the "truth" of Shakespeare's play and the historical figure it encodes, the "palpable device" of the long-prepared indictment and the apparent hasting of Hastings's demise opens the question of authority. Which comes first, the event or the ghost writer?

So far is Richard from being merely the passive psychological victim of his deformity, he early on becomes deformity's theorist and manipulator, not only "descanting" upon it, but projecting and displacing its characteristics onto others. The death of Clarence is a good example of how this works in the play. Clarence is imprisoned at Edward's order, but at the instigation of Richard. The two murderers who go to the Tower to carry out the execution bear Richard's warrant for entry. And Edward is nonplussed when, at the worst possible time from a political standpoint, Clarence's death is announced. "Is Clarence dead?" he asks, "The order was reversed." "But he, poor man, by your first order died," says Richard. "And that a winged Mercury did bear;/Some tardy cripple bare the countermand,/That came too lag to see him buried" (2.1.87–91).

The phrase "tardy cripple" spoken by the crippled Richard is doubly ironic. He himself is represented in this account not by the cripple, but by "winged Mercury," fleet of foot, who bears the message of execution – here, in fact, made possible by Richard's forged warrant. The "tardy cripple," coming "too lag" to save Clarence, is Richard's displacement of deformity onto the foiled intentions of his well-formed brother the King.

An even more striking instance of this crippling or deforming of the world outside Richard occurs in the scene at Baynard's Castle (3.7) in which Richard enters aloft between two bishops, "divinely bent to meditation" (62), and Buckingham stages a public entreaty to persuade him to accept the throne. Buckingham describes Richard as the rightful heir, with "due of birth" and "lineal glory," (120–1), able to prevent the resigning of the crown "to the corruption of a blemish'd stock" (122). But his description of the present state of governance is oddly pertinent (and impertinent) to the man he is apparently addressing:

> The noble isle doth want her proper limbs;
> Her face defac'd with scars of infamy,

>Her royal stock graft with ignoble plants,
>And almost should'red in the swallowing gulf
>Of dark forgetfulness and deep oblivion. (125-9)

Here the cripple is England, wanting "proper limbs" (compare Richard's own ironic description of "me that halts and am misshapen thus" as "a marv'llous proper man" in the eyes of the Lady Anne [1.2.250-4]). "Defac'd" and especially "should'red" make the transferred anatomical references unmistakable.

In the final scene of *3 Henry VI* an ambitious and disgruntled Richard had murmured aside, "yet I am not look'd on in the world./ This shoulder was ordain'd so thick to heave,/And heave it shall some weight, or break my back" (5.7.22-4). In the scene of the wooing of Anne, Richard protests that Queen Margaret's slanderous tongue "laid their guilt upon my guiltless shoulders" (*Richard III* 1.2.98), again mischievously calling attention to his own physical deformity; later he is twitted by young York to the same effect ("Because that I am little like an ape/He thinks that you should bear me on your shoulders" [3.1.130-1]). Richard's deformed shoulder is what "shoulders" the noble isle of England into near oblivion, but in Buckingham's anatomy of the deformed state the "proper man" is the well derived Richard, who will restore the kingdom to its wonted shape. In both of these cases a condition of deformity is transferred, to the hypothetical messenger or the diseased polity.

Deformity as a self-augmenting textual effect, contaminating the telling of Richard's story as well as Richard's story itself, has been associated with his literary presence almost from the first. More's account of the notorious sermon of Dr Shaa is a good example. Dr Shaa had been persuaded to preach a sermon in which he would impute the bastardy of Edward's sons and point out Richard's physical resemblance to his father the Duke of York. He was to have intoned these sentiments, comparing Richard's visage and behavior to those of the admired Duke, at the point when Richard himself appeared in the congregation. Richard, however, was late, and the key passage already past when he did turn up. Seeing him enter, Dr Shaa, in a flurry of discomfiture, began to repeat his point for point comparison, but "out of al order, and out of al frame,"[24] to the consternation of the audience. The "shamefull sermon" having backfired, Shaa fled to his house and was forced to "kepe him out of sight lyke an owl," and soon "withered away" of shame.

In this little story Dr Shaa sees himself as a writer of predictive history, predicating the future on a repetition of the past (the second Richard an image of the first). But his narrative, out of all order and out of all frame, like Richard's own misshapen body, becomes in

More's retelling the perversion and distortion of its intended form and design. Moreover, Dr Shaa himself is contaminated by the rhetorical force of the prevailing mythology about Richard. In the course of More's account Shaa himself becomes deformed, or "withered," as if by the disseminated agency of his ignoble association with Richard, whose own arm is "like a with'red shrub" (3 Henry VI 3.2.156), "like a blasted sapling, with'red up" (Richard III 3.4.69). The figure of Richard keeps escaping its own boundaries, to appear uncannily replicative in the authors of his twisted history.

Other putative sources for Shakespeare's play have suffered the same suggestive narrative contamination. Francis Seager's complaint, Richard Plantagenet, Duke of Gloucester, one of the tragedies published in the 1563 Mirror for Magistrates, is described by a prose commentator in the volume as appropriate to its subject. The roughness of the meter was suitable, since "kyng Rychard never kept measure in any of his doings . . . it were agaynst the decorum of his personage, to use eyther good Meter or order."[25] The "decorum of his personage" seems also to have affected the Arden editor, Antony Hammond, who describes this same poem as "a dull, lame piece of verse."[26]

Such observations reflect the powerful ghostly presence of the lame and halting Richard. E. M. W. Tillyard, writing of the first tetralogy, remarks upon "the special shape in which the age of Elizabeth saw its own immediate past and its present political problems," and again of "the shape in which the War of the Roses appeared to Shakespeare's contemporaries."[27]

That "special shape" is Richard's. Images of "the beauty of virtue and the deformity of vice" were commonplace in Tudor writings (this particular phrase comes from the second preface to Grafton's Chronicle at Large [1569], probably written by Thomas Norton, the author of Gorboduc); but when the subject turned explicitly to Richard, the correspondence of physical, moral, and poetic or stylistic deformity seems particularly overdetermined.

Bacon's essay "Of Deformity," reads like a description of Richard III, though it may have been provoked more directly by Robert Cecil:

Deformed persons are commonly even with nature; for as nature hath done ill by them, so do they by nature; being for the most part, as the Scripture saith, 'Void of natural affection,' and so they have their revenge of nature. Certain there is a consent between the body and the mind, and where nature erreth in the one, she ventureth in the other. . . . Whosoever has anything fixed in his person that doth induce contempt, hath also a perpetual spur in himself, to rescue and deliver himself from scorn; therefore all deformed persons are extreme bold . . . Also it stireth in them industry, . . . to watch and observe the weakness of others that they may have somewhat to repay. Again, in their superiors it quencheth jealousy and it layeth their competitors and emulators asleep; as never believing they should be in possibility of advancement, till they see them in possession. So that, upon the matter, in a great wit deformity is an advantage to rising. . . . they will, if they be of spirit, seek to free themselves from scorn, which must be either by virtue or malice.[28]

Samuel Johnson cites these sentiments with approbation in his notes on *3 Henry VI*, making explicit their relevance to Richard ("Bacon remarks that the deformed are commonly daring, and it is almost proverbially observed that they are ill-natured. The truth is, that the deformed, like all other men, are displeased with inferiority, and endeavour to gain ground by good or bad means, as they are virtuous or corrupt").[29] And, indeed, this too may be an instance of overdetermined contamination. Dr Johnson's stress on "deformities" reflects his own self-consciousness of deformation. Suffering from scrofula as an infant, Johnson was marked throughout life by "scars on the lower part of the face and on the neck"[30] which he sought to conceal in his portraits by presenting the better side of his face to the painter's view. Until the age of six he bore on his arm an open, running sore, or "issue," cut and left open with the idea of draining infection. This, and the partial blindness also induced by tuberculosis in infancy, produced in him a "situation so appalling," writes Walter Jackson Bate, that "we are naturally tempted to speculate on the psychological results."[31]

But Johnson's most striking observations about deformity in Shakespeare occur in another connection. "We fix our eyes upon his graces, and turn them from his deformities, and endure in him what we should in another loathe or despise." The subject of these comments, astonishingly, is not Richard III, but Shakespeare himself – and the "deformities" are those of literary and dramatic creation. "I have seen," he continues, "in the book of some modern critic, a collection of anomalies, which shew that he has corrupted language by every model of depravation, but which his admirer had accumulated as a monument of honour."[32] "Anomalies," "corrupted language," "model of depravation" – all this sounds very like Richard III as he is received by a reluctantly admiring audience. Not only does Richard theorize his own deformity, he generates and theorizes deformity as a form of power.

II

In a response to a recent collection of essays on *"Race," Writing, and Difference*, Houston A. Baker, Jr. discusses Shakespeare's Caliban as an example of what he calls "the deformation of mastery," the way in which a representative of the indigenous population finds a voice within the colonialist discourse of the master, Prospero.[33] Caliban, the "hooting deformed of Shakespeare's *The Tempest*," provides for Baker an opportunity to describe "a drama of deformation" as it is articulated by the indigenous Other that advertises itself through a phaneric mask of display. Caliban's metacurses, his deployment of language against language, are a result of his conscription by Western culture, his "willingness to barter his signs for the white magician's language."[34] His physical deformity and his curses are alike indices of this double bind. What Baker proposes – and he is here troping the present-day Afro-American scholar's discourse on Caliban's – is a " 'vernacular' invasion and transcendence of fields of colonizing discourse in order to destroy white male hegemony."[35] Unable to go back to a pre-lapsarian or pre-Prosperian innocence (another impossible and hypothetical origin only fantasized in retrospect by the play) Caliban and his twentieth-century heirs must find a solution to the double bind in a "triple play" of what Baker calls "supraliteracy," the deployment of the vernacular, "hooting" phaneric deformities that are the sign of the slipped noose, of the freed, independent, and victorious subject.

What Baker is here calling for, in an elegant phaneric display of his own, is essentially a rhetoric and a politics of deformation. His word "hoot," which he takes from an ethological description of gorilla display, nowhere appears in *The Tempest*, but it suggests the "mimic hootings" of Wordsworth's Boy of Winander, and even the phaneric "hoos" of Stevens' Chieftain Iffucan of Azcan.

The "deformed slave" who is Caliban has lately been taken as the site of deformation for a number of contemporary debates. Thus we might consider Caliban not only as a figure for the colonized subject, but also as a figure for mixed genre, as Paul Howe has suggested,[36] or (on the model of Frankenstein's monster) as a figure for woman. And this kind of deformation, too, has potential relevance for Richard III. Because in the course of Shakespeare's play Richard himself develops what is in effect a rhetoric of deformation, calling attention to the novelties of his physical shape and the ways in which that shape liberates him from the constraints of conventional courtly deportment. "Cheated of feature by dissembling nature," Richard himself feels free to cheat and dissemble; "deformed, unfinished," he freely descants on his own deformity.

"Man," writes Nietzsche in his essay "The Use and Abuse of History," "braces himself against the great and ever greater pressure of what is past: it pushes him down or bends him sideways, it encumbers his steps as a dark invisible burden which he would like to disown."[37] So Richard "Crook-back" (*3 Henry VI* 1.4.75; 2.2.96; 5.5.30) is bent not only by specific historical distortions but by the intrinsic distortion of history, which Richard bears, like an ape, on his shoulders. Again, as *Titus Andronicus* particularizes in its decapitations and cutting off of hands the dismembering of historiographical writing, so *Richard III* anatomizes the dangers of re-membering, of history as an artifact of memory.

Writing of what he describes as "monumental history," Nietzsche argues that

> as long as the soul of historiography lies in the great stimuli that a man of power derives from it, as long as the past has to be described as worthy of imitation, as imitable and possible for a second time, it of course incurs the danger of becoming *somewhat distorted*. . . . there have been ages, indeed, which were quite incapable of distinguishing between a monumentalized past and a mythical fiction . . . . Monumental history deceives by analogies: with seductive similarities it inspires to fanaticism; and when we go on to think of this kind of history in the hands of gifted egoists and visionary scoundrels, then we see empires destroyed, princes murdered, wars and revolutions launched and the number of historical "effects in themselves," that is to say, effects without sufficient cause, again augmented.[38]

"Gifted egoists and visionary scoundrels"; "wars and revolutions launched"; "princes murdered"; the past "somewhat distorted" in the direction of mythical fiction – Nietzsche is uncannily describing not only monumental history but also Richard III – and *Richard III*. Moreover, Richard himself in his opening soliloquy articulates the process of monumental history:

> Now are our brows bound with victorious wreaths,
> Our bruised arms hung up for monuments,
> Our stern alarums chang'd to merry meetings,
> Our dreadful marches to delightful measures. (1.1.5–8)

This is the description of something completed and assimilated, something finished – against which Richard remains defiantly incomplete and imperfect: "curtail'd of this fair proportion,/Cheated of feature by dissembling nature,/Deform'd, unfinish'd, sent before

my time/Into this breathing world scarce half made up" (18–21).
Yet Nietzsche, too, writes of the consciousness of history as
something that reminds man of "what his existence fundamentally is
– an imperfect tense that can never become a perfect one."[39] So the
imperfect and unperfected Richard stands over against "the phrase
'it was'."[40]

It is in the multiple narratives of birth that Richard comes most
clearly to stand as an embodiment of the paradoxical temporality of
history. On the one hand, he is premature: "Deform'd, unfinish'd,
sent before (his) time." Yet on the other, he is born too late, "held
for two years in his mother's womb, emerging with teeth,"
overdeveloped and overarmed. Both Robert N. Watson and Janet
Adelman[41] have identified, in psychoanalytic terms, another birth
scene, a fantasized one in which the "unlick'd bear-whelp" carves
his own way out of the womb, making a birth canal where none
exists:

> Seeking a way, and straying from the way,
> Not knowing how to find the open air,
> But toiling desperately to find it out –
> Torment myself to catch the English crown;
> And from that torment I will free myself,
> Or hew my way out with a bloody axe.
>
> (3 Henry VI 3.2.176–81)

Figuratively, this may be seen as a process of violently willful
biological birth; politically, it presents itself as a birth of historical
process. Premature, Protean, fully and functionally toothed, Richard
here hews out an historical path, the way to the crown (and to the
chronicles). The violence of his act is inseparable and indistinguish-
able from that act itself. His use of history is simultaneously and
necessarily its abuse.

There is another retelling of the birth story in *Richard III*, this
one by the Lady Anne:

> If ever he have child, abortive be it,
> Prodigious, and untimely brought to light,
> Whose ugly and unnatural aspect
> May fright the hopeful mother at the view,
> And that be heir to his unhappiness!
>
> (1.2.21–5)

This passage, too, can be conceived as a description of autogenesis.
The fantasy child who is to be the only offspring of Richard and
Anne is Richard himself.[42] A different construction, or reconstruc-
tion, of Anne's speech, however, might read this predictive curse as

the birth of history. History – the historical subject and the synthetic Shakespearean history play – is the prodigious and untimely result of the union of chronicle and drama. Anne's imagined scene of the mother's dismay (she does not, of course, envisage *herself* as the "hopeful mother" of his child) strongly recalls King Henry VI's account of the birth of Richard: "Thy mother felt more than a mother's pain,/And yet brought forth less than a mother's hope" (*3 Henry VI* 5.6.49–50).

As I have argued elsewhere,[43] recent critical displacements of the once-fashionable notion of "providential history" by a politically self-conscious, ideologically determined reshaping of historical "fact" have foregrounded the degree of belatedness intrinsic to and implicit in Elizabethan history plays. The "now" of these plays is always preeminently the "now" of the time of their literary genesis – the time is manifestly out of joint, and the retrospective reconstruction of history ("to tell my story," to pursue Hamlet's own chronicling of the process) is the only means of shaping time at either the protagonist's or the dramatist's command. "May not an ass know when the cart draws the horse?" asks Lear's Fool (*King Lear* 1.4.223), but the cart, or tumbril, of historical events inevitably draws the hero's charger in its wake. Thus the repudiation of the fiction of historical accuracy or "objectivity," the self-delusive and far from benign assumption that the past can be recaptured without contamination from the present, has become a crucial starting point of both the Foucauldian and the deconstructive projects. For history is always in the process of deconstructing itself – of becoming, as it always was, "his-story," the story that the teller imposes upon the reconstructed events of the past.

This is not new news to the chroniclers of chroniclers. Sidney's famous description of the historian in his *Apologie for Poetrie* characterizes him as "loaden with old mouse-eaten records, authorizing himself (for the most part) upon other histories, whose greatest authorities, are built upon the notable foundation of hearsay, having much ado to accord differing writers, and to pick truth out of partiality."[44] The historian is constrained by his burden of facts; "Many times he must tell events, whereof he can yield no cause; or if he do, it must be poetical"[45] – must, that is, make the move from "fact" to fiction, "for that a feigned example, hath as much force to teach, as a true example." One of the best known passages in the *Apologie* addresses the question of theatrical fictions, mimesis, and allegoresis.

> What child is there, that coming to a play, and seeing Thebes written in great letters upon an old door, doth believe that it is

Thebes? If then a man can arrive, at that child's age, to know that the poet's persons and doings, are but pictures what should be, and not stories what have been, they will never give the lie, to things not affirmatively, but allegorically, and figuratively written. And therefore, as in history, looking for truth, they go away full fraught with falsehood; so in poesy, looking for fiction, they shall use the narration, but as an imaginative groundplot of a profitable invention.[46]

This quotation, often cited, is frequently truncated by the omission of the last sentence. Its sense seems to be that poesy – which here includes drama – is less culpable of distortion than history, because it does not pretend to objectivity. Or, to put the position somewhat differently, its distortion is the product of design. A very similar position is adumbrated in "The Use and Abuse of History," in Nietzsche's argument that the only possible "objectivity" in the framing of history comes in the work of the dramatist, who alone writes history *as* an expression of the "artistic drive" rather than as a putatively authoritative and objective record of *what was*. For drama, in Nietzsche's terms, offers

an artistically true painting but not an historically true one. To think of history objectively in this fashion is the silent work of the dramatist; that is to say, to think of all things in relation to all others and to weave the isolated event into the whole: always with the presupposition that if a unity of plan does not already reside in things it must be implanted into them. Thus man spins his web over the past and subdues it, thus he gives expression to his artistic drive – but not to his drive towards truth or justice. Objectivity and justice have nothing to do with one another.[47]

By contrast to drama all other modes of historical writing are fundamentally unsatisfactory, constructive in some ways but destructive in others. Since they are written by historical subjects in effect created by the very history they seek to document, there can be no objective or authoritative vantage point for their observations. And this point is oddly but firmly insisted upon by both Sidney and Nietzsche. Thus Sidney claims that "the best of the historian is subject to the poet; for whatsoever action, or faction, whatsoever counsel, policy, or war strategem, the historian is bound to recite, that may the poet (if he list) with his imitation make his own."[48] And Nietzsche writes that the human subject must situate himself or herself *"against history"*;[49] "if you want biographies, do not desire those who bear the legend 'Herr So-and-So and his age,' but those upon whose title-page there would stand 'a fighter against his age'."[50]

The title page of *biographies*; "the *history* of great men."[51] It is often asked about Shakespeare's *Richard III*, as about other pivotal works in the Shakespeare canon (e.g. *Julius Caesar*): is it a tragedy or is it a history? Is it, as both Quarto and Folio title pages call it, "the tragedy of Richard III," or, as the Folio classifies it, generically to be listed under the histories? Nietzsche has here uncannily provided an answer to the question of *why* this is a question: the birth of history can only be presented as the birth of tragedy.

"The Use and Abuse of History" (1874) is indeed in some sense a coda or extrapolation of Nietzsche's great study of the rise and fall of the tragic vision in ancient Greece, *The Birth of Tragedy* (1871). In that work, as Hayden White has noted, Nietzsche "lamented the decline and fall of ancient tragedy, and named the modern historical consciousness as its antitype."[52] "The Use and Abuse of History" continues this exploration of what has gone wrong, of what has been lost with the loss of the classical tragic vision.

But Nietzsche's remarks are not confined to the Greeks alone. There is another dramatist who haunts Nietzsche's text, and that dramatist, perhaps unsurprisingly, is Shakespeare. Twice he takes as his starting point what someone else has said about Shakespeare's intersection with the modern historical world. Quoting Franz Grillparzer, Nietzsche critiques the contemporary German's sensibility, developed, so he says, "from his experience in the theater. 'We feel in abstractions,' [Grillparzer] says, 'we hardly know any longer how feeling really expresses itself with our contemporaries; we show them performing actions such as they no longer perform nowadays. Shakespeare has ruined all of us moderns.' "[53] Shortly thereafter, Nietzsche quotes Goethe:

> Goethe once said of Shakespeare: "No one despised outward costume more than he; he knew very well the inner human costume, and here all are alike. They say he hit off the Romans admirably; but I don't find it so, they are all nothing but flesh-and-blood Englishmen, but they are certainly human beings, human from head to foot, and the Roman toga sits on them perfectly well."

Nietzsche takes this opportunity to condemn present-day literati and officials, who could not be portrayed as Romans

> because they are not human beings but only flesh-and-blood compendia and as it were abstractions made concrete . . . creations of historical culture, wholly structure, image, form

without demonstrable content and, unhappily, *ill-designed form* and, what is more, *uniform.* And so let my proposition be understood and pondered: *history can be borne only by strong personalities, weak ones are utterly extinguished by it* .... He who no longer dares to trust himself but involuntarily asks of history 'How ought I to feel about this?' finds that his timidity gradually turns him into an actor and that he is playing a role, usually indeed many roles and therefore playing them badly and superficially.[54]

"*Ill-designed form* and, what is more, *uniform.*" For Nietzsche the modern politician's failure lies precisely in his conformity to unthinking standards of political correctness, what Nietzsche scornfully calls "objective" standards, as if any strong personality, in his view, could be "objective" or subscribe to an "objective" reading of history. "Ill-design" for Nietzsche is thus the obverse of what it is for *Richard III.* In Shakespeare's play Richard's physical appearance, his ill-design, perversely glories in its difference from the usual, the uniform, the fully formed.

The famous scene in which he woos and wins the Lady Anne ("and will she yet abase her eyes on me ... On me, that halts and am misshapen thus?/My dukedom to a beggarly denier,/I do mistake my person all this while!/Upon my life she finds (although I cannot)/Myself to be a marv'llous proper man./I'll be at charges for a looking glass ..." [1.2.2.246–55]) displays a Richard whose narcissistic posturing translates ill-design ("misshapen thus") into "proper" or handsome appearance – and thus to *proprietary* and *appropriative* behavior, made possible by his flouting of the conventional *proprieties.*

Shakespeare appears a third time in this relatively short essay, when Nietzsche is offering a critique of the "philosophy of the unconscious" of Eduard von Hartmann. Von Hartmann's description of the "manhood of man" is ironically disparaged by a citation from Jaques's celebrated speech in *As You Like It* on the seven ages of man – a citation that not surprisingly encodes the word "history".[55]

> Last scene of all,
> That ends this strange, eventful history,
> Is second childishness, and mere oblivion,
> Sans teeth, sans eyes, sans taste, sans every thing.
>
> (2.7.163–66)

The Richard who comes into the world already provided with teeth is an apt counter-image to this toothless historical deterioration.

Yet, as these citations make clear, the power of drama as a historical force can be enfeebling as well as enabling, reducing men to actors in the very act of raising history to drama. "Overproud European," writes Nietzsche in an apostrophe that neatly deconstructs Pico's *De dignitate hominis*,

> you are raving! Your knowledge does not perfect nature, it only destroys your own nature. Compare for once the heights of your capacity for knowledge with the depths of your capacity for action. It is true you climb upon the sunbeams of knowledge up to Heaven, but you also climb down to chaos. Your manner of moving, that of climbing upon knowledge, is your fatality; the ground sinks away from you into the unknown; there is no longer any support for your life, only spider's threads which every new grasp of knowledge tears apart. – But enough of this seriousness, since it is also possible to view the matter more cheerfully.
>
> The madly thoughtless shattering and dismantling of all foundations, their dissolution into a continual evolving that flows ceaselessly away, the tireless unspinning and historicizing of all there has ever been by modern man, the great cross-spider at the node of the cosmic web – all this may concern and dismay moralists, artists, the pious, even statesmen; *we* shall for once let it cheer us by looking at it in the glittering magic mirror of a *philosophical parodist* in whose head the age has come to an ironical awareness of itself.[56]

Self-irony, proclaimed by a philosophical parodist eying history (and the construction of the human subject) in a glittering magic mirror. It is a stunning evocation of Richard III. "Shine out, fair sun, till I have bought a glass,/That I may see my shadow as I pass" (*Richard III* 1.2.262–3). Over and over again, Shakespeare's Richard Crook-back is compared to a spider, spinning plots. Queen Margaret refers to him as a "bottled spider,/Whose deadly web ensnareth thee about" (1.3.241–2), and the hapless Queen Elizabeth recalls her warning when it is too late: "O, thou didst prophesy the time would come/That I should wish for thee to help me curse/That bottled spider, that foul bunch-back'd toad!" (4.3.80–1). The Lady Anne likewise classes him with "spiders, toads,/Or any creeping venom'd thing that lives" (1.2.19–20) – even as she succumbs to his designs. Indeed Richard's father, the Duke of York, his predecessor in vengeful soliloquy, had claimed for himself the same identification: "My brain, more busy than the laboring spider,/Weaves tedious snares to trap mine enemies" (*2 Henry VI* 3.1.339–40).

Is the present afflicted or instructed by the power of tragedy to "weave the isolated event into the whole?" Can the "tireless unspinning and historicizing of all there has ever been by modern man, the great cross-spider at the node of the cosmic web" – occupied with weaving "spider's threads which every new grasp of knowledge tears apart"[57] – be seen as that which cripples as well as empowers the observer who would profit from historical models, historical example, historical textualizations? This is perhaps the question Shakespeare forces us to ask of our own ambivalent fascination with "that bottled spider/Whose deadly web ensnareth [us] about": Richard III – and *Richard III* – as the dramatization of the power of deformity inherent in both tragedy and history.

3

A Rome of one's own

"When in Rome, do as the Greeks"
Kenneth Burke, *Counter-Statement*

I begin with two modified or "fractured" quotations – quotations
that presume upon a suppressed or at least unexpressed original that
the present phrase undertakes to revise – quotations, that is, that
take the form of a pun. "A Rome of one's own"; "When in Rome,
do as the Greeks." Even without such punning superscription,
however, the use of quotation is itself always already doubled,
already belated, since it cites a voice or an opinion that gains force
from being somehow absent, authority from the fact of being set
apart. Used always "in quotation," as there and not there, true and
not true, the real thing and yet a copy, the quotation occupies the
space of a memorial reconstruction in the present plane of
discourse. Notice that we put "in quotation" in quotation marks.
This is a pictogram of how the palimpsest of authority in discourse
works. Quotation, then, is a use of history, since in a quotation
tradition and authority are simultaneously instated and put in
question. In the same way, a quotation is a ghost: a revenant taken
out of context, making an unexpected, often disconcerting appearance – the return of the expressed. Thus Walter Benjamin, perhaps
the most assiduous modern collector of quotations, writes that
"Quotations in my works are like robbers by the roadside who
make an armed attack and relieve an idler of his convictions."[1]
Surveying a world suffering the loss of both authority and tradition,
he argued that the function of quotations was "not the strength to
preserve but to cleanse, to tear out of context, to destroy."[2] The
quotation by its very presence offers a critique of the context into
which it is summoned. It stands as a qualification of the circumstances for which it is apparently so suited as to be cited in the first
place. A quotation is *always* "in quotation," always *in*appropriate
for its proper place.

What I would like to suggest here, and what has already been
suggested implicitly by the two quotations with which I began, is
that the idea of Rome is itself such a quotation. Like any instated
view of a civilization and its artifacts, the idea of Rome is from the

first belated, already a nostalgic and edited memory when it first appears.

Consider the success of a failed analogy in Freud's *Civilization and Its Discontents*. In attempting to explain the "problem of preservation in the sphere of the mind" he offers as an example "the history of the Eternal City."[3] Were a visitor to go to Rome today, he suggests, furnished with the most complete historical and geographical details of the city's past, he (or she) might find some vestiges of the oldest periods combined with later ruins, but in a place where one set of buildings had been razed to build another, there would stand only the most recent structures. Sites of ancient temples remain, mingled with the monuments of Renaissance and post-Renaissance cultures. "This is the manner in which the past is preserved in historical sites like Rome."[4]

"Now let us, by a flight of imagination, suppose that Rome is not a human habitation but a psychical entity with a similarly long and copious past – an entity, that is to say, in which nothing that has once come into existence will have passed away and all the earlier phases of development continue to exist alongside the latest one."[5] Thus the Palazzo Caffarelli would stand once more on the same site as the Temple of Jupiter Capitolinus, without either having to be removed. "Where the Coliseum now stands we could at the same time admire Nero's vanished Golden House."[6]

After elaborating this spatial/temporal fantasy for a few more sentences, Freud abandons it as a seemingly "idle game," meant to show how impossible it is to represent the characteristics of mental life in pictorial terms. Moreover, he points out, a further objection to his model might be considered. "The question may be raised why we chose precisely the past of a *city* to compare with the past of the mind."[7] In order to preserve its past intact, the mind must be undamaged by trauma or illness; but cities undergo processes of demolition and urban renewal that are very like the destructive influences of illness. "A city is thus *a priori* unsuited for a comparison of this sort with a mental organism."[8] Then why make it? Why does Freud create this elaborate comparison, then put its validity in question, and finally "bow" to his own "objection," "abandoning" the attempt to draw a striking contrast. Might it be not the general case of a city, but rather the particular case of Rome, that leads him to his analogy in the first place? For the "flight of imagination" he urges upon us is not, after all, so far-fetched. Rome *is* "not [only] a human habitation but a psychical entity," an embodiment of fantasy and desire.

We will shortly see that Freud's own writings are haunted, most specifically, by the uncanny reappearance of *Julius Caesar*. It will come as no surprise to learn that Freud himself once played the part of Brutus,[9] the introspective hero for whom "between the acting of a dreadful thing/And the first motion, all the interim is/Like a phantasma or a hideous dream./The Genius and the mortal instruments are then in council" (*Julius Caesar* 2.1.63–7).[10] This apparently gratuitous and quickly discarded idea of Rome comes to Freud in the context of a work, *Civilization and Its Discontents*, that stages the conflict between instinct and civilized repression, between the aggressive, egoistic demands of the individual and the socially and psychically nurtured sense of guilt that safeguards a civilized world. We are on the site of *Julius Caesar*, a locus to which the superego, the ghost of Caesar, comes too late to a horrified Brutus – too late to prevent the assassination and its anarchic consequences: "Now let it work" (*Julius Caesar* 3.2.260). One of the archaeological layers of Freud's Rome is Shakespeare's Rome. And in Shakespeare's plays "Rome" is self-evidently "in quotation," already idealized, historicized, and put in question.

We might consider, as an example, the specific literal quotation embedded in Shakespeare's *Julius Caesar*. "*Et tu, Brute?*" "You too, Brutus?" – or, as the Riverside edition more archaically puts it, "and thou, Brutus?" Every schoolchild knows this line, yet it is found nowhere in the works of classical authors. A passage in Suetonius (*Julius Caesar*, 82) describing the events of the assassination contains a similar sentiment, again set off by linguistic difference; in Suetonius' account, written in Latin, Caesar reproaches Brutus in Greek ("καὶ σὺ τέκνον"; "And thou, my son"). But "*Et tu, Brute?*" as a phrase is apparently a coinage of Elizabethan, rather than of Roman, culture. It first appears, perhaps significantly, in *The True Tragedie of Richard Duke of Yorke* (printed 1595): "Et tu, Brute, wilt thou stab *Caesar* too?" This same line appears in Nicholson's *Acolastus his Afterwitte* (1600), and Malone suggests that the Latin phrase was used in a lost work, the *Epilogus Caesaris Interfecti*, written by Richard Edes and acted at Oxford in 1582. "Indeed," as T. S. Dorsch suggests, "it seems to have become something of a stage commonplace."[11] Ben Jonson makes a joke of it in *Every Man Out of His Humour* (5.6.79); *Caesar's Revenge* (c.1594) has "What, Brutus too?"; and in the tragic story of Julius Caesar added to *A Mirror for Magistrates* in 1587[12] there occurs a version of the same line: "And Brutus thou my sonne (quoth I) whom erst I loued best?" Shakespeare makes sure that his own audience will be ready for this famous floating tag line, not only by the dramatic situation, but also by providing Caesar with a tongue twister of a lead-in: "Doth not Brutus bootless kneel?" (3.1.75).

When it is finally uttered in Shakespeare's play, the quotation "*Et tu, Brute?*" thus appears to be a survival, a remnant of authentic Romanness, a sign of origin. Yet, as we have just noticed, it is precisely *not* that. "*Et tu, Brute?*" is a quotation of a quotation, a quotation which has *always* been "in quotation," ultimately a quotation of nothing. It is instead a back-formation from Elizabethan literary culture, a "genuine antique reproduction."

We could make much the same observation about another key moment in the text, a moment which, like "*Et tu, Brute?*," is from the first in quotation. I refer, of course, to the dramatic reenactment of the assassination in after years as it is envisaged by Brutus and Cassius immediately before the act takes place on the stage. Here the genuine antique reproduction is imagined as re-production, as a restaging of this scene by later actors, for later audiences – like the one that first attended Shakespeare's *Tragedy of Julius Caesar.*

Brutus.	Stoop, Romans, stoop,
	And let us bathe our hands in Caesar's blood
	Up to the elbows, and besmear our swords;
	Then walk we forth, even to the market-place,
	And waving our red weapons o'er our heads,
	Let's all cry, Peace, freedom, and liberty!
Cassius.	Stoop then, and wash. How many ages hence
	Shall this our lofty scene be acted over
	In states unborn and accents yet unknown!
Brutus.	How many times shall Caesar bleed in sport,
	That now on Pompey's basis lies along
	No worthier than the dust!
Cassius.	So oft as that shall be,
	So often shall the knot of us be call'd
	The men that gave their country liberty.

(3.1.105–18)

Jonathan Goldberg comments on this much-noticed scene that

the 'now' in this performance demands that it refer to the real event, not the stage one. Yet, in fact, the lines are about that performance, too, and the claims upon an audience that they can make. They can make us believe that the staged event is real. The 'acting over,' the representation before our eyes, may be taken for the act itself; and perhaps what the perfect reciprocity of the metaphor hints is that history itself may be a series of representations. The acts on the stage of history in Brutus' formulation embody power in a form of transcendent constancy; events recur but do not change, unique events are acted over.[13]

Julius Caesar shows us the second time, and not the first, a representation of a representation. The "now" of Shakespeare's play already points to a ghostly "then." Brutus and Cassius imagine a time when their words, gestures and actions will be both quoted and imitated, and they imagine, as well, the context and effect of that quotation. Within the play this is immediately ironic; they are not portrayed, nor are they immediately received, as men who give their country liberty. But the subversiveness of this moment within the play undergoes a double reversal in history, following the function ascribed to quotation by Benjamin: "not the strength to preserve but to cleanse, to tear out of context, to destroy." To see how this works in history, to see how great Caesar's ghost is set loose by the play's own contextualizing gestures, it may be helpful to return for a moment to Walter Benjamin.

One of Benjamin's "Theses on the Philosophy of History" begins with a quotation from Karl Kraus that also bears on this discussion: "Origin is the goal." Benjamin then goes on to assess the belatedness of historical constructions and the particular consuming passion of the French Revolution for the idea of Rome.

> History is the subject of a structure whose site is not homo-geneous, empty time, but time filled by the presence of the now [*Jetztzeit*]. Thus, to Robespierre ancient Rome was a past charged with the time of the now which he blasted out of the continuum of history. The French Revolution viewed itself as Rome reincarnate. It evoked ancient Rome the way fashion evokes costumes of the past. Fashion has a flair for the topical, no matter where it stirs in the thickets of long ago; it is a tiger's leap into the past. This jump, however, takes place in an arena where the ruling class gives the commands. The same leap in the open air of history is the dialectical one, which is how Marx understood the revolution.[14]

Notice Benjamin's phrase, "Rome reincarnate." The ghost of ancient Rome, the dislocation into history of the assassinated Caesar presents itself as at once an uncanny *flâneur* of revolution and a revenger *of* – as well as *from* – the past. The appropriation of Rome by the French Revolution, and particularly the appropriation of the moment of the assassination by self-styled "men who gave their country liberty" is an old story. But it was an old story even when it was new.

"How Marx understood the revolution" – dialectically. Marx begins *The Eighteenth Brumaire of Louis Bonaparte* with a famous observation about history and genre: "Hegel remarks somewhere that all facts and personages of great importance in world history occur, as it were, twice. He forgot to add: "the first time as tragedy, the second as farce."[15] Farce is the *Aufhebung* of tragedy. Marx encodes the theatrical metaphor:

> Men make their own history, but they do not make it just as they please; they do not make it under circumstances chosen by themselves, but under circumstances directly encountered, given and transmitted from the past. The tradition of all the dead generations weighs like a nightmare on the brain of the living. And just when they seem engaged in revolutionizing themselves and things, in creating something that has never yet existed, precisely in such periods of revolutionary crisis they anxiously conjure up the spirits of the past to their service and borrow from them names, battle cries and costumes in order to present the new scene of world history in this time-honoured disguise and this borrowed language.[16]

Here, and in the passages that follow in *The Eighteenth Brumaire*, Marx might almost be directly commenting on the scene from Shakespeare's *Julius Caesar* which we have just considered, the scene in which Cassius and Brutus foresee the reenactment of their own revolutionary deed, and its interpretation in the eyes of history. Like Benjamin, Marx stresses the role of costume and role, not only of the heroes, but also of the "parties and the masses of the old French Revolution, [who] performed the task of their time in Roman costume and with Roman phrases."[17]

> The new social formation once established, the antediluvian Colossi disappeared and with them resurrected Romanity – the Brutuses, Gracchi, Publicolas, the tribunes, the senators, and Caesar himself . . . unheroic as bourgeois society is, it nevertheless took heroism, sacrifice, terror, civil war and battles of peoples to bring it into being. And in the classically austere traditions of the Roman republic its gladiators found the ideals and the art forms, the self-deceptions that they needed in order to conceal from themselves the bourgeois limitations of the content of their struggles and to keep their enthusiasm on the high plane of the great historical tragedy. Similarly, at another stage of development, a century earlier, Cromwell and the English people had borrowed speech, passions, and illusions from the Old Testament for their bourgeois revolution.[18]

The insistent presence of the theatrical metaphor throughout this passage is suggestive. Desiring to represent their actions in terms of historical tragedy, bourgeois revolutionaries – according to Marx's script – costume themselves in the roles of historical precedent, the trappings and the suits of woe – and of wonder. Throughout this section of *The Eighteenth Brumaire*, Marx's references are uncannily pertinent to Shakespeare's English history plays, and also – indeed, particularly – to *Julius Caesar*.

> Thus the awakening of the dead in those revolutions served the purpose of glorifying the new struggles, not of parodying the old; of magnifying the given task in imagination, not fleeing from its resolution in reality; of finding once more the spirit of revolution, not of making its ghost walk about again.
>   From 1848 to 1851 only the ghost of the old revolution walked about . . .[19]

In Marx, the calling up of the spirits of Rome (Brutus, etc.) to authorize a revolution is a repetition, but the rhetorical calling up of such personified spirits of Rome is already what Brutus is doing in Shakespeare. In other words, the so-called original is already a figure.

Something very similar happens in the way Nietzsche regards Julius Caesar – not so much as a historical, but rather as a literary personage, and specifically, a Shakespearean construct. As Alexander Nehamas observes,

> When [Nietzsche] writes that in the greatest human beings we find the most powerfully conflicting instincts under control, his example is none other than Shakespeare – that is to say, Shakespeare's plays (*The Will to Power*, 966). Even when he praises Julius Caesar as the "most beautiful type" of the character that contains "inexorable and fearful instincts that provoke the maximum of authority and discipline among themselves" (*Twilight of the Idols*, IX, 39) we must not assume without question that he is thinking of Caesar as a historical figure. Rather, we must recall that he writes, "When I seek my ultimate formula for *Shakespeare*, I only find this: he conceived of the type of Caesar" (*Ecce Homo*, II, 4), who therefore turns out to be himself a literary character.[20]

Here, once again, a ghostly, hypothetical, and contingent idea of "Shakespeare" informs and begets a literary construction of Julius Caesar, a construction so powerful that it displaces, in Nietzsche's own writing, the merely historical, the putative original. Shakespeare "conceived of the type of Caesar"; Nietzsche conceives of the type of Shakespeare who possesses the "authority and discipline" to do so.

"Why com'st thou?" demands a terrified Brutus in Shakespeare's play, and the Ghost replies, "To tell thee thou shalt see me at

Philippi" (4.3.282–3). This is the counter-plot, the plot of the new author taking charge, the "ghost of the old revolution," already dislocated, set loose. Brutus's impassioned apostrophe at the death of Cassius, "O Julius Caesar, thou art mighty yet!/Thy spirit walks abroad, and turns our swords/In our own proper entrails" (5.3.94–6), marks the recognition of the Ghost as the true author of this play of historical differences. The apostrophe conjures the appearance of the Ghost even when its form is not physically present, conjures it in fact *because* it is not present, marking presence through absence. Were Caesar alive he would not provide the motivation for these suicides, the revenge against the self that actuates both Brutus and Cassius. "The ghost of Caesar hath appear'd to me/Two several times by night," Brutus advises his friends, "at Sardis once,/And this last night, here in Philippi fields./I know my hour is come" (5.5.17–20). Caesar, and not Caesarism, is the playwright of Shakespeare's *Tragedy of Julius Caesar*, a play whose revisionary, self-revising generic status remains tantalizingly in question. What is the *Aufhebung* between tragedy and history? Does the play not present itself *initially* as farce – as, that is, an already belated tragedy, a tragedy in quotation? Visualize once again the spectacle of Brutus and Cassius waving their bloody hands about, as they intone "Peace, freedom and liberty." The ghost of the old revolution is present before the ghost of Caesar ever appears.

The ghost of Caesar. "Great Caesar's ghost!" – another quotation that is not a quotation, a phrase that appears nowhere in Shakespeare's play. The phrase, of course, is that of Perry White, the editor of *The Daily Planet*, a twentieth-century Globe. And what does editor White see in his mind's eye when he invokes the name of Caesar? Why, a situation that calls for – perhaps has already called for – Superman. It is not surprising to find Nietzsche, like Marx, concerned with the dramatization of revolution, and the specific model of Rome as exemplar of the way in which the concept of historical reenactment can inhibit the development of a pragmatic sense of historical possibility in the present. If we look once again at the passage cited in Chapter 2, in which Nietzsche quotes Goethe on Shakespeare and the Romans, we will notice that he adds a further qualification to Goethe's critique:

Goethe once said of Shakespeare: "No one despised outward costume more than he; he knew very well the inner human costume, and here all are alike. They say he hit off the Romans admirably; but I don't find it so, they are all nothing but flesh-and-blood Englishmen, but they are certainly human beings, human from head to foot, and the Roman toga sits on them

perfectly well." Now I ask whether it would be possible to
represent our contemporary men of letters, popular figures,
officials or politicians as Romans; it simply would not work,
because they are not human beings but only flesh-and-blood
compendia and as it were abstractions made concrete... not
men, not gods, not animals, but creations of historical culture ...
Gradually all congruity between the man and his historical
domain is lost; we behold pert little fellows associating with the
Romans as though they were their equals."[21]

"You blocks, you stones, you worse than senseless things!" the
tribune Marullus excoriates the plebeians. "O you hard hearts, you
cruel men of Rome,/Knew you not Pompey?" (*Julius Caesar*
1.1.35–7) Nietzsche's uniform and superficial "creations of historical
culture" are already present here in Shakespeare's "men of Rome,"
the plebeians so easily swayed by the political passions and fashions
of the moment, forgetful of the recent past and of their previous
allegiances. We might observe that Mark Antony will flatter these
same plebeians from the rostrum at Caesar's funeral by reversing
this very formulation, almost as if he has overheard the opening
scene: "It is not meet you know how Caesar lov'd you;/You are not
wood, you are not stones, but men;/And being men, hearing the
will of Caesar,/It will inflame you, it will make you mad"
(3.2.141–4). Nietzsche distinguishes at least in part between the
strong personalities of history, the Antonys and Cassiuses (and
Caesars), and "pert little fellows associating with the Romans as
though they were their equals." But in Shakespeare's play even the
Romans – even the *noble* Romans – are pert little fellows playing
many roles. Brutus and Cassius posture for posterity, and mis-
conceive their audience. The heroic motivations each is so anxious
to attach to his deed of murder are already undercut by previous
events, previous ruminations, in the play.

The more we observe this entire phenomenon of the belatedness
of the idea of Rome, the clearer it becomes that it is closely tied to
the figure of the ghost of Caesar – with that "strong personality," to
use Nietzsche's phrase, who can bear history rather than being
extinguished by it. There is a sense in which the ghost of Caesar *is*
the idea of Rome, dislocated in its very act of coming into being,
deriving its power from the very fact of its retrospection. The ghost
of Caesar is always lurking in any configuration of Romanness,
always on the margins of any Roman representation, unflappable,
imperturbable, robustly absent.

Always absent. The ghost of Caesar is in a sense absent from the
beginning, since its identity is far from clear even in Plutarch.

North's translation speaks of "the ghost that appeared unto Brutus" at the beginning of the *Life of Caesar*, but the narrative itself deliberately eschews precise identification in favor of spectral suggestiveness. Brutus, lying awake,

> thought he heard a noise at his tent-door, and looking toward the light of the lamp that waxed very dim, he saw a horrible vision of a man, of a wonderful greatness and dreadful look, which at the first made him marvellously afraid. But when he saw that it did him no hurt, but stood by the bed-side and said nothing; at length he asked him what he was. The image answered him: "I am thy ill angel, Brutus, and thou shalt see me by the city of Philippes." Then Brutus replied again, and said, "Well, I shall see thee then." Therewithal the spirit presently vanished from him .... The second battle being at hand, the spirit appeared again unto him, but spake never a word. Thereupon Brutus, knowing that he should die, did put himself to all hazard in battle .... [22]

The *Life of Brutus* repeats the same story almost verbatim:

> Brutus, lying in his tent, saw a wonderful strange and monstrous shape of a body coming towards him, and said never a word. So Brutus boldly asked what he was, a god or a man, and what cause brought him thither? The spirit answered him, "I am thy evil spirit, Brutus, and thou shalt see me by the city of Philippes." Brutus being no otherwise afraid, replied again unto it: "Well, then I shall see thee again." The spirit presently vanished away; and Brutus called his men unto him, who told him that they heard no noise, nor saw anything at all. Thereupon Brutus returned again to think on his matters as he did before. [23]

The word "ghost" itself, although it is found in the speech-prefixes of the Folio, appears only twice in the spoken text of *Julius Caesar*, and in its first instance (Cassius's despairing observation that the army lies "ready to give up the ghost" [5.1.88]) does not refer to the spectral figure of Caesar. It is only on the eve of Brutus's death, at the very end of the play, that the nocturnal visitant is identified, and read as an omen of death: "The ghost of Caesar hath appear'd to me/Two several times by night," says Brutus, "At Sardis once, and this last night, here in Philippi fields./I know my hour is come" (5.5.17–20). By delaying the appearance of the word "ghost" until the eleventh hour, the play emphasizes its questionable nature. *Is* it the ghost of Caesar? What does it mean, that it should call itself "thy evil spirit, Brutus"? Are the two things, as they seem to be, the same? The nature of ghosts is to be thus in question, to serve as catalysts for doubt, guilt, self-examination. But the degree to which this ghost is an embodiment (or disembodiment) of Brutus's own guilty conscience raises, as well, the whole question of the uncanny – the return of the repressed. "For this uncanny is in reality nothing new or foreign, but something familiar and oldestablished in the mind that has been estranged only by the process of repression."[24] And *Rome*, Caesar's Rome, is the "something repressed which recurs."

In his essay on "The Uncanny," Freud goes out of his way to explain that theatrical ghosts are *not* necessarily manifestations of the peculiar and disorienting phenomenon he is describing.

> The souls in Dante's *Inferno*, or the ghostly apparitions in *Hamlet, Macbeth*, or *Julius Caesar*, may be gloomy and terrible enough, but they are no more really uncanny than is Homer's jovial world of gods. We order our judgment to the imaginary reality imposed on us by the writer, and regard souls, spirits and spectres as though their existence had the same validity in their world as our own has in the external world. And then in this case too we are spared all trace of the uncanny.[25]

Here Freud is making an important distinction between fictional constructs that occupy the same imaginative terrain, constructs not more or less imagined because they are termed ghosts rather than men or women, and true uncanniness, which arises from a slippage in expectation. "As soon as the writer pretends to move in the world of common reality," he says, "he takes advantage, as it were, of our supposedly surmounted superstitiousness; he deceives us into thinking that he is giving us the sober truth, and then after all oversteps the bounds of possibility."[26] If the ghost breaks or oversteps the frame, violating the implicit contract with reader or audience, then it becomes – or might become – uncanny. If, on the other hand, the characters identified as ghosts have neither more nor less fictional "reality" than their purportedly living counterparts, there can be no slippage, and therefore, no sensation of the return of the repressed, of the unconscious stalking the reader or spectator. Thus "in fairy-stories feelings of fear – including uncanny sensations – are ruled out altogether."[27] If the ground rules encode fantasy, the fantastic will not take us aback.

Like Horatio's reassurance to the terrified sentries, "Tush, tush, 'twill not appear" (*Hamlet* 1.1.30), this would, however, be more compelling as a universal distinction if the ghost did not immediately make his appearance, forcing Horatio to acknowledge that "this thing" (22) is "something more than fantasy" (54).

What happens when the ghost, safely ensconced in his play as a dramatic character among others, not only strikes those that look upon him with fear, but breaks the bounds of his play? Brutus describes the uncanny sensation of the conspirators when he learns of the deaths by suicide of Cassius and Titinius: "O Julius Caesar, thou art mighty yet!/Thy spirit walks abroad, and turns our swords/In our own proper entrails" (*Julius Caesar* 5.3.94–6). Although the ghost may not appear immediately as uncanny to the audience in the theater – since it is one costumed actor among others – it does raise the whole question of uncanniness: it puts the uncanny in quotation.

That the ghost of Caesar *is* in Freud's sense uncanny to Brutus seems clear from the first interchange between them in Brutus's tent neare Sardis, in Act 4 scene 3. Shakespeare borrows much of his language from North's Plutarch, but adds some characteristic markers of uncanniness associated with such spectral confrontations in other plays:

Brutus.	Ha! Who comes here?
	I think it is the weakness of mine eyes
	That shapes this monstrous apparition
	It comes upon me. Art thou any thing?
	Art thou some god, some angel, or some devil,
	That mak'st my blood cold, and my hair to stare?
	Speak to me what thou art.
Ghost.	Thy evil spirit, Brutus.
Brutus.	Why com'st thou?
Ghost.	To tell thee thou shalt see me at Philippi.
Brutus.	Well; then I shall see thee again?
Ghost.	Ay, at Philippi.
Brutus.	Why, I will see thee at Philippi then
	[Exit Ghost]
	Now I have taken heart thou vanishest.
	Ill spirit, I would hold more talk with thee.
	(4.3.275–87)

Like Horatio and the sentries, Brutus calls the apparition a "thing"; like Macbeth imagining the "horrid image" of the murder of Duncan, he feels his hair begin to stare. His physiological rationalization ("I think it is the weakness of mine eyes/That shapes this monstrous apparition") half-discloses the truth, that this "thing" is "thy evil spirit, Brutus," generated in some sense by his actions and his guilt. Earlier Cassius had engaged him in a politic discussion of optics that diagnosed this "weakness of [the] eyes": "Tell me, good Brutus, can you see your face?" *Brutus.* "No,

Cassius; for the eye sees not itself/But by reflection, by some other things" (1.2.51–3). Cassius elected for himself the role of Brutus's "glass," to "modestly discover" to him "That of yourself which you yet know not of" (69–70). But the "other things" that can inform the eye include the ghost of Caesar, a figment not yet dreamt of in Cassius's philosophy.

Freud has direct recourse to Shakespeare's *Julius Caesar* on another occasion, and once again his responses and observations are directly germane to the question of the uncanny absent presence of the ghost as a figure for the elusive and desirable idea of Rome. The context is a dream he recounts in *The Interpretation of Dreams*. Freud describes sitting at a small table with two friends, one of whom he knew in his waking mind to be dead at the time of the dream's occurrence. The first friend fell to discussing his sister, describing her as recently dead, and making some such remark as "that was the threshold." When the second friend failed to respond, Freud (in the dream) attempted to explain that he was unable to do so because he was not alive. But Freud spoke in Latin, and misspoke, saying "*non vixit*" ("he did not live") rather than "*non vivit*" ("he is not living"). He then gave the deceased man a piercing look, under which glance he melted away, and (in the dream) he realized that the other man, too, was a revenant, an apparition, one who has returned from another place, and that "people of that kind only existed as long as one liked and could be got rid of if someone else wished it."[28]

Through a characteristic series of interpretative moves, Freud then recalls that the word "*vixit*" was inscribed on the Kaiser Josef Memorial, lamenting the Kaiser's untimely death. The dead friend in the dream was also named Josef, and also died young after a brilliant early career in science. He traces an ambivalence in himself toward this friend, which he finds perfectly expressed in Brutus's speech of self-justification in Shakespeare's *Julius Caesar* (3.2.), "As Caesar loved me, I weep for him; as he was fortunate, I rejoice at it; as he was valiant, I honour him; but, as he was ambitious, I slew him." Freud then observes that he had been playing the part of Brutus in his dream, and connects the name of *Kaiser* Josef with Caesar, and the month in which the dream was set, July, with the name of Julius. "Strange to say," he goes on, "I really once did play the part of Brutus. I once acted in the scene between Brutus and Caesar from Schiller [*Die Räuber*] before an audience of children." Reconstructing this memory, Freud recalls that his acting partner was a nephew, one year older than himself. "He had come to us on a visit from England; and he, too, was a *revenant*, for it was the playmate of my earliest years who had returned in him." A further association leads to the recovery of a linguistic link between "*non vixit*" and the word "*wichsen*," ("to hit") uttered about his nephew in childhood, and the dream of the dead man at the table is uncovered as, at least in part, a story about his childhood. Perhaps significantly, in reassessing his relationship with the nephew, Freud writes that "There must have been times when he treated me very badly and I must have shown courage in the face of my *tyrant*."[29]

Now, this dream about the formidable figure who not only was not living but did not, or had never, lived ("*non vixit*") suggests something interesting about the status of the revenant, the one who returns. It is intrinsically the *idea* of such a person, in contradistinction to his palpable or historical reality, that exercises so powerful an effect upon the memory. Though Freud does not say so in so many words, the ghost of Caesar is another revenant here, "slain" by Freud's piercing glance in the dream, the "tyrant" rival vanquished for his ambition, desiring what the young Freud had also desired. The dead friend and the long-lost nephew are both imagined as revenants who "only exist for just so long as one likes and should be removable at a wish."[30] The latent content of his dream leads his mind in two contrary directions: "No one is irreplaceable!" on the one hand, and on the other, "There are nothing but *revenants*: all those we have lost come back!"[31] In formulating these two thoughts, he places himself once more in the role of Brutus. The first sentiment is that of Brutus before the assassination; the second the experience of Brutus after Caesar's death. But where Freud in his dream is able to be the instrument of the annihilation of the revenant-rival, in Shakespeare's play the annihilating gaze works in the opposite fashion, and Caesar's ghost vanquishes the "weakness of [Brutus's] eyes," the sight of the revenant disheartens the living friend, and leads him ultimately to suicide.

We might consider in this context the personification of the idea of Rome produced by Brutus's reading of the letter thrown in at his closet window in 2.1.46–8. As I have discussed above (Chapter 1) Brutus's "piec[ing] out" of the lacunae in the letter reflects his own desire to be the object of Rome's general and disinterested affections, not the comrade of a mortal, identifiable, and therefore potentially fallible and envious co-conspirator like Cassius, who has in fact caused these "writings" "in several hands" (1.2.318; 316) to be inscribed and anonymously delivered. Brutus's language, as he reads and rereads the letter, sounds curiously like that of a lover who has received a much-desired request for service: "O Rome, I make thee promise,/If the redress will follow, thou receivest/Thy full petition at the hand of Brutus!" (56–8). The "hand" of Brutus, the writing hand that fills in the blanks, the crucial absences in the text, will enable him to become Rome's champion. His wife Portia is not entirely mistaken when she complains that he "ungently/Stole from [her] bed" (237–8). There *is* another passion in his life. Brutus's other symptoms, as Portia reports them, likewise resemble those of a lovesick adolescent almost as much as they do a man of troubled conscience; at supper he "suddenly arose, and walk'd about,/Musing and sighing, with [his] arms across" (238–40), he "walk[s] unbrac'd and suck[s] up the humors of the dank morning" (262–3). His behavior, in other words, recalls that of other Shakespearean heroes rightly or wrongly diagnosed as suffering from the pangs of love – Hamlet, whose "unbraced" appearance was read by Polonius, as "the very ecstasy of love" (2.1.99); and even Romeo, wandering at dawn, "adding to clouds more clouds with his deep sighs" (*Romeo and Juliet* 1.1.133). But Brutus's letter reading might remind us, as well, of another Shakespearean recipient of an anonymous letter, one who likewise imagines himself to be the chosen beloved, fulfilling his fondest dream of passion and power: Malvolio. The gaps in Mavolio's letter are as easily pieced out as are the ones left for Brutus to supply; all that is needed is a conviction about the author's identity and intention. Apparently written within a year or two of one another, *Twelfth Night* and *Julius Caesar* offer two very similar scenes of reading, which are also, simultaneously, scenes of writing – of ghost writing. Malvolio, too, thinks he can identify the "sweet Roman hand" (*Twelfth Night* 3.4.28). The crucial factor in each is the beloved's absence. For in the case of Brutus there can be no mistake; Rome is his beloved, his fantasy object, always just out of reach. It is only when he kills Caesar that Rome is finally reified for him, and appears to reproach him. That Rome *is* the ghost of Caesar – that the ghost of Caesar embodies in disembodied form the idea of Rome – is Brutus horrified discovery, and his undoing.

Earlier in the play Cassius, ruminating on the power of names, had sought to convince Brutus that *his* name, with its crucial history, its noble Roman predecessor, was as powerful a talisman as Caesar's:

> Brutus and Caesar: what should be in that "Caesar"?
> Why should that name be sounded more than yours?
> Write them together, yours is as fair a name:
> Sound them, it does become the mouth as well;
> Weigh them, it is as heavy; conjure with 'em,
> "Brutus" will start a spirit as soon as "Caesar." (1.2.142–7)

But will they come when you do call to them? The irony here

would seem to be that Cassius errs so disastrously in this last point –
that the name of "Caesar" does start a spirit: his own. Yet is it
"Caesar" or "Brutus" that starts the spirit – "thy evil spirit,
Brutus?" The openness of the question – what does the "thing," the
"monstrous apparition" look like? why does it identify itself not as
Julius Caesar but as Brutus's evil spirit? Is it some god, some angel
or some devil? – the play's deliberate refusal to close and foreclose
these open questions until the eve of Brutus's death increases the
horror of the experience for both Brutus and the audience, but it
does something else as well: it reifies the ghost *as* absence, as the
space of phantasm, undecidability, desire, and dread.

A Rome of one's own. The homonym *room/Rome* occurs twice
in the play. Cassius complains passionately to Brutus, "When could
they say, till now, that talk'd of Rome,/That her wide walks
encompass'd but one man?/Now is it Rome indeed and room
enough,/When there is in it but one only man" (1.2.154–7). After
the assassination, Antony sends word to the man who will become
the new Caesar: "here is a mourning Rome, a dangerous Rome,/No
Rome of safety for Octavius yet" (3.1.288–9). G. L. Kittredge
remarks of Cassius's play on words, "Here (as often) the pun
expresses contempt: 'Rome!' ay, it is rightly named *Room*, for
there's only one MAN in it!' "[32] But the room to roam, indeed the
license to roam, in Rome and beyond, is precisely the prerogative
taken by the ghost of Caesar. The dislocation of the ghost begins
with the assassination – and with it begins the dislocation of Rome.

It is Brutus, after all, who declares so forcefully to the
conspirators the inseparability of body and spirit:

> We all stand up against the spirit of Caesar,
> And in the spirit of men there is no blood;
> O that we then could come by Caesar's spirit
> And not dismember Caesar! But, alas,
> Caesar must bleed for it! (2.1.167–70)

To come by Caesar's spirit will, as he is shortly to discover, be all
too easy. The dismemberment of Caesar, however, configures itself
not only in the discourse of politics (dis-membering the body
politic, denying precisely that equality of membership the conspirators are eager to safeguard) but also in the language of the uncanny.
"Dismembered limbs, a severed head, a hand cut off at the wrist, all
these have something peculiarly uncanny about them, especially
when . . . they prove able to move of themselves in addition."[33]

The canny conspirators urge that Caesar's death be also the
occasion for the death of Mark Antony, and Brutus roundly
disputes with them:

> Our course will seem too bloody, Caius Cassius,
> To cut the head off and then hack the limbs –
> Like wrath in death and envy afterwards;
> For Antony is but a limb of Caesar . . . .
> And for Mark Antony, think not of him;
> For he can do more than Caesar's arm
> When Caesar's head is off. (2.1.162–5; 180–3)

"To cut the head off and then hack the limbs"; "For he can do no more than Caesar's arm/When Caesar's head is off." We may remember that the place of the assassination, the Capitol, was said to have received its name from the circumstance of a human head (*caput*) being discovered at its summit when the foundations were laid for the Temple of Jupiter. The dismemberment puns that literalize themselves so appallingly in *Titus Andronicus* ("And help to set a head on headless Rome," 1.1.186) may be in part provoked by this same archaeological and etymological circumstance.[34] Decapitated at the Capitol, Caesar in his death brings to a head all the disaffection that lies just beneath the surface in Rome. The head cut off, Brutus's rhetorical display instigates the process of Caesar's uncanny reappearance; not only his "spirit" but his "limb" will take on a life of its own, in Antony's moving oration, and in his anarchic pleasure in further dismemberment:

> A curse shall light upon the limbs of men;
> Domestic fury and fierce civil strife
> Shall cumber all the parts of Italy;
> Blood and destruction shall be so in use,
> And dreadful objects so familiar,
> That mothers shall but smile when they behold
> Their infants quartered with the hands of war;
> All pity chok'd with custom of fell deeds;
> And Caesar's spirit, ranging for revenge,
> With Ate at his side come hot from hell,
> Shall in these confines with a monarch's voice
> Cry "Havoc!" and let slip the dogs of war . . . . (3.1.262–73)

"Caesar's spirit, ranging for revenge" thus is let slip by the action of the conspirators. After his death, and only then, can Caesar with impunity declare himself "with a monarch's voice." Ironically the conspirators achieve exactly the converse of their object. By killing Caesar they achieve his dissemination through "all the parts of Italy," and free him as well to play many parts, not only in this play, or indeed in other Shakespearean plays, but throughout history.

Once dead, the disembodied spirit of Julius Caesar cannot be contained. Dismembered, it becomes a cast member in numerous other plays. As the monstrous apparition that appears in his tent is uncanny to Brutus, so the ghost of Caesar leaves its uncanny trace all over the Shakespearean corpus. " 'Tis here, 'tis here, 'tis gone."

The ghost, not surprisingly, precedes the play that bears its name. It is from the first belated. The first part of *Henry VI* begins with the funeral of the previous and much lamented monarch, and at once his eulogist, the Duke of Bedford, links the king's ghost with that of Caesar:

> Henry the Fifth, thy ghost I invoke.
> Prosper this realm, keep it from civil broils,
> Combat with adverse planets in the heavens!
> A far more glorious star thy soul will make
> Than Julius Caesar or bright – (1.1.52–5)

At this point, perhaps inevitably, a messenger arrives with the news that France has been lost. We might encode a stage direction "[Enter Ghost]." The Duke of Gloucester remarks despairingly that "If Henry were recall'd to life again,/These news would cause him once more yield the ghost" (65–7). The assassination of Caesar is in fact invoked throughout the first tetralogy as the benchmark of treacherous action used to measure the enormity of the murders of Suffolk and of Margarete's son, the Prince of Wales.

A more palpable trace of Julis Caesar, at once, to use Freud's phrase, a "human habitation and a psychical entity," is invested in the relic he *is* said to have left behind him in England – the Tower of London. Thus in *Richard III* Buckingham and the young Prince Edward engage in an edifying discussion of historical record and the currency of rumor – just the kind of rumor "let slip" by Caesar's own life, career, and death. The young Prince has just been consigned to the Tower by his uncle, Richard of Gloucester, and he protests:

Prince.	I do not like the Tower, of any place. Did Julius Caesar build that place, my lord?
Buckingham.	He did, my gracious lord, begin that place, Which, since, succeeding ages have re-edified.
Prince.	Is it upon record, or else reported Successively from age to age, he built it?
Buckingham.	Upon record, my gracious lord.

Prince.   But say, my lord, it were not register'd,
                 Methinks the truth should live from age
                 to age,
                 As 'twere retailed to all posterity,
                 Even to the general all-ending day . . . .
Prince.   That Julius Caesar was a famous man:
                 With what his valor did enrich his wit,
                 His wit set down to make his valure live.
                 Death makes no conquest of this con-
                 queror,
                 For now he lives in fame though not in
                 life. (*Richard III* 3.1.68–78; 84–8)

Prince Edward is on his way to becoming a murdered martyr, much as befell Caesar. Caesar "lives in fame though not in life," ("O Julius Caesar, thou art mighty yet") just as will the princes in the tower. The discussion of historical transmission ("registered" – i.e., written down, versus "reported," i.e., passed on orally from age to age) is another model for the survival of Caesar's ghost. Shakespeare's tragedy of *Julius Caesar* may have begun the edification of the Caesar story, and in quite a different way from that envisaged by Cassius and Brutus in Act 3 scene 1, but the dissemination of great Caesar's ghost through history – in, for example, the writings of Marx and Nietzsche – has re-edified his spirit "in succeeding ages."

The Tower of London makes its baneful appearance again in *Richard II*, where the Queen calls it "Julius Caesar's ill-erected tower," the place to which King Richard is briefly sent before he is redirected to Pomfret and to his death. By the time of *Cymbeline*, where the context is ancient Britain rather than the recent history of England, the ghostly authority of Julius Caesar is fully instated. As many commentators have pointed out, the events of *Cymbeline* are framed by the Incarnation, the "time of universal peace" when, under the Emperor Augustus, the Christ child is born. The memory of "Julius Caesar (whose remembrance yet/Lives in men's eyes, and will to ears and tongues/Be theme and hearing ever)" (*Cymbeline* 3.1.2–4) haunts both the generals of Augustan Rome and the Britons, though Cymbeline's Queen cites with scorn Caesar's most celebrated act of political self-promotion: "A kind of conquest/Caesar made here, but made not here his brag/Of "Came, saw, and overcame" (3.1.22–4). Like Rosalind, who also finds occasion to cite this "thrasonical brag" (*As You Like It* 5.2.31–2) the queen establishes Caesar's dominance as a coiner of military slogans and a chronicler of his own history – as, in essence, his own self-inscriber. Caesar as ghost, and Caesar as ghost writer, together haunt the precincts of these plays.

As we might expect, the prowess of "Julius Caesar,/Who at Philippi the good Brutus ghosted" (*Antony and Cleopatra* 2.6.12–13) ghosts the young men of the succeeding generation in *Antony and Cleopatra*. Egypt is the place where "Julius Caesar/Grew fat with feeding" (*Antony and Cleopatra* 2.6.64–5); "Apollodorus carried . . . A certain queen to Caesar in a mattress" (68–70); and Cleopatra's power is measured by the fact that "she made great Caesar lay his sword to bed" (2.2.227). Julius Caesar, as father, sexual rival, political precursor, is everywhere in these young men's imaginations; he is the powerfully invisible figure against whom not only young Pompey but also Octavius and Antony assess themselves. As Janet Adelman points out, "however much Shakespeare may have challenged the grandeur of Julius Caesar in *Julius Caesar*, he is 'great Caesar' or 'broad-fronted Caesar' in this play, an almost mythic figure who towers over the generation of his heir."[35] Manifestly, Caesar is more powerful in his absence than in his presence.

When, as happens in several of Shakespeare's plays, the name of Caesar becomes a synonym for "ruler" (e.g., *3 Henry VI* 3.1.18; *The Merry Wives of Windsor* 1.3.9–10; *2 Henry IV* 2.4.166), Cassius's and Brutus's notion of the verdict of history ("so often shall the knot of us be call'd/The men that gave our country liberty") is given the lie. For in the historical transmission carried on not only by but also within Shakespeare's plays themselves, Julius Caesar is mighty yet. He inspires the prologue in *Henry V* to compare the return of that warrior king to the welcome "conqu'ring Caesar" received from senators and plebeians in "th'antique Rome" (5. Prologue. 26–8). His name gives point to the otherwise pointless-seeming name of the bawd Pompey in *Measure for Measure* ("Pompey, I shall beat you to your tent, and prove a shrewd Caesar to you" 2.1.248–9). He forms the standard of martial valor for Iago's mischievous rhetoric (*Othello* 2.3.122). Whether as conqueror, as author of the commentaries (*2 Henry VI* 4.7.60), as legendary architect of the Tower of London, as hero, lover, or slain martyr, the figure of Julius Caesar "ghosts" these plays as persistently as he ghosted Brutus at Philippi.

Yet of all Shakespeare's plays, it is perhaps in *Hamlet* that we feel most the ghostly, dislocated presence and pressure of Julius Caesar. Chronologically this makes good sense; Shakespeare was steeped in the Julian materials when he came to write *Hamlet*. Analogies have often been made between Brutus's apparent irresolution and Hamlet's, while the magisterial figure of Old Hamlet on the battlements, described at the outset as "this thing" (1.1.21) and a "fair and warlike form" (47) is reminiscent of the monstrous apparition Brutus confronts in his tent. If, as tradition holds, Shakespeare himself played the Ghost in *Hamlet*, thus becoming doubly his own ghost writer, we may imagine the ghost of Caesar as another haunting presence on the boundaries and margins of this play. Horatio, taking note of what Barnardo calls the "portentous figure" of Old Hamlet, draws the inevitable classical analogy:

> In the most high and palmy state of Rome,
> A little ere the mightiest Julius fell,
> The graves stood tenantless and the sheeted dead
> Did squeak and gibber in the Roman streets. (1.1.113–16)

This phenomenon is reported in *Julius Caesar* both by Casca ("this dreadful night,/That thunders, lightens, opens graves" [1.3.73–74]) and by Calphurnia ("graves have yawn'd and yielded up their dead . . . And ghosts did shriek and squeal about the streets" [2.2.24]). Shakespeare's sources here go back to Plutarch, Ovid, Virgil, and Lucan's *Pharsalia*, but the intertextual relationship between *Hamlet* and *Julius Caesar* suggests another kind of "ghosting," as well. The well-recorded circumstances of omens and portents auguring Caesar's death is repeated in Denmark:

> Even the like precurse of fear'd events,
> As harbingers preceding still the fates
> And prologue to the omen coming on,
> Have heaven and earth together demonstrated
> Unto our climatures and countrymen (1.1.123–28).

The auguries of the Roman catastrophe have "ghosted" even the Ghost in *Hamlet*. The "high and palmy state of Rome," soon to be disrupted by the assassination of its paternal ruler, foreshadows a similar development in Denmark. Even the itinerant players are preceded and heralded by a Roman ghost, for as Polonius rushes to tell Hamlet the "news," Hamlet forestalls him with "news" of his own – old news. "When Roscius was an actor in Rome – " (2.2.391–2). Hamlet's mention of Quintus Roscius Gallus, the most celebrated of Roman comic actors, lets Polonius know that he already expects the arrival of the players – themselves now displaced and forced to roam by the success (and the "succession" [351]) of children "tyrannically clapp'd" (341) for their performance. From Roscius to Polonius – o what a falling off was there.

We noted that Brutus received the "writings" thrown in at his closet window and created from them a script, a closet drama – a play whose reception he intends to encode even as he writes his stage directions. Polonius, too, is in his way a closet dramatist, hidden away in the Queen's closet, stabbed when Hamlet's sword thrusts through the arras, breaking the plane of the stage, becoming an actor rather than the playwright he intends. But this is not the first time Polonius has acted, or "enacted."

For though Freud may have played Brutus, it is Polonius who by his own account "did enact Julius Caesar. I was kill'd i' th'Capitol," he says, "Brutus killed me" (*Hamlet* 3.2.103–4). This Caesar, like his "imperious" namesake, shortly to be invoked by Hamlet, is likewise turned to clay. And in Polonius's enactment of Julius Caesar we see already in place Nietzsche's dire and ironic prediction.

> Now I ask whether it would be possible to represent our contemporary men of letters, popular figures, officials or politicians as Romans; it simply would not work . . . all congruity between the man and his historical domain is lost; we behold pert little fellows associating with the Romans as though they were their equals.

If it is true that all roads lead to Rome, that is because they never get there.

4

Freud's choice:
"The Theme of the Three
Caskets"

Analysis is not a matter of discovering in a particular case the differential features of the theory, and in doing so believe that one is explaining why your daughter is silent – for the point at issue is to *get her to speak*, and this effect proceeds from a type of intervention that has nothing to do with a differential feature.

Analysis consists precisely in getting her to speak. It might be said, therefore, that in the last resort, it amounts to overcoming the barrier of silence, and this is what, at one time, was called the analysis of resistances.

The symptom is first of all the silence in the supposed speaking subject.

Lacan, *The Four Fundamental Concepts of Psycho-Analysis*

Up to this point, we have been invoking Freud and other modern theorists to enable a reading of Shakespeare – as ghost writer of modern theory. In this chapter, it is Shakespeare who will reveal Freud to be subject to the uncanny causality of the literary – within life.

In 1913, shortly after the publication of essays on "A Special Type of Object Choice Made by Men" (1910) and "The Most Prevalent Form of Degradation of Erotic Life" (1912) Sigmund Freud took up a literary critical question that seems far removed from these clinical concerns. In "The Theme of the Three Caskets" (1913)[1] Freud sets out to address a certain morphological similarity between two works by an author whose plays often inform his writings: "Two scenes from Shakespeare," he writes, "one from a comedy and the other from a tragedy, have lately given me occasion for setting and solving a little problem."[2] The phrase "little problem" is characteristic of Freud the literary man; as if concerned to be seen as dabbling in a field in which he is clearly an amateur, rather than an expert (or a professor), he trivializes his detective work at the outset. The problem, and, perhaps, the solution, are negligible, a scientist's excursion into the world of poetry, and also, as he will shortly point out, into the world of myth – a world more closely related to his own expertise in the interpretation of dreams. In his private correspondence during the period of the essay's composition Freud goes out of his way to dismiss its importance. Writing to Ludwig Binswanger he characterizes it as "a trifle," something "pleasant enough to discuss . . . at length during a walk along the lake, but not important enough to write about" in a letter to a fellow psychoanalyst.[3] A "trifle"; a "little problem."

Here is the problem, as Freud sets it out: Portia's father's will ordains that she must take as her husband only the one suitor who chooses correctly among three caskets of gold, silver, and lead. Why is the right answer the lead casket, which seems to be so much less prepossessing than the others, and about which its chooser – Bassanio – has so much less to say in its praise than do Morocco and Arragon in choosing the flashier caskets of gold and silver? Freud traces the "origin" of the "oracle of choosing a casket" to a tale from the *Gesta Romanorum*, and thence to an Estonian folk-epic which is itself an "astral myth," a story about sun, moon, and star youths.[4] As Freud points out, somewhere in its transmission this myth seems to have undergone a reversal, so that, instead of a young woman choosing among three potential husbands, we have in *The Merchant of Venice* a very different choice: "a man chooses between three caskets."[5] Drawing on his researches into dream symbolism, Freud points out that caskets, like boxes and baskets, are "symbols of the essential thing in woman," and removes the veil of interpretation: "With one wave of the hand, such as usually happens only in fairy-tales, we have stripped the astral garment from our theme; and now we see that the subject is an idea from human life, a man's choice between three women."[6]

It is interesting that a woman's choice between three men does not present itself to Freud (or to the myth-critics he consults) as "an idea from human life," but rather as an allegory that demands interpretation. But let us put this peculiarity aside for a moment, and go back to Freud's reading. For he now introduces the second Shakespearean scene, which is, of course, that of Lear's division of the kingdom: "Is not this once more a scene of choosing between three women, of whom the youngest is the best, the supreme one?"[7] Here again analogues from fairy tale and myth come to Freud's mind: the choice of Paris; the story of Cinderella; Apuleius' tale of Cupid and Psyche. Though Cinderella, Aphrodite and Psyche are all contemplated as *brides* by their male choosers, Freud cautions that the apparent disparity in *Lear* (that the King is choosing among *daughters*) "must not lead us astray."[8] Lear is old; in fact, Freud insists, *he has to be old*, and therefore his choice must lie among daughters, rather than among wives or brides:

> The three women, of whom the third surpasses the other two, must surely be regarded as in some way alike if they are represented as sisters. It must not lead us astray if in *Lear* the three are the daughters of him who makes the choice; this means probably nothing more than that Lear has to be represented as an old man. An old man cannot very well choose between three women in any other way: thus they become his daughters.[9]

There are a number of curious things here to which we might give our attention. Why the odd insistence on Lear's advanced age? Why does he *have to be* represented as an old man? A phrase like "it must not lead us astray" almost always points toward a tempting byway; is the path of straying, as in romance, or in Freud's own essay on "The Uncanny," not in fact the path that leads us where we unconsciously want or need to go? But let us for a moment bracket these matters – that Lear has to be old, that his choice must lie between daughters – let us not be led "astray," but return to the straight and narrow path of Freud's argument.

Freud notes in both Portia's third, leaden casket and Cordelia's obstinate refusal to speak, the characteristic of "dumbness," or silence, and observes that "psychoanalysis has to say that dumbness is in dreams a familiar representation of death,"[10] as is a "striking pallor,"[11] like that of lead. The third woman, then, is a dead woman, or rather, the Goddess of Death herself. The three sisters, says Freud, are "the Fates, the Moerae [sic], the Parcae, or the Norns." But how, he asks, can we see Portia, "the fairest and wisest of women,"[12] or Cordelia, the "one faithful daughter," as death? "Can a contradiction be more complete?"[13]

What is the contradiction here? Freud sees a contradiction in the fact that the desirable woman, the third sister, the object of choice, is death. "Every time in this theme of ours there occurs a free choice between the women, and if the choice is thereupon to fall on death – that which no man chooses, to which by destiny alone man falls a victim"[14] – if this is the case, a contradiction "is certainly forthcoming" – indeed, "the acme of contradiction."

Why does Freud go to such lengths to equate a desirable woman with death? "Can a contradiction be more complete?" He explains this "contradiction" between death and desirability by the mechanism of reaction-formation. "Man" – the universal subject is Freud's locution, Freud's choice – "man overcomes death, which in thought he has acknowledged. No greater triumph of wish-fulfillment is conceivable. Just where in reality he obeys compulsion, he exercises choice; and that which he chooses is not a thing of horror, but the fairest and most desirable thing in life."[15] Creating in his imagination a Goddess of Love to replace the unwelcome reality of the Goddess of Death, "man," in Freud's interpretation, makes the third who always walks beside him into a desired choice rather than a repellent fate. "The fairest and the best, she who has stepped into the place of the Death-goddess, has kept characteristics that border on the uncanny, so that from them we might guess at what lay beneath."[16] Moreover, in *Lear*, Freud argues, Shakespeare takes a step toward disclosing this subtext. For Lear is not only an old man; he is a dying man. The extraordinary project of dividing the inheritance thus loses its strangeness. "The poet," says Freud

> brings us very near to the ancient idea by making the man who accomplishes the choice between the three sisters aged and dying. The regressive treatment he has thus undertaken with the myth, which was disguised by the reversal of the wish, allows its original meaning so far to appear that perhaps a superficial allegorical interpretation of the three female figures in the theme becomes possible as well.[17]

These three figures are, for Freud, the mother, the "companion of his bed and board," and "the destroyer" – or, alternatively,

> the three forms taken on by the figure of the mother as life proceeds: the mother herself, the beloved who is chosen after her pattern, and finally the Mother Earth who receives him again. But it is in vain that the old man yearns after the love of woman as once he had it from his mother; the third of the Fates alone, the silent Goddess of Death, will take him into her arms.[18]

So ends Freud's essay, eloquently and with pathos. With pathos, and with the mother, who is suddenly everywhere in the fable, the final solution to the "little problem." Marianne Krüll, in her recent study *Freud and His Father*[19], reads this final passage as auto-biographical commentary, as a longing for "the traditional mother figure who affords her child protection and warmth."[20] "The actual mother," writes Krüll, "is the model for the beloved, for whose love the old man (in 1913 Freud was fifty-seven years old) yearns in vain."[21] Freud, then, nostalgically re-imagines "man's" choice as the choice of the mother, speaking now from the subject position of the "old man" he has become.

But there is more than one old man in this story – and in Freud's story. We may recall his deflection of the image of Lear as suitor: "An old man cannot very well choose between three women in any other way; thus they become his daughters."[22] In a patient Freud might well read this as the evasion, or displacement, it appears to us to be. For there *is* an old man as suitor in the Freud family romance, and the old man is his own father, Jacob. "How did it come about," writes Krüll, "that Jacob, aged forty, married the 'virgin' Amalie Nathansohn, who was not yet twenty?"[23] – Amalie Nathansohn, who was to become the mother of Sigmund Freud. "It is," asserts Krüll, "possible that Jacob tried to prove to himself by this marriage that he was not yet an old man, still sexually potent and virile, perhaps because he had no wish to allow his grown-up sons to usurp his position."[24] Furthermore, at least according to recent research (by Krüll, and others),[25] Amalie seems to have been Jacob Freud's *third* wife; he had previously been married to Sally Kanner, who died in 1852, and to a mysterious woman called Rebekka, who appears to have been someone different from Sally, whose name is recorded in a register of Jews resident in Freiberg in 1852 ("Jakob Freud, 38 yrs. Wife Rebekka 23")[26] and also recorded (though then struck out) in a passport register in Freiberg in the same year. Most Freud biographers accept the existence of Rebekka and the authenticity of the marriage, although alternative interpretations have been proposed: Rebekka was another name for Sally, and her age was also altered for some unknown reason; Jacob pretended to be married to Rebekka to get her a residence permit in Moravia. But if – as seems likely – Rebekka did exist and was married to Jacob, the motif of the old man choosing a third young enough to be his daughter is all the more pointed. Amalie Nathansohn Freud is Jacob's daughter-wife – "our joy, although our last and least" (*King Lear* 1.1.83–4). The deflection of the personal (the substitution of the regal Lear for the Jewish Shylock) thus leads uncannily back to the personal, to the father. We may recall that the patriarch on whom Shylock calls for his own example, repeatedly evoking him by name, is Jacob, whose sharp business dealings with his father-in-law arouse Shylock's admiration. (And Amalie's father as well as her husband was named Jacob.)

As Max Schur, among others, has noticed,[27] Freud, in his famous letter to Fliess of 21 September 1897, renouncing the seduction theory, makes a curious joke about a woman named Rebekka – a joke that is really about himself. "One of the stories from my collection occurs to me," he writes, "Rebekka, you can take off your wedding-gown, you're not a *Kalle* [a bride] any longer."[28] Freud himself has ceased to be a "bride," full of pleasure at his exciting discovery – but as Schur asks, "Why just this joke at this time? Why a joke in which Freud identifies himself with a disgraced woman? And a joke, the punch line of which contains the name of this mysterious second wife of his father?"[29] Marianne Krüll speculates that Rebekka was Jacob's great secret, to which the son was told in a famous dream to close his/an eye(s) (see below Chapter 6). She inquires, "did Freud perhaps remember her name in his renunciation letter because it was on her account that he had to stop his search into his father's past, a search his seduction theory would have forced him to continue?"[30]

Freud's father died in October, 1896. In his letters to Fliess the son repeatedly refers to him as "the old man."[31] "The old man's condition does not depress me. I do not begrudge him the well-deserved rest that he himself desires" (2 November, 1896). In a celebrated remark in the preface to the second edition of *The Interpretation of Dreams* Freud wrote that the book was of a special significance for him because it was "a portion of my own self-analysis, my reaction to my father's death – that is to say, to the most important event, the most poignant loss, of a man's life."[32] The poignancy and the ambivalence of the loss of "the old man" – his last days attended, Cordelia-like, by Freud's "unmarried sister" who, Freud wrote to a friend, "[was] nursing him and suffering in the process"[33] – suggest some relevance to *Lear*. For, as we have seen, in the "Three Caskets" essay Lear is repeatedly, insistently characterized as an "old man":

> Lear is an old man. We said before that this is why the three sisters appear as his daughters. The paternal relationship, of which so many fruitful dramatic situations might arise, is not turned to further account in the drama. But Lear is not only an old man; he is a dying man. . . . Eternal wisdom, in the garb of the primitive myth, bids the old man renounce love, choose death and make friends with the necessity of dying.[34]

The father in this visualization is not a sexually powerful figure but one who must "renounce love," must "choose death." A version of the Oedipal drama is here recognizably acting itself out. Jacob Freud is not to be imagined as choosing a young wife (Freud's mother, the desirable woman) but rather as choosing – or realizing that he has to choose – death. But is this the only Oedipal drama encoded in Freud's "little problem"? Can the "problem" be double-read in Freud's own life and writings? Does Freud write himself into this essay, this problem, this choice-which-is-not-a-choice, not only in the subject position of the child, but also in the subject position of the husband, the woman-chooser, the father? As we are beginning to see, the essay on the "Three Caskets" is really an essay about substitution that enacts substitution as its own methodology. The essay, in other words, has the structure of displacement and occlusion, the structure of a dream. What is being occluded? What is being displaced? And onto – into – what?

For one thing, the desire of the old man for a woman ("the companion of his bed and board") has been displaced onto the paternal relation ("An old man cannot very well choose between three women in any other way; thus they become his daughters").

For another thing, the filial relationship between the author and the "old man" has been displaced onto the relationship between the author and mythic or archetypal "man" ("one might say that the three inevitable relations man has with woman are here represented"). In other words, the threatening paternal figure has been occluded, and stands revealed instead as a figure for the son. The story is not about an old man who chooses something (someone) the son would like to choose ("the mother herself, the beloved who is chosen after her pattern"), but instead about the choices available to the son, since the father has been forced to "renounce love, choose death and make friends with the necessity of dying."[35] The desiring subject is "man" – Bassanio, Lear, or Freud. We have returned to the "idea from human life, a man's choice between three women." Let us look then at Freud as suitor, and Freud as father.

In 1883 Sigmund Freud, then twenty-seven years old, wrote an affectionate letter to his fiancée, Martha Bernays, in which he addressed her playfully as "my Cordelia-Marty." "Why Cordelia?" he teases. "That will be explained later."[36] Norman Holland finds the "explanation" in the letter's next sentence, which consoles Martha on her sore throat.[37] Presumably this condition rendered her unable to speak, or at least left her with the voice "ever soft,/ Gentle and low" that Lear finds "an excellent thing in woman" (5.3.273–4). (It may be of some interest that Lear's observation comes as he strains to hear words he fancies to come from the lips of the *dead* Cordelia). But Freud's naming of his wife "Cordelia" has other "explanations," as well. In a further paragraph in the same letter he quotes a conversation he had with his then-mentor, Josef Breuer. Breuer told him in confidence some intimate details about his own family life, which were only to be repeated to Martha once she and Freud were married.

> And then I opened up [wrote Freud to Martha] and said: "This same Martha who at the moment has a sore throat in Dustern-brook, is in reality a sweet Cordelia and we are already on terms of closest intimacy and can say anything to each other." Whereupon he said he too always calls his wife by that name because she is incapable of displaying affection to others, even including her own father. And the ears of both Cordelias, the one

of thirty-seven and the other of twenty-two, must have been ringing while we were thinking of them with serious tenderness.[38]

Freud's comment to Breuer, as he reports it to Martha, seems to suggest that for him "Cordelia" is a woman outwardly silent, but actually warm and expressive ("we . . . can say anything to each other"). Breuer's wife is also called "Cordelia" because she is not demonstrative. She is, in fact, "incapable": "incapable of showing affection to others, even her own father." But once again, we may ask, who is in the subject position of the father here? Who is "Cordelia's" father, to whom she does not, cannot, declare her love? Breuer's wife, jealous of her husband's patient "Anna O." (Bertha Pappenheim) insisted that he give up his treatment of her in 1882, a year before this letter was written. Breuer himself, fourteen years older than Freud and something of a father-figure to him at this stage of their careers, collaborated with Freud in the writing of *Studies on Hysteria*. Freud himself, as he wrote to "Cordelia-Marty," "opened up," spoke, made what was inside him available to Breuer in the course of this conversation. What forged a bond between these two men, one a generation older than the other, was the silence – the adorable silence – of the women they had chosen to marry.

That both men unselfconsciously and without any sense of inappropriateness describe their wives (in Freud's case, his wife-to-be) as daughters – daughter–wives thought of in their absence "with serious tenderness" *because of* their supposed reticence – suggests that there is considerable slippage between the paternal and the conjugal relation here. This is not particularly surprising, in and of itself, given the nineteenth-century middle-class European culture in which both men lived. What *is* somewhat surprising is the text's resistance, in "The Theme of the Three Caskets," to any such ambiguity, the foreclosure of an ambiguous or ambivalent paternal/spousal role: "an old man cannot very well choose between three women in any other way, thus they become his daughters." For as a much younger man – thirty years before – Freud had apparently experienced no difficulty in seeing "Cordelia" as a *wife's* name, and a *wife's* role. In the "Three Caskets" essay he writes that Lear "should have recognized the unassuming, speechless love of the third and regarded it,"[39] as he and Breuer congratulated one another (and themselves) for doing. "Cordelia masks her true self, becoming as unassuming as lead. She remains dumb. She 'loves and is silent.' "[40] The same traits he praises and boasts of in "Cordelia-Marty" are present here. Lear should have known better.

(Interestingly, this same configuration – a sore throat, a "pale" woman, a group of three men conflated in one dream figure – is repeated with what seems uncanny precision in one of Freud's most famous dreams, the dream of Irma's injection.[41] The "white patch" he sees in Irma's throat reminds him "of a serious illness of my eldest daughter's."[42] The characteristics of the woman in the dream remind him of not one but three women in his life: "and now three similar situations came to my recollection involving my wife, Irma, and the dead Mathilde."[43] The sore throat, in the dream associated with the female genitals, is examined by a group of male doctors. Freud interprets his own dream as an allegory of wish-fulfillment, an allegory of analysis: "Its content was the fulfillment of a wish and its motive was a wish."[44] This is quite a good reading, not only of the dream of Irma's injection, but also of Freud's appropriation of "The Theme of the Three Caskets" to "solve" a problem in his own mental life. In the dream Freud takes Irma aside "to reproach her for not having accepted my 'solution' yet."[45] In the same way in the "Three Caskets" he sets and solves the "little problem," offering – or imposing – his own "solution." Irma is at fault if she will not accept Freud's reading of her condition: "If you still get pains, it is really only your fault.")[46]

Moreover, "Cordelia-Marty," the quiet and faithful Martha Bernays, was not, as it happens, an only child. She had a sister, Minna, described by Krüll as "a more stimulating conversational partner than his wife."[47] Minna Bernays came to live with the Freuds in 1896, and she and Freud often travelled together. It is claimed by many of Freud's biographers (most recently and persuasively by Peter Swales) that Minna and Sigmund Freud had an affair in 1900 that resulted in a pregnancy and an abortion.[48]

But Freud's essay tells us that man always chooses, emblematically, between *three* women. Amalie the mother, Martha the wife, and – Minna, the stimulating conversationalist? Or is there someone else? Who is the third? And what does *she* displace or occlude? Mother, wife, and Death-goddess, says Freud in his essay. Or mother, wife, and – child? The choice, "man's" choice, lights on the third. And Freud's choice, in interpreting his own essay, lights on Anna Freud – on the woman who is, although he does not say so, his *third* and youngest daughter.

In 1913, the year "The Three Caskets" was published, Freud wrote to Sandor Ferenczi to congratulate him on reaching his fortieth birthday. This was a highly charged question for Freud; he himself had been convinced that he would die on his own fortieth birthday, 6 May 1896.[49] In the letter to Ferenczi he does not mention his own fear of dying at forty. He does, however, refer to the other necessary choice mentioned in the "Three Caskets" essay, the choice that, he argues, "man" substitutes for death: the choice of a woman.

"Your recent letter," he wrote, "reminded me of my own fortieth birthday." Ferenczi, however, was a luckier man – not lonely like the forty-year-old Freud, who felt himself at that age abandoned by old friends, lacking new ones, unrecognized by the professional world, sustained only by his own defiance and by the beginning of what was to be his landmark work, *The Interpretation of Dreams*. But in one way Freud at forty was better situated than Ferenczi: "One possession of which I felt sure at your age you haven't yet acquired."[50] As the footnote to Ernst Freud's edition of the letters points out, the "possession" is "that of a wife." A wife is thus something to be possessed, like a jewel (or a casket). "For each of us fate assumes the form of one (or several) women," he writes to Ferenczi, "and your fate bears several unusually precious features." The parenthetical interpolation, "one (or several) women," is of some interest here. For "each of us [men]," Freud suggests, there are several women, several choices or fates. As he does in the "Three Caskets" essay when he refers, in that passage we have had several occasions to notice, to "an idea from human life, a man's choice between three women," Freud here again unselfconsciously employs the universal subject ("each of us") to refer to the gendered subject, "man," occluding the possibility of a woman's choice, or "fate." The woman for Freud in this letter, and in the essay published in the same year, is the possession, that which is chosen, that which denotes love or death for "man" – not the chooser, not one "of us," confronting her own death, or her own love, or fate.

At this point in the letter to Ferenczi, in fact, Freud refers directly to his essay on the "Three Caskets." And when he does so, he discloses – or makes as if to disclose – the essay's secret, or riddle, that which is contained in *its* casket. He is, he says, about to set off for a holiday at Marienbad, "free of analysis" – unburdened (like Lear). There, he writes, "my closest companion will be my little daughter, who is developing very well at the moment (you will long ago have guessed the subjective condition for the 'Choice of the Three Caskets')." Ferenczi will long ago have "guessed," like the hopeful suitors for Portia's hand, "whereof who chooses his meaning chooses you" (*Merchant of Venice* 1.2.31). The "little problem" posed by the essay has for him, according to Freud, been demystified, already both set and solved. "The Theme of the Three Caskets" is provoked by a "subjective condition" concerning the third woman, "my little daughter," Anna Freud, then almost eighteen years old.

Now, what, precisely, do we know about Anna Freud? We know that she was Freud's third and last daughter, and his youngest child.[51] She was "the only one of his children to continue his work, who never left him."[52] She became a child analyst; she did not marry. Here is how he describes her in a letter to the writer Arnold Zweig: "it cannot have remained concealed from you that fate has granted me as compensation for much that has been denied me, the possession of a daughter who, in tragic circumstances, would not have fallen short of Antigone."[53] This letter was written in 1934, twenty years after the "Three Caskets" essay, but we might notice how close it is in tone and content to the letter to Ferenczi of 1913. Again there is a secret, a secret the confidant-correspondent will have guessed: "it cannot have remained concealed from you." Again we have "fate," a wistful lament for recognition and rewards denied to Freud by the world, and a "possession," who turns out to be a woman: "a daughter who, in tragic circumstances, would not have fallen short of Antigone." Of Antigone – or of Cordelia? We have already seen that Freud refers to a *wife* as a possession, and to Martha Bernays as "Cordelia-Marty." Now, a generation later, the treasured female possession is a daughter. A year after his first "Antigone" letter to Zweig he again refers to Anna as "my faithful Anna-Antigone."[54] Antigone – Oedipus' daughter, who retired with the blind Oedipus to Colonnus where he died in banishment, in exile. It is reasonable, I think, to see Antigone here as a figure not unlike Cordelia, with whom Lear wished to retire from an antagonistic world, "away to prison," to "sing like birds i' th' cage" (5.3.8–9). The blind Oedipus is himself a figure who resembles both the oppressed Lear (to whom Kent had cried, "see better," 1.1.157) and the blinded Gloucester. Anna-Antigone-Cordelia, if we may so name her, is indeed the third daughter of the old man's choice. Freud, in despair at the ascendancy of Hitler and the Nazis, writes sadly to Zweig about his inability to leave Vienna ("For where should I go in my state of dependence and helplessness?";[55] "My idea of enjoying spring on Mt. Carmel with you [Zweig had emigrated to Palestine] was, of course, only a fantasy. Even supported by my faithful Anna-Antigone I could not undertake the journey."[56]) He ends his letter with an allusion that makes it clear that Shakespeare is – as so frequently – in his mind. "The times are dark, fortunately it is not my task to put them right." He is not a Hamlet, though in earlier essays and letters he has been one. But in these letters about Anna-Antigone, written to the man who addresses him as "Father Freud," we can again see something of Lear.

In "The Theme of the Three Caskets" Freud subjects Shakespeare's plays to the same analytic scrutiny he uses on the dreams and narrative of his patients. To his experienced ears Bassanio's choice of the lead casket seems to be couched (if I may use that word) in an unpersuasive way: "What he finds to say in glorification of lead as against gold and silver is but little and has a forced ring about it. If in psychoanalytic practice we were confronted with such a speech, we should suspect concealed motives behind the unsatisfying argument."[57] The reading of the "Three Caskets" essay I have been offering here starts off from similar suspicions, and from an argument that seems similarly unsatisfying. Why does Freud set himself this "little problem"? Why compare these two scenes of choice from Shakespeare's plays, eliding or omitting as he does so some of the most striking dramatic characters of *The Merchant of Venice*, the play with which he ostensibly begins his enquiry? Why displace both Shylock and Portia, the Jew and the independent woman, the woman who inherits money from her dead father and goes on to dress herself in men's clothing and to solve a riddle?

In his own life Cordelia–Marty and Anna–Antigone, the two faithful daughter–wives, stay with the patriarch to the end. They are as different as can be imagined from the rebellious Jessica, Shylock's daughter, who leaves the Jew's house, "transformed to a boy" (*Merchant of Venice* 2.6.39), taking with her a casket full of money that she tosses heedlessly to her Christian lover ("Here, catch this casket, it is worth the pains" (33)). Portia, the benefactress to both Jessica and Bassanio, a woman not only dressed but also empowered like a man, derives her power initially from the *death* of the patriarch, the death of the father who ordains – who "sets," in Freud's terms – the "little problem" of the casket choice.

When Freud says "this theme of ours," what does he mean? He means this theme of *his*. The "little problem" he sets up at the beginning of his essays – sets up *and* solves, as he tells us in the first sentence, as if the two operations were virtually the same – this "little problem" is a problem only for him. It is certainly far from clear, in the history of Shakespeare criticism, that this "little problem" has occasioned much concern. The essay is called "The Theme of the Three Caskets," yet, as Norman Holland comments, "oddly enough, the essay [does] not say a great deal about *The Merchant of Venice*."[58] Readers who turn to it eagerly in search of Freud's wisdom on Shakespeare (for this is the source of the text's authority, that it represents one of the few moments in which Freud *announces* in his published works a reading of Shakespeare) are often disappointed – or at least surprised – to find *The Merchant of Venice* so quickly elided, and *King Lear* so quickly substituted for it. And yet *The Merchant of Venice* would seem to have, for Freud the Jewish psychoanalyst, the most profound and immediate relevance. Is this why it is so quickly deflected and displaced?

By turning the Jew into the patriarch, Shylock into Lear, Freud universalizes and ennobles his own patriarchal position, no longer Jewish, marginal, contestatory, other. Man – mythic, universal man – must be the chooser; woman the chosen, the object of choice. In the one work in which he explicitly confronts his own Jewishness, *Moses and Monotheism* (1939), Freud grapples with both the powerful father and the idea of choosing and being chosen. The Jews are the "chosen people"[59] and Freud expresses great ambivalence about being in the position of the chosen rather than the chooser. To be the chooser is to be the father, to be the God. (He finds "astonishing" "the conception of a god suddenly 'choosing' a people, making it 'his' people and himself its own god."[60] And the sign of being chosen, the sign of submission to the father, was circumcision. ("Circumcision is the symbolical substitute of castration, a punishment which the primeval father dealt his sons long ago out of the fullness of his power; and whosoever accepted this symbol showed by so doing that he was ready to submit to the father's will."[61]) To be the chosen is to be disempowered, circumcised, castrated. The great success of Saint Paul, Freud thought, was in large part "due to his having given up the idea of the chosen people and its visible sign – circumcision. This is how the religion could become all-embracing, universal."[62] For Freud, then, arguably, the very act of choosing was masculine, empowering, paternal.

By turning *The Merchant of Venice* into *King Lear* Freud occludes Portia and her own scene of choice, when, dressed like a man, she chooses between two men, two symbolic castrates, Antonio the "tainted wether of the flock" (4.1.114) and Shylock the circumcised Jew.[63] Is *this* the problem – the *big* problem – which the setting and (simultaneous) solving of this "little problem" solves for Freud? – the problem of the two things he does not want to think of, the two things that remain on the periphery of the essay on "The Three Caskets," discreetly offstage and off-page, the two figures central to *The Merchant of Venice*: the cross-dressed woman and the Jew?

5

Macbeth: the male Medusa

Who is the author of Shakespeare's plays? For *Macbeth*,[1] at least, the answer seems clear: it is Lady Macbeth. Here is the scene in which her astonished audience, a doctor and a gentlewoman, describe her as she writes, seals, and performs the play – repeatedly, night after night.

> *Gentlewoman.* Since his Majesty went into the field, I have seen her rise from her bed, throw her night-gown upon her, unlock her closet, take forth paper, fold it, write upon't, read it, afterwards seal it, and again return to bed; yet all this while in a most fast sleep.
>
> *Doctor.* A great perturbation in nature, to receive at once the benefit of sleep and do the effects of watching! In this slumb'ry agitation, besides her walking and other actual performances, what, at any time, have you heard her say?
>
> *Gentlewoman.* That, sir, which I will not report after her. (5.1.4–14)
>
> *Lady Macbeth.* Out, damn'd spot! out, I say! one – two – why then 'tis time to do't. Hell is murky. Fie, my lord, fie, a soldier, and afeard? What need we fear who knows it, when none can call our pow'r to accompt? Yet who would have thought the old man to have had so much blood in him? (35–40)
>
> *Doctor.* Go to, go to; you have known what you should not.
>
> *Gentlewoman.* She has spoke what she should not. (46–8)
>
> *Doctor.* My mind she has mated, and amaz'd my sight. I think, but dare not speak. (78–9)[1]

Is *Macbeth*, then, a tale told by a sleepwalker, capable of striking its audience blind and dumb? What can be made of this *mise en abyme*, this uncanny reenactment of the play's composition and "actual performances," which repeat but do not exorcise its traumatic events?

What is striking about this scene is not only that it offers a perfect miniature of the play's action and the audience's response, but that it represents the medium of representation itself as a sleepwalker – someone who, in the very act of dramatic composition and performance, personifies the transgression of a boundary. *Macbeth* is, of course, a play *about* things "unnatural,/Even like the deed that's done" (2.4.10–11) – the murder of a king, the slaughter of innocent women and children, bearded women who know the future, a moving grove, a child not born of woman, horses that eat each other ("to th'amazement of mine eyes/That look'd upon it" (2.4.19–20). But to what extent can the play itself be seen as transgressive? Is this a mere figure of the play's power to unsettle, or does the play *literally* let something loose that stalks with uncanny sureness, compelled to repeat what it can neither repress nor cure? Let us look at stage history.

"towards his design
Moves like a ghost"

By the superstitious on and off the stage, *Macbeth* has always been considered an unlucky play. Actors have been known to refuse to wear a cloak or carry a sword that has been used in a *Macbeth* production.[2] Inside the theatre, it is said, even in the wings and dressing rooms, they will not mention the name of the play, or the names of any of its characters. They call it "the Scottish play" or "that play" or "the unmentionable." Macbeth's death is referred to as "the death," and Lady Macbeth as "the Queen." T"   ho unwittingly or carelessly break these unspoken rules, and quote from the "Scottish play" behind the scenes, are obliged to perform a time-honored ritual to remove the "curse." The offender must go out of the dressing room, turn around three times, spit, knock on the door three times, and beg to be admitted. It may be that this ceremony of exorcism derives in some way from the knocking at the gate in the Porter scene (2.3), or from the witches' custom of cursing in threes, or perhaps from the incantation of those same witches when Macbeth approaches them on the heath: "By the pricking of my thumbs,/Something wicked this way comes./Open, locks,/Whoever knocks!" (4.1.44–47). An alternative method of removing the curse is said to be to quote from *The Merchant of Venice* – especially Lorenzo's benison to the departing Portia: "Fair thoughts and happy hours attend on you!" (3.4.41). *Merchant* is considered a particularly lucky play, and thus to provide an antidote for the malign powers of *Macbeth*.

Interestingly enough, if we are to believe in stage history, those powers seem to have been considerable. In the first production of the play outside England, in 1672, the Dutch actor playing Macbeth was at odds with the actor playing Duncan over the affections of the latter's wife – who was cast in the role of Lady Macbeth. One evening the murder scene was particularly bloody, and "Duncan" did not appear for his curtain call. Afterwards it was discovered that a real dagger had been used. The former "Macbeth" served a life sentence for murder.

In more modern times the curse has apparently been equally lively. Laurence Olivier played the title part in 1937. First he lost his voice. Then the sets were found to be far too large for the stage. Finally he narrowly escaped death when a heavy weight plummeted from above and demolished the chair in which he had just been sitting. The show went on.

In the 1942 production starring – and directed by – John Gielgud there were no fewer than four fatalities. Two of the witches, the Duncan, and the scenic designer all died in the course of its run. The set was then repainted and used for a light comedy, whereupon the principal actor of that play promptly died.

Orson Welles filmed the play in 1946. When the film was finished, he discovered that the Scots accent he had insisted his actors acquire was totally incomprehensible to the audience. The entire sound track had to be recorded again.

When Charlton Heston played the part he had a serious motorcycle accident during rehearsals, after which there was much backstage murmuring about the "curse." The production was staged outdoors, and Heston was required to ride a horse in the opening scene. At the first performance he rushed from the stage, clutching his tights and whispering urgently, "Get them off me. Get them off me." The tights, it seemed, had been dipped in kerosene, either accidentally or on purpose, so that the heat from the horse inflicted painful burns. To add insult to injury, the audience responded to the play as if it were a comedy, laughing uproariously throughout the last act, and redoubling their laughter when Macduff appeared with Macbeth's severed head, which had been closely modeled on Heston's own.

Actors have occasionally been tempted to defy the curse, chanting lines from the play in unison in their dressing rooms just to see what would happen. This occurred in 1974 at the Bankside Theater, which was then performing in a tent. The result was a huge and sudden rainstorm, which short-circuited the electricity and made the entire stage a deathtrap. Then the canvas roof of the tent collapsed – fortunately just after the audience had made its way out. The entire theatrical season for the following year had to be cancelled.

On another occasion the young actress playing Lady Macbeth declared shortly after the dress rehearsal that she did not believe in the curse. The next day she decided she had been playing the sleepwalking scene wrong, keeping her eyes open when they ought properly to be shut. At the first performance she entered with her eyes closed and fell fifteen feet into the orchestra pit. She climbed back to the stage and continued the scene.

But the show has not always gone on. The great Russian director Constantin Stanislavski, who greatly admired *Macbeth*, mounted an elaborate production for the Moscow Arts Theater. During the dress rehearsal the actor playing Macbeth forgot his lines and – as was the custom in the Russian theater – came down to the prompt box at the front of the stage to get his cue. There was no word from the prompter. Irritably he tried again; still no word. A third try; nothing. At last he peered into the box, only to find the aged prompter dead – but still clutching the script. Stanislavski, no less a fatalist than his countrymen Chekhov and Dostoevsky, cancelled the production immediately. It – like the prompter – was never revived.

Stories of this kind are legion. People have been injured or killed, and productions seriously disrupted. The play is not only thought to be unlucky – on the face of things it actually has been unlucky, and actors today continue to believe in the curse. Recently, a tourist visiting the Stratford Festival in Ontario, Canada, innocently mentioned the name of the play while standing on the stage; the tour guide, a member of the company, quickly crossed himself.

What is there about Shakespeare's *Macbeth* that provokes so strong a response, and so heightened a defense? The answer is not hard to locate, for the play is itself continually, even obsessively, concerned with taboo, with things that should not be heard and things that should not be seen, boundaries that should not be crossed – and are. One of the principal themes of *Macbeth* is the forbidden, the interdicted, that which a man (or woman) may not with safety see or do. As much as it seeks to repress this acknowledgment, the play's *subject* is the uncanny and the forbidden – and its ancillary, covering subject is the need to repress or deny that fact. There *is* something uncanny going on here. Thus attempts to explain away the evidence of stage history have about them an engagingly overdetermined air of rationalization – a deliberate insistence upon finding the "facts" – as if these would dispel the numinous effect. Thus it is asserted that the role of Macbeth is so large, and the stage action so busy, with swordfights, entrances and exits (especially at the end of the play, when Birnam Wood comes to Dunsinane) that accidents are just bound to happen – an explanation that explains nothing at all.

"Research" has also been brought to bear on the suppression of this troubling history of performance. We are informed, for example, that the witches' brew concocted in Act IV was based on an actual recipe known to the witches of Shakespeare's native Warwickshire – a region famous for its practice of witchcraft.[3] Since the public enunciation of these secret ingredients – "fillet of a fenny snake," "eye of newt and toe of frog," not to mention "liver of blaspheming Jew" and "finger of birth-strangled babe" – would constitute a kind of inverse blasphemy, like the use of Christian artifacts in the Black Mass, disastrous or "unlucky" events might well ensue.

Ingenious "solutions" of this kind, with their spurious but reassuring documentation (the "real" recipe; the "original" witches, now safely dead) invite us to take refuge in the happy bromide that "accidents are bound to happen," as if such uncomfortable formulae could, by their very familiarity, produce comfort – or at least eliminate the sneaking suspicion that there is more going on in *Macbeth* than is dreamt of in anyone's philosophy. But such deferrals will not stay in place. The play is itself transgressive, and insists upon the posing of pertinent thought-troubling questions.

What is the relationship of the play to its stage history? In what sense can *Macbeth* be said to be about this kind of transgression and dislocation? Are these seeming "accidents" part of the play's affect – and also of its subject? – something let out to wander, to cross the borders between safety and danger, play and "reality," like a sleep-walker or a persistent wandering ghost: Lady Macbeth's somnam-bulistic nightmare, or Banquo's unsettling, extraneous and persistent presence at the banquet? The more we wish to pack her safely offstage and thus to bed, to banish him from his usurped place at table the more we see how much the play resists such easy resolutions, such comfortable conclusions about the dramatic role of dramatic presentations. The story *of* the play reflects the story *in* the play.

"wicked dreams abuse

The curtain'd sleep"

Macbeth presents us with what is in effect a test case of the limits of representation. The boundary between what is inside the play and what is outside it (in its performances, in its textual resonances) is continually transgressed, and marked by a series of taboo border crossings: sleep/waking, male/female, life/death, fair/foul, heaven/hell, night/morning. It is perhaps no accident that the Porter scene, itself a theatrical presentation of the transgressive limit or boundary, has aroused so much critical interest. It may indeed be the case that all stories about the uncanny are stories about the repression of the uncanny. In his essay on "The Uncanny" Freud discusses the strategy of the writer who lulls his reader into a false sense of security which he then deliberately transgresses or violates: "He takes advantage, as it were, of our supposedly surmounted superstitiousness; he deceives us into thinking that he is giving us the sober truth, and then after all oversteps the bounds of possibility."[4] Something of the same emotion is reflected in De Quincey's famous remarks "On the Knocking at the Gate in *Macbeth*" (1823), and even more acutely in Mallarmé's, "La Fausse Entrée des Sorcières dans *Macbeth*" which takes De Quincey as a point of departure. Mallarmé is fascinated by the witches' uncanny presence, so different from the bold transgressive knock at the gate. "*Rien, en intensité, comparable aux coups à la porte répercutés dans la terreur; mais ici, au contraire, un évanouissement, furtif, décevant la curiosité.*"[5] "Something comes only to vanish, furtive, disappointing all curiosity." He lays stress on the fact that the witches do not *enter*, are not described as entering the scene in the ordinary way of actors – instead they *appear: extra-scéniquement*, uncannily present.

> *Overture sur un chef-d'oeuvre: comme, en le chef-d'oeuvre, le rideau simplement s'est levé, une minute, trop tôt, trahissant des menées fatidiques.*
>
> *Cette toile qui sépare du mystère, a, selon de l'impatience, prématurement cédé–admis, en avance sur l'instant réglementaire, la cécité commune à surprendre le geste éffarouché de comparses des ténèbres – exposé, dans une violation comme fortuite, pour multiplier l'angoisse, cela même qui parassait devoir rester caché, tel que cela se lie par derrière et effectivement à l'invisible: chacun scrute et dérange, parmi l'éclair, la cuisine du forfait, sans le chaudron futur aux ingrédients pires que des recommandations et un brusque au revoir.*

[The overture to a masterpiece: as if, in the masterpiece, the curtain had simply risen a minute too soon, betraying fateful goings-on.

That canvas that separates mystery off has somehow, through some impatience, prematurely given way – admitted, anticipating upon the regulation moment, the common blindness to surprise the startled gesture of the cronies of darkness – exposed, in a seemingly fortuitous violation, so that anxiety is compounded, the very thing that seemed to have to remain hidden, such that *that* is knotted up from behind and effectively ·· the invisible; everyone examines and disturbs, in the lightning, the kitchen in which the deed is cooking, without the future cauldron with its ingredients worse than recommendations, admonitions, prophecies and a brusque vow to meet again.]

In Mallarmé's vision of the scene, we have a *theatrical* transgression – the curtain lifts too soon, the witches and their malign powers are prematurely exposed in a "fortuitous violation." Like an antemasque, the first encounter of the witches seems indecently to invite the spectator behind the scenes, into the kitchen, to the source of creative energy and dramatic power before it unfolds in its proper place. "The very thing that seemed to have to remain hidden" is revealed, examined, and disturbed. The spectator sees – indeed is compelled to see, by the timely-untimely lifting of the curtain – what should not be seen. *Une violation comme fortuite* – a fortuitous, but also a somehow fortunate violation.

Macbeth is full of such moments of transgressive sight and concomitant, disseminated violation. Repeatedly the play – through its chief protagonist – theorizes about the uncanny, while at the same time resolutely determining to ignore it, to cover it over or repress it.

> This supernatural soliciting
> Cannot be ill; cannot be good. If ill,
> Why hath it given me earnest of success,
> Commencing in a truth? I am Thane of Cawdor.
> If good, why do I yield to that suggestion
> Whose horrid image doth unfix my hair
> And make my seated heart knock at my ribs,
> Against the use of nature? Present fears
> Are less than horrible imaginings:
> My thought, whose murther yet is but fantastical
> Shakes so my single state of man that function
> Is smother'd in surmise, and nothing is
> But what is not. (1.3.13–42)

"Supernatural soliciting"; "function . . . smother'd in surmise"; "nothing is but what is not." Yet in the next moment Macbeth resolves that "If chance will have me king, why, chance may crown me/Without my stir" (143–4). Notice that it is a horrid "image" that transfixes him (by "unfixing" his hair and setting his heart to "knocking" – a physiological anticipation of the unnatural knocking in the Porter scene). The boundary between a thing and its reflection is constantly being transgressed, here and elsewhere in the play. Good/ill; natural/supernatural; single/double; function/surmise; is/is not. "Nothing," a present absence, emerges from this internal debate as the one palpable substantive. But as much as Macbeth tries to contain these speculations, to know and dissemble the uncanny, it will out. Murder will out.

Consider another key passage about boundary transgression,

knowledge and identity. Prior to the murder of Duncan, Macbeth is still vacillating, debating the trajectory of murder and the priority of particular taboos: against slaying a kinsman; against slaying a king; against slaying a guest; tacitly against parricide, the double murder of king and father.

> If it were done, when 'tis done, then 'twere well
> If were done quickly. If th'assassination
> Could trammel up the consequence, and catch
> With his surcease, success; that but this blow
> Might be the be-all and the end-all – here,
> But here, upon this bank and shoal of time,
> We'ld jump the life to come. But in these cases
> We still have judgment here, that we but teach
> Bloody instructions, which, being taught, return
> To plague th'inventor. This even-handed justice
> Commends th'ingredience of our poison'd chalice
> To our own lips. He's here in double trust:
> First, as I am his kinsman and his subject,
> Strong both against the deed; then, as his host,
> Who should against the murtherer shut the door,
> Not bear the knife myself. (1.7.1–16)

"Shut the door"; but it is precisely this door, this portal, threshold, or boundary, which cannot be shut. The keen knife that, in Lady Macbeth's pregnant phrase, must "see not the wound it makes" (1.5.52) will pierce the blanket of the dark – and the limits of the stage. The stage history of the play is in effect the acting out of the play's own preoccupation with boundary transgression. It is not extrinsic or anecdotal; it is the matter of the play itself.

A particularly striking instance of this transgressive violation occurs, as we have noticed, in the sleepwalking scene, which encodes an onstage audience: Lady Macbeth's Waiting-Gentle-woman, horrified by the events of previous nights, has called a Doctor of Physic to observe her lady's actions. "What, at any time, have you heard her say?" asks the Doctor (5.1.12–13). "That, sir," replies the Waiting-Gentlewoman, "which I will not report after her" (15–16). "Neither to you," she answers, "nor any one, having no witness to confirm my speech" (17–18). What she has heard is unspeakable, unrepeatable. At this point the sleeping Lady Macbeth appears, tries to wash invisible blood from her hands, and in half a dozen other words and actions reveals that she and her husband are guilty of the murders. Not only Duncan, but Banquo and the family of Macduff have all been their victims. And the response of the

Doctor and Waiting-Gentlewoman is once again expressed in terms of taboo. "You have known what you should not," he reproaches her (46–7), and she replies roundly, "She has spoke what she should not. I am sure of that. Heaven knows what she has known" (48–49). Notice "should not" here – not "cannot." The unspeakable knowledge is transgressive, interdicted. The audience in the theater, which has experienced these horrors once, now relives them through new eyes and ears. As the scene closes the Doctor confirms the sense of impotent dismay that is felt by both audiences, onstage and off, declaring, "My mind she has mated, and amaz'd my sight./I think, but dare not speak" (78–9).

"My mind she has mated" – that is, checkmated, stunned, stupefied – "and amaz'd my sight." Consider how very frequently in the play this kind of perturbation in nature takes place. As we have seen, Macbeth is paralyzed when he contemplates the murder of Duncan. Having committed the murder, he cannot bear to look upon his victim: "I am afraid to think what I have done;/Look on't again I dare not" (2.2.48–9). The vision of the dagger he sees before him (2.1.), the blood-boltered ghost of Banquo (which, like the dagger, is invisible to everyone on the stage save Macbeth himself), and the apparitions produced by the witches are all literally amazing sights, sights that are taboo, forbidden, dangerous. "Seek to know no more" (4.1.103) counsel the witches. But Macbeth is deaf to their instruction. "I will be satisfied. Deny me this,/And an eternal curse fall on you!" (104–5). With extraordinary hubris he threatens to lay a curse upon the very creatures who themselves possess the power of malediction. And when they ironically comply with his demands he misinterprets what he sees and hears, and brings upon himself defeat and death. The whole play is in one sense at least a parade of forbidden images gazed upon at peril, and it inscribes an awareness of this, a preoccupation with it. Through "the sightless couriers of the air" it "blow(s) the horrid deed in every eye" (1.7.24). "My mind she has mated, and amaz'd my sight." There is one dramatic moment, early in the play, in which the act of gazing on the taboo is explicitly described, and it is a moment which I think has a crucial significance for the pattern and meaning of Shakespeare's play. I refer to the moment – and the manner – in which Macduff announces the death of Duncan.

The time is early morning. Macduff and Lennox, two loyal liegemen, have arrived to see the King at his request. They knock on the Porter's door, waking him and prompting the famous and disquieting comparison of Macbeth's castle to hell itself. "If a man were porter of Hell Gate, he should have old turning the key" (2.3.2–3). For Macduff and Lennox the crossing of this threshold is a transgressive act, a fatal journey from the familiar to the forbidden, a rite of dreadful passage from which they will return greatly changed.[6]

Admitted, they are welcomed by their host, Macbeth, who shows them the way to the king's chamber. And it is from that chamber that Macduff emerges, a moment later, with words of horror on his tongue. "O horror, horror, horror! Tongue nor heart/Cannot conceive nor name thee!" (64–5). Again the event is said to be unspeakable – it cannot be told. But equally important, it cannot be looked upon.

> Approach the chamber, and *destroy your sight*
> *With* a *new Gorgon.* Do not bid me speak;
> See, and then speak yourselves.
>   Awake, awake!
> Ring the alarum-bell! Murther and treason!
> Banquo and Donalbain! Malcolm, awake!
> Shake off this downy sleep, death's counterfeit,
> And look on death itself! Up, up, and see
> The great doom's image! Malcolm! Banquo!
> As from your graves rise up, and walk like sprites
> To countenance this horror! Ring the bell (2.3.71–80)

The Gorgon of classical mythology turned those who looked upon her to stone. To Macduff the sight of the dead king is a "new Gorgon" that will do the same to Duncan's subjects – a monstrous vision that will amaze their sight. What is this reference to "a new Gorgon" doing in the play?

"our rarer monsters"

The most famous of the Gorgons was Medusa, one of three sisters in Greek mythology, whose hair was said to be entwined with serpents, whose hands were brass, their bodies covered with scales, their teeth like boars' tusks.[7] When gazed upon, they turned the onlooker to stone. The first two Gorgons, Stheno ("The Mighty One") and Euryale ("Wide-leaping") were immortal, and seem to have nothing really to do with the myth beyond multiplying the fearsome power of the terrible and petrifying female image from one to the favorite number for monstrous females, three (seen above, Chapter 4) as with the Graiai, or Spirits of Eld; the Moirai, or Fates; and the Charities, or Graces. The two supernumerary Gorgons disappear almost immediately from most accounts, leaving the focus on the third, the mortal Gorgon, Medusa, whose name – significantly enough for *Macbeth* – means "The Queen."

I arrive to talk about Medusa at a moment when considerable attention has been paid to this myth – particularly by Freud and by theorists influenced by him. I will therefore first run briefly through the myth in such a way as to highlight those aspects of it that are important for my purposes, then touch upon the readings of Freud and others, and how they pose, or counterpose, some difficulties and unresolved questions in contextualizing the Medusa story within *Macbeth*. Once again I hope to show that the unresolved questions are precisely at issue in the play. Specifically, the initial difficulty of applying Freud's reading of the Medusa head as a fearful sighting of the female genitals indicates a site of resistance and underscores the way in which gender undecidability and anxiety about gender identification and gender roles are at the center of *Macbeth* – and of Macbeth.[8]

In classical mythology the story of Medusa is one of the exploits of the hero Perseus, the son of Zeus and of a mortal woman, Danae. For reasons that need not concern us here mother and son were exiled from their native country and came to the land of a certain king, Polydectes. Polydectes lusted after Danae, and sent her inconvenient son Perseus off to fetch the head of Medusa, hoping – and expecting – that he would never return from this dangerous exploit. But Perseus was favored by the gods, especially Athena, the virgin goddess of wisdom and war, who advised him how to proceed. To gain access to the Gorgons (still described as three, although only Medusa's head was his object) he first visited another triad of figures, the Graiai, who are thought to be either the sisters or the sentries of those Gorgons. The Graiai, gray-haired from birth, are considered by modern commentators to represent the personified spirits of old age. They had only one eye and one tooth among them, and by trickery Perseus stole both, agreeing to return them only when he received in exchange a magic cap, which made him invisible; magic shoes, which made him swift; and a magic wallet, in which he might carry the severed head. When the time came he approached Medusa with his back turned, looking at her image as it was reflected in his shield rather than directly, and was thus able to decapitate her without being turned to stone. Once he achieved this feat he made use of the head as a weapon, turning to stone those who dared to oppose him. Ultimately he gave the head to his patroness, Athena, who wore it thereafter on her aegis.

Thus the head of Medusa, so horrible in life, becomes in death an apotropaic talisman, a means of warding off evil. Throughout Greek and Roman art the Medusa head – with grinning mouth, staring eyes, and protruding tongue – appears as a protective ornament, whether worn on armor, carved on statues of Athena, or incised on tombstones. In fact the head as a talisman seems to have preceded the myth, and perhaps to have generated it. Jane Ellen Harrison writes persuasively that

> in her essence Medusa is a head and nothing more; her potency only begins when her head is severed; she is in a word a mask with a body later appended. The primitive Greek knew that there was in his ritual a horrid thing called a Gorgoneion, a grinning mask with glaring eyes and protruding beast-like tusks and pendant tongue. How did this Gorgoneion come to be? A hero had slain a beast called the Gorgon, and this was its head. Though many other associations gathered round it, the basis of the Gorgoneion is a cultus object, a ritual mask misunderstood. The object comes first; then the monster is begotten to account for it; then the hero is supplied to account for the slaying of the monster."[9]

Thus Homer speaks of the Gorgon as a disembodied head, whether he is describing an ornament or an actual monster. Agamemnon carries a shield embossed with the staring face of the Gorgon (*Iliad* 11.36), Hector glares with the Gorgon's stark eyes (*Iliad* 8.349), and Odysseus fears lest Persephone send a Gorgon-head from deeper hell to afright him, and flees to his ship (*Odyssey* 11.634).

If the Gorgon's heads in effect precede and preempt the bodies that support them, in what sense can we say of Macbeth that *his* real potency only begins when his head is severed, and he becomes an apotropaic object? Before we come to consider the terrifying heads of Shakespeare's *Macbeth*, it may be useful to consider what some of his contemporaries thought of the Medusa myth, and the degree to which there was a consciousness of that myth in Western Europe, and especially in England.

Renaissance mythographers, when they contemplated the story of Medusa, saw plainly allegorical meanings. The influential Italian mythographer Caesare Ripa, in his *Iconologia*, interpreted the head of the Medusa as "a symbol of the victory of reason over the senses, the natural foes of 'virtu,' which like physical enemies are petrified when faced with the Medusa."[10] The real battle was within the warring elements of the self. Thus Mantegna represents *Philosophia* in the form of Minerva with a shield bearing a Medusa mask, to represent wisdom's control of the senses.[11] The degree to which this interpretation accords with the spirit of *Macbeth* is made manifest in the two speeches we have already considered: Macbeth's first long aside, which begins, "This supernatural soliciting/Cannot be ill, cannot be good" (1.3.130–1), and the remarkable soliloquy that begins Act 1 scene 7, ("If it were done when 'tis done, then 'twere well/It were done quickly" [1–2]). Like Lady Macbeth's open eyes and closed sense in the sleepwalking scene, this speech refuses to look where it is going, to see where it is headed – and so in effect it beheads itself, and "falls on th'other" (28), yielding to the very transgressive energy it struggles so hard to contain.

Francis Bacon, in a treatise called *De sapientia veterum*, or *The Wisedome of the Ancients*, titled his interpretation of the Medusa story "Perseus, or Warre." The Medusa was an emblem of tyranny, against which the just warrior should fight.

> There must bee a care that the motives of Warre bee just and honorable; for that begets an alacrity . . . in the soldiers that fight . . . . But there is no pretence to take up arms more pious than the suppression of Tyranny, under which yoake the people loose their courage, and are cast downe without heart and vigour, as in the sight of Medusa."[12]

Bacon also has interesting things to say about the Graiai, whom he identifies as "treasons which may be termed the Sisters of Warre." They are "descended of the same stocke, but far unlike in nobilities of birth; for Warres are generall and heroicall, but Treasons are base and ignoble."[13] "Perseus [Bacon continues] therefore was to deale with these Greae for the love of their eye and tooth. Their eye to discover, their tooth to sowe rumors and stirre up envy, and to molest and trouble the minds of men."[14] Once again, we have forbidden sight and forbidden language. The Graiai in this reading bear a suggestive resemblance to the weird sisters, similarly consulted, and similarly – though again reluctantly – helpful to the hero in his quest. The Old English word *wyrd* means Fate, and it has been conjectured by Holinshed and others that the weird sisters may represent the "goddesses of destiny"; Holinshed also reports that they resembled "creatures of elder world."[15] In any case the threeness of the witches, (and indeed the murderers) calls to mind the ritual trios of Graiai and Gorgons, all relentless and unrepentant in their dealings with mortal men.

Another English mythographer, Alexander Ross, sees Medusa as an emblem of the dangerous power of women: "the sight of these Gorgones turned men into stones; and so many men are bereft of their sense and reason, by doting too much on women's beauty."[16] Ross also comments on the fact that not only Perseus but his entire family were made into constellations, remarking that by this fact it was possible to see "how one worthy person doth enoble a whole family."[17]

For James I the allegorization of the Medusa story would have had potentially disquieting political – and personal – implications. In his political writings James continually recurred to the image of the King as head of state: thus he writes in the *Basilikon Doron* of the King as a "publicke person" to whose "preseruation or fall, the safetie or wracke of the whole common-weale is necessarily coupled, as the body is to the head";[18] in a speech to the first English Parliament (19 March 1603) he declared, "I am the Husband, and the whole Isle is my lawfull Wife; I am the Head, and it is my Body",[19] and in *The Trew Law of Free Monarchies* (1598) he likewise articulates, and embellishes, this figure:

> And for the similitude of the head and the body, it may very well fall out that the head will be forced to garre cut off some rotten members (as I haue already said) to keep the rest of the body in integritie: but what state the body can be in, if the heade, for any infirmitie that can fall to it, be cut off, I leaue it to the readers iudgement."[20]

The decapitation of the state, the severing of the head from the body politic, was at the same time unimaginable, and offered to the reader (or audience) to imagine. Yet in James' own recent memory. there had been such a beheading and such a severance, of a monarch "set upon a skaffolde" – or, as later editions of the *Basilikon Doron* would emend the phrase, "on a stage, whose smallest actions and gestures, all the people gazingly doe behold":[21] the public beheading of his mother, Mary Queen of Scots, on February 8, 1587. The fate of Mary haunts the *Basilikon Doron*, so much so that in his introduction to later editions the King felt it necessary to excoriate the "malicious" critics who claimed that "in some parts [of the *Basilikon Doron*] I should seeme to nourish in my minde, a vindictive resolution against *England*, or at the least, some principals there, for the Queene my mothers quarrell";[22] in the treatise itself he urges Prince Henry to pay particular heed to the Fifth Commandment, to honor his father and his mother, alluding to the just retribution that had fallen upon "all them that were chiefe traitours to my parents . . . I mean specially by them that serued the Queene my mother."[23] (The editor of James' political writings comments without irony that the religious and civil disorders of the time "had been brought to a head by the execution of Mary Stuart in 1587."[24])

In the *Basilikon Doron*, addressed to his son as presumptive heir, James distinguishes – in passages that have often been linked to *Macbeth* – between the characteristics of the "good King" and those of the "vsurping Tyran."[25] For James, a usurping tyrant like

Macbeth, who deserves to have his head struck off and exhibited to the people ("live to be the show and gaze o' th' time! . . . painted upon a pole, and underwrit,/'Here may you see the tyrant.' " 5.8.24–7) would indeed be a sort of male Medusa. The play covers over and represses or displaces the figure of the decapitated Mary, so offensive and so omnipresent to the King's imagination, "set high upon a skaffolde," and substitutes for it the appropriate and politically necessary decapitation of Macbeth: "Behold where stands/Th'usurper's cursed head" (5.9.20–1).

Not only mythographic and political but also archaeological evidence speaks to these questions. The architectural remains of Roman Britain include a remarkable number of Medusa heads.[26] Coffins, tombstone pediments, antefixes, floor mosaics and pottery all bear Medusa masks, as do bronze jugs, jug-handles, and visor-masks, skillets intended for religious and sacrificial use, rings, coins, pendants, and *phalerae* (small glass or metal disks, often awarded as gifts to soldiers of the Roman armies) – to say nothing of statues and relief carvings of the goddess Minerva (the Roman counterpart of Athena) with the head of Medusa displayed on her aegis. The function of these decorations, like those of their Greek predecessors, is in most cases clearly apotropaic; the figured jet pendants, for example, were obviously intended to ward off evil from their wearers, the *phalerae* to protect the soldiers in battle, and the tomb and coffin Medusas to safeguard the dead.

But among these numerous Medusas there were a few which differed crucially from the traditional representation, for they are manifestly *male*. Three certain examples of the male Medusa have been found in England, and others have been tentatively identified. Carved on a pediment for a tombstone at Chester is a bearded and moustached male head with severely patterned hair and eight writhing snakes framing its face. "It is, in fact," writes J. M. C. Toynbee, "a kind of male Medusa."[27] An antefix or roof ornament from Dorchester bears the mask of another bearded Medusa, and coins from the reign of Tincommius (ca. 20 B.C.–5A.D.) carry full-faced Medusa masks which are "very probably bearded."[28] But the most celebrated of the British male Medusas is the second or third century sculpted pediment on the Temple of Sulis-Minerva at Bath. Toynbee, cataloguer of the 1961 London Exhibition of Art in Roman Britain, asserts

That the glaring mask on the boss of the central, dominating shield of the Bath pediment is, to some extent, at any rate, intended, despite its masculinity, to depict the Medusa of Minerva is certain. Of this the wings and snakes in the hair are

clinching evidence; the owl beside the shield was specifically
Minerva's bird; the temple was dedicated to her as conflated with
the Celtic Sulis; and to Minerva, as the child of Jupiter, oak-
wreaths are appropriate. The Bath face, with its trap-like mouth,
lined, scowling brows, and huge, deeply drilled, and penetrating
eyes, is, indeed, very different from the normal, feminine Medusa
of Hellenistic and Roman art. All the same, wild, glowering,
frowning faces, sometimes set on round shields, were not
unknown in Roman art in Mediterranean lands."[29]

Indeed, other representations of the male Medusa are to be found in
the Mediterranean area, specifically at Rome, Petra, and Hatra in
Mesopotamia (now Al Hdr, Iraq).[30]

Toynbee's description of the striking mouth, brows, and eyes on
the pediment at Bath bring sharply to mind another decorative
architectural motif that also involves a glaring male beard, often with
gaping mouth and protruding tongue. I refer to the foliate head or
leaf mask which gained enormous popularity in England and
throughout Western Europe during the Romanesque and medieval
periods. These remarkable images, with leaves sprouting from their
faces, can be found virtually everywhere in English medieval
churches, from fonts to tombs, corbels and capitals to arm rests.
Known in Britain chiefly as the Green Man, this often sinister and
frightening figure appears among other places, in Exeter, Ely,
Lincoln, and Winchester Cathedrals, and in the Church of the Holy
Trinity in Coventry, Warwickshire – not a great distance from
Shakespeare's home in Stratford-upon-Avon.[31] The Green Man,
although he seems in some ways an odd choice for ecclesiastical
ornamentation, in fact embodies a warning against the dark side of
man's nature, the devil within: "For all flesh is as grass, and all the
glory of man as the flower of grass. The grass withereth, and the
flower thereof falleth away" (1 Peter 1:24).

Foliate head and Medusa head, one monster with hair and beard
of leaves, the other with snaky locks; both are in effect conquered,
tamed, and appropriated as symbols by religions to which they were
originally antipathetic. Medusa was considered Athena's antitype,
"a hostile Pallas who could sometimes be united with her . . . and
sometimes regarded as an antagonist being detested by the goddess
herself."[32] So closely are they associated that Euripides calls Athena
"Gorgon" twice in his plays. The rational goddess can also be an
irrational monster; wisdom can be transformed to war: "There's no
art/To find the mind's construction in the face" (*Macbeth* 1.4.11–
12). As for the Green Man, a type of the male Medusa, he is
terrifying precisely because he is, and is not, man. And, as I hope to

show, Macbeth too becomes a male Medusa. To see why, it may be helpful to return to Freud.

"Bloody instructions, which, being taught, return To plague th'inventor"

Freud's essay on "The Uncanny" is uncannily pertinent to *Macbeth*, although – as we have already seen – Freud repeatedly denies or represses that pertinence by disclaiming any direct relationship between the literary appearance of ghosts and apparitions and the *Unheimlich* or uncanny. The affect of uncanniness, we have noted, is for Freud a kind of "morbid anxiety" that derives from "something repressed which *recurs*"; this uncanny is in reality nothing new or foreign, but "something familiar and old-established in the mind that has been estranged only by the process of repression."[33] Thus he is moved to agree with Schelling that the uncanny is something which ought to have been kept concealed but has nonetheless come to light – something concealed because of the protective mechanism of repression.

Associated with such sensations as intellectual uncertainty whether an object is alive or not, the fear of the evil eye and of "the omnipotence of thoughts,"[34] instantaneous wish-fulfillment, secret power to do harm, and the return of the dead,[35] the uncanny is nothing less than the thematized subtext of Shakespeare's *Macbeth*. For example, the "moving grove," Birnan wood en route to Dunsinane, is precisely the kind of phenomenon about which it is difficult to judge – is it animate or inanimate, natural or unnatural? The audience knows, because it is told directly in Act 5 scene 4, that the soldiers have hewn down boughs, and carry them before them – not as an uncanny spectacle but as military camouflage, that they may better scout out the numbers of the enemy, and hide their own troop strength. The rational explanation is given to us directly, and apparently explains the strategem. But does it? With the witches' prophecy inevitably in mind, we may count the ironic fulfillment as itself uncanny. Macbeth's appalled presentiment of doom identifies the moving grove as a reified, dramatized catachresis.

> I pull in resolution, and begin
> To doubt th'equivocation of the fiend
> That lies like truth. "Fear not, till Birnan wood
> Do come to Dunsinane," and now a wood
> Comes toward Dunsinane. (5.5.41–5)

The uncanny, says Freud, is also linked to the well-documented phenomenon of the double – whether through telepathic communication between persons, so that one "identifies himself with another person, so that his self becomes confounded, or the foreign self is substituted for his own" – as in the case of Macbeth and Lady Macbeth – or through the "constant recurrence of similar situations, a same face, or character-trait, or twist of fortune, or a same crime, or even a same name recurring throughout several consecutive generations." Manifestations of the uncanny appear in the witches' riddling prophecies, the puzzling, spectacular apparitions, the walking of trees and sleepers, the persistent sense of doubling that pervades the whole play: two Thanes of Cawdor; two kings and two kingdoms, England and Scotland themselves doubled and divided; two heirs apparent to Duncan; the recurrent prefix "Mac" itself which means "son of"; the sexually ambiguous witches replicated in the wilfully unsexed Lady Macbeth; Macbeth and Banquo on the battlefield "As canons overcharg'd with double cracks, so they/Doubly redoubled strokes upon the foe" (1.2.37–8); Duncan as the Macbeths' guest, "here in double trust" (1.7.12), their ostentatious hospitality as Lady Macbeth points out, "in every point twice done, and then done double" (1.6.15). Macbeth believes the witches' prophecies (and believes that he interprets them correctly), but he will "make assurance double sure" by killing Macduff, thus bringing down sure disaster upon himself. The witches or weird sisters, he will later assert, are "juggling fiends" "that palter with us in a double sense," (5.8.19; 20), and we hear them chant their litany of "double, double, toil and trouble" (4.1.10; 20; 35). The mode of involuntary repetition, which we saw embodied in Lady Macbeth's futile acting out of the events of the play, determines dramatic action from Macbeth's first reported action to his death at the close. In Act 1 scene 2 a "bloody man," the sergeant just returned from battle, reports Macbeth's valiant victory over a traitorous rebel, "the merciless Macdonwald." "Brave Macbeth," says the sergeant,

> (well he deserves that name),
> Disdaining Fortune with his brandish'd steel,
> Which smok'd with bloody execution,
> (Like Valor's minion) carv'd out his passage
> Till he fac'd the slave;
> Which nev'r shook hands, nor bade farewell to him,
> Till he unseam'd him from the nave to th'chops,
> And fix'd his head upon our battlements. (16–23)

The play thus begins with the (offstage) head of a rebel fixed upon the battlements, as it will end with another rebellion, another battle, and "the usurper's cursed head" held aloft by Macduff. The sergeant's phrase, "bloody execution" encapsulates the doubleness, since execution here means both deed and death, and points ahead to the "If it were done" soliloquy (1.7.1). Thus, Macbeth performs in the first, offstage battle what might be aptly described as "bloody instructions, which, being taught, return/To plague th'inventor" (1.7.9–10), imagistically "carv[ing] out" the patterns of his own retributive death.

Significantly, Freud singles out as well a series of metonymic objects, dislocated body parts – several of which appear as prominent stage properties in Elizabethan and Jacobean drama: "Dismembered limbs, *a severed head*, a hand cut off at the wrist, feet which dance by themselves – all these have something peculiarly uncanny about them . . . As we already know, this kind of uncanniness springs from its association with the castration-complex."[36] For Freud, indeed, the castration-complex is intrinsic to uncanniness wherever it appears. The severed head so central to *Macbeth* (and its Medusa associations) is only one instance of this pervasive pattern of underlying meaning. Doubling, too, is linked to castration anxiety: "the 'double' was originally an insurance against destruction of the ego . . . This invention of doubling as a preservation against extinction has its counterpart in the language of dreams, which is fond of representing castration by a doubling or multiplication of the genital symbol."[37] Again, he comments that "It often happens that male patients declare that there is something uncanny about the female genital organs."[38] Later, in his essay on "Medusa's Head" (1922), he will point out that the representation of Medusa's hair by snakes in works of visual art is another manifestation of the castration complex:

> however frightening they may be in themselves, they nevertheless serve actually as a mitigation of the horror, for they replace the penis, the absence of which is the cause of the horror. This is a confirmation of the technical rule according to which a multiplication of penis symbols signifies castration.[39]

The "Medusa's Head" essay has achieved a certain prominence in recent theoretical discussions, in part because of Neil Hertz's provocative article "Medusa's Head: Male Hysteria under Political Pressure" in the Fall 1983 issue of *Representations*, and the replies to it by Catherine Gallagher and Joel Fineman in the same issue of that journal.[40] The key passage here is Freud's explanation of "the horrifying decapitated head of Medusa":

> To decapitate = to castrate. The terror of Medusa is thus a terror of castration that is linked to the sight of something. Numerous

analyses have made us familiar with the occasion for this: It occurs when a boy, who has hitherto been unwilling to believe the threat of castration, catches sight of the female genitals, probably those of an adult, surrounded by hair, and essentially those of his mother.

The hair upon Medusa's head is frequently represented in works of art in the form of snakes, and these once again are derived from the castration complex. It is a remarkable fact that, however frightening they may be in themselves, they nevertheless serve as a mitigation of the horror, for they replace the penis, the absence of which is the cause of the horror. This is a confirmation of the technical rule according to which a multiplication of penis symbols signifies castration.

The sight of Medusa's head makes the spectator stiff with terror, turns him into stone. Observe that we have here once again the same origin from the castration complex and the same transformation of affect! For becoming stiff means an erection. Thus in the original situation it offers consolation to the spectator: he is still in possession of a penis, and the stiffening reassures him of the fact.

If Medusa's head takes the place of a representation of the female genitals, or rather if it isolates their horrifying effects from the pleasure-giving ones, it may be recalled that displaying the genitals is familiar in other connections as an apotropaic act. What arouses horror in oneself will produce the same effect upon the enemy against whom one is seeking to de.   oneself. We read in Rabelais of how the Devil took to flight when the woman showed him her vulva.

The erect male organ also has an apotropaic effect, but thanks to another mechanism. To display the penis (or any of its surrogates) is to say: "I am not afraid of you. I defy you. I have a penis." Here, then, is another way of intimidating the Evil Spirit.[41]

The desire to rewrite the female first as castration then as erection has seldom been so clearly expressed. In *Macbeth*, too, gender assignments are constantly in doubt, in flux, and in the way.

We may note that the brief 1922 piece on "Medusa's Head," the 1927 essay on "Fetishism," and the longer essay on "The Uncanny" (1919) all return or double back upon this fear of castration and its relationship to the sight of the female genitals, the mythologized version of which is Medusa's severed head. In this context it is particularly interesting to take note of Freud's own implicit strategy of repression or denial in "The Uncanny" as manifested in his gentle but firm correction of E. Jentsch's interpretation of Hoffmann's tale with which "The Uncanny" begins. Jentsch had maintained, in what is described as "a fertile but not exhaustive paper,"[42] that uncanny effects in literature are produced by uncertainty as to whether a particular figure in the story is a human being or an automaton. This, says Freud, is not in fact what produces uncanniness in "The Sand-Man." It is not, or not only,"the theme of the doll, Olympia, who is to all appearance a living being" that gives Hoffmann's tale its "quite unparalleled atmosphere of uncanniness," but rather "the theme of the Sand-Man who tears out children's eyes,"[43] and the Sand-Man's association with fears of castration and the castrating father. Yet when he turns to the subject of other imaginative literature, Freud makes a similar move in the direction of a misleading detail. Twice in his essay he specifically mentions Shakespeare's plays, and prominent among them, *Macbeth*; on both occasions, as we have seen, he denies that the presence of "spirits, demons and ghosts"[44] or "ghostly apparitions" in themselves impart to the play an aspect of the play's uncanniness. I quote again:

> The souls in Dante's *Inferno* or the ghostly apparitions in *Macbeth* or *Julius Caesar*, may be gloomy and terrible enough, but they are no more really uncanny than is Homer's jovial world of gods. We order our judgement to the imaginary reality imposed on us by the writer, and regard souls, spirits and spectres as though their existence had the same validity in their world as our own has in the external world. And then in this case too we are spared all trace of the uncanny.[45]

What Freud in effect denies here, in the case of Shakespeare, is the real uncanniness at the center of the play, which is provoked not by the ghosts and apparitions in *Macbeth* but rather by the "morbid anxiety" produced by "something repressed which *recurs*"[46] – an idea, fear, or fantasy that is continually undergoing a process of repression or denial. "This uncanny is in reality nothing new or foreign, but something familiar and old-established in the mind that has been estranged only by the process of repression."[47] Summing up his findings, Freud catalogues them, and in doing so names practically every major theme in *Macbeth*: "animism, magic and witchcraft, the omnipotence of thought, man's attitude to death, involuntary repetition, and the castration-complex comprise practically all the factors which turn something fearful into an uncanny thing."[48] By the terms of this anatomy, *Macbeth* is *the* play of the uncanny – the uncanniest in the canon.[49]

For Macbeth the dramatic character, uncanniness, the "something repressed which recurs," is figured not only in the witches and

Banquo's ghost, but also, perhaps most strikingly, in the fear of castration, which he repeatedly expresses in the form of gender anxiety:

> *Macbeth.*   I dare do all that may become a man;
> Who dares do more is none.
> *Lady Macbeth.*   What beast was't then
> That made you break this enterprise to me?
> When you durst do it, then you were a man;
> And to be more than what you were, you would
> Be so much more the man. (1.7.46–51)

Lady Macbeth's sexual taunts here and elsewhere in the play have about them the painful familiarity of an old story, an efficacious and destructive strategy of attack upon his masculinity, his male identity.[50] "You would/Be so much more the man." But what is *more* than man? Is it, in this play of border transgressions, equivalent to being woman? or some androgynous combination of the genders, like the bearded witches or the "unsexed" Lady Macbeth herself?

This same conversation repeats itself in a yet more agonized form when Macbeth is confronted by the Medusa head of Banquo at the banquet in Act 3 scene 4.

> *Macbeth.*   Thou canst not say I did it; never shake
> Thy gory locks at me ... (49–50)
> *Lady Macbeth.*   – *Are you a man?*
> *Macbeth.*   Ay, and a bold one, *that dare look on that*
> *Which might appall the devil.*
> *Lady Macbeth.*   O proper stuff!
> This is the very painting of your fear;
> This is the air-drawn dagger which you said
> Led you to Duncan. O, these flaws and starts
> (Impostors to true fear) would well become
> *A woman's story at a winter's fire,*
> *Authorized by her grandam.* Shame itself,
> *Why do you make such faces?* When all's done
> You *look* but on a stool. (57–67)

> *Macbeth (to Ghost):* Avaunt, *and quit my sight!* let the earth
> hide thee!
> Thy bones are marrowless, thy blood is cold;
> *Thou hast no speculation in those eyes*
> *Which thou dost glare with!*

Lady Macbeth (to assembled lords): Think of this, good peers,
              But as a thing of custom. 'Tis no other;
              Only it spoils the pleasure of the time.
Macbeth.   *What man dare, I dare.*
              Approach thou like the rugged Russian bear,
              Th'armed rhinoceros, or th'Hyrcan tiger,
              Take any shape but that, and my firm nerves
              Shall never tremble. Or be alive again,
              And dare me to the desert with thy sword;
              If trembling I inhabit them, protest me
              The baby of a girl. Hence, horrible shadow!
              Unreal mock'ry, hence!   (Exit Ghost)
                   Why, so; *being gone*
              I am a man again. (92–106)

Macbeth (to Lady Macbeth):   You make me strange
              Even to the disposition that I owe,
              When now I think you can behold such sights,
              And keep the natural ruby of your cheeks
              When mine is blanch'd with fear. (111–15)

"Daring" here becomes the play's trope of transgression, and also
Macbeth's desperate and self-defeating rhetorical equivalent of
masculinity in action. Lady Macbeth taunts him with "Letting 'I
dare not' wait upon 'I would,'/Like the poor cat in th'adage"
(1.7.44–5), giving the word an aphoristic context; the "poor cat"
contrasts ironically with the "beast" that broke the murder plan to
her, and also to the Hyrcan tiger, the Russian bear and the armed
rhinoceros, just as "the baby of a girl" contrasts with the bold
"man" he claims to be. Lady Macbeth's scathing reference to female
storytelling, womanish narrative, and female authority and lineage
neatly encapsulates all his fears, providing a devastating alternative
to the bold male historical chronicle in which he would like to act,
as well as to the paternal authority symbolized by Duncan, by the
desire for heirs to the throne, and by the tacit and powerful figure of
the father-king James I. Likewise the references to proliferation of
dangerous gazings and forbidden sights in this scene ("never shake
thy gory locks at me"; "a bold one, that dare look on that/Which
might appall the devil"; "Avaunt, and quit my sight"; "Thou hast no
speculation in those eyes/Which thou dost glare with"; "take any
shape but that, and my firm nerves/Shall never tremble"; "Hence,
horrible shadow!/Unreal mock'ry, hence!"; "you can behold such
sights,/And keep the natural ruby of your cheeks,/When mine is
blanch'd with fear") calls attention to the underlying theme of the

Medusa complex. Notice that Lady Macbeth can, in his view, look with impunity on that which reduces him to unmanned fright. Why? Because she is "unsexed"? Because she is a woman? Because she has no "manhood" to protect?

"Unsex me here"

With its gaping mouth, its snaky locks and its association with femininity, castration, and erection, Medusa's head ends up being the displacement upward neither of the female nor of the male genitals but of gender undecidability as such. *That* is what is truly uncanny about it, and it is that uncanniness that is registered in the gender uncertainties in *Macbeth*. Yet Freud (along with virtually all other commentators on Medusa as well as on *Macbeth*, including recent feminist critics) enacts the *repression* of gender undecidability. Freud's text is positively acrobatic in its desire to reassign decidable difference, to read the Medusa figure in terms of castration anxiety and penis display, and to locate fetishism as an identifiable variant of this same anxious and repressive process. Shakespeare's play, however, resists such assignment, resists even the present-day tendency to see the play in terms of male homosocial bonding or anxiety about female power.[51] Power in *Macbeth* is a function of neither the male nor the female but of the suspicion of the undecidable. The phallus as floating signifier is more powerful than when definitely assigned to either gender.

The presence of gender anxiety and its contiguity to border crossings and boundary transgressions has been evident from the opening moments of the play, when the three witches, the weird sisters, gloatingly plot their revenge upon the sailor's wife through their designs upon her husband, the "master o' the Tiger." The witches, who physically exhibit signs of their gender undecidability, as Banquo notes ("you should be women,/ And yet your beards forbid me to interpret/That you are so" [1.3.45–7]), are in a sense pluralized, replicative dream-figures for Lady Macbeth. Both they and she whisper plots and hint at the glorious future for Macbeth, goading him on to "dare." We may remember also that Medusa, whose name means "the Queen," was originally one of three. Wherever Macbeth goes, to the castle or to the heath, he encounters the same powerful female presence that lures him to destruction.

As for the witches, their language early in the play is what we might now recognize as Medusa language, the language of gender undecidability and castration fear. "Like a rat without a tail" the First Witch will "do"; in glossing this zoological peculiarity the eighteenth-century editor George Steevens noted a belief of

Shakespeare's time "that though a witch could assume the form of any animal she pleased, the tail would still be wanting, and that the reason given by some old writers for such a deficiency was, that though the hands and feet by an easy change might be converted into the four paws of a beast, there was still no part about a woman which corresponded wtih the length of tail common to almost all our foot-footed creatures."[52] Again the woman comes up short – a Renaissance witch, it seems, could not even aspire to mimetic rathood, but instead had to content herself with a curtailed or foreshortened version of that condition. The gleeful assertion, "I'll drain him dry as hay" (1.3.18) may refer to unslakable thirst, a common affliction of sailors, but it is also plausibly a description of a man exhausted ("drained dry") by excessive sexual demands made upon him. "Sleep shall neither night nor day/Hang upon his penthouse lid. . . Weary sev'nights, nine times nine,/Shall he dwindle, peak and pine" (1.3.19–23).[53] The transgressive and usurping androgynous power of the witches seems to justify, indeed to invite, a reading of these lines as sexually invasive and demeaning; the drained husband will not, unlike the weird sisters, be capable of "doing." "Look what I have," the First Witch cries delightedly.

2 *Witch.*	Show me, show me.
1 *Witch.*	Here I have a pilot's thumb,
	Wrack'd as homeward he did come. *Drum within*
3 *Witch.*	A drum, a drum!
	Macbeth doth come (26–31)

This dismembered "pilot's thumb" culminates the implicit narrative of sexual disabling and castration. The repetition of the word "come" to describe the progress of both Macbeth and the hapless "pilot" reinforces the metonymic association of the two figures, especially since Macbeth is also on his way home to be "wrack'd." (He uses the word in a similar context of storm and disaster just before his own decapitation at the play's close: "Blow wind, come wrack,/At least we'll die with harness on our back!" [5.5.50–1]) Nor can we entirely ignore the possibility that "look what I have" can function as a gleeful, childlike announcement of sexual display. Just as the Medusa head incorporates the elements of sexual gazing (scopophilia) and its concomitant punishment, castration, so the First Witch's exhibition of a prize, coming as it does in the narrative just after the account of the "drained" sailor, invites a similar transgressive sight. The morphological similarity between thumb and phallus needs no elaboration, and the possession by the witches of a thumb/phallus as a fetishistic object would emphasize their ambiguous, androgynous character, shortly to be remarked by

Banquo. The witches' chortling exchange, aptly described by Coleridge as exhibiting "a certain fierce familiarity, grotesqueness mingled with terror,"[54] introduces the entrance of Macbeth and Banquo, and marks Banquo's questions of them as appropriate descriptions of the uncanny:

> What are these
> So wither'd and so wild in their attire,
> That look not like th'inhabitants o' th' earth,
> And yet are on't? Live you? or are you aught
> That man may question? . . .
> You should be women,
> And yet your beards forbid me to interpret
> That you are so. (1.3.39–47)

The "Medusa complex," if we may continue to call it that, persists throughout the play, from Macduff's horrified cry to the final scene. Macbeth's first act is to display a severed head. Even before the murder there is a muted anticipation of the myth, in an image that seems localized but will recur: Macbeth's curious insistence on the phenomenon of his hair standing on end as if it were alive. Learning that he is Thane of Cawdor, and therefore that the witches' other prophecies may come true, he contemplates the murder of Duncan and is terrified at the thought. "Why," he wonders aloud,

> do I yield to that suggestion
> Whose horrid image doth unfix my hair
> And make my seated heart knock at my ribs
> Against the use of nature? (1.3.134–7)

The word "horrid" comes from a Latin word meaning "to bristle with fear," and is used to mean "bristling, shaggy," throughout the Renaissance. Metaphorically, at least, Macbeth's hair stands on end, "unfixed" by the "horrible imaginings" that flood his mind. Significantly, his imagined physiological response occurs in a key passage about undecidability and the sensation of the uncanny. The "supernatural solicitings" are the text of transgressive doubt, when "nothing is but what is not."

Much later in the play he makes use of the same image, this time to emphasize not his emotional distraction but the numbness that has succeeded it. Hearing the distressful cry of women, he speculates on its source, but does not otherwise respond.

> I have almost forgot the taste of fears.
> The time has been, my senses would have cool'd
> To hear a night-shriek, and my fell of hair

> Would at a dismal treatise rouse and stir
> As life were in't. I have supp'd full with horrors. (5.5.9–13)

Notice "as life were in't." Hair that stands on end is occasionally mentioned elsewhere in Shakespeare, notably when Brutus beholds the ghost of Caesar and addresses it as a "monstrous apparition." "Art thou any thing?" he asks. "Art thou some god, some angel, or some devil,/That mak'st my blood cold, and my hair to stare?" (*Julius Caesar* 4.3.278–80). Never, however, does this figure appear with the imaginative intensity that it does in *Macbeth*. Occurring once near the beginning of the play and once near the end, the picture of the man with horrid, bristling hair frames the dramatic action in an oddly haunting way.

Like Brutus, Macbeth is also visited by the ghost of a man he has murdered, and that encounter provides the opportunity for another, more substantial evocation of the Medusa story. On this occasion Macbeth is the horrified onlooker, and the ghost of Banquo the instrument of his petrification.

The scene is the banqueting-hall, where the Scottish lords are gathering to feast with their new king. Macbeth has just learned of the successful murder of Banquo – "his throat is cut" (3.4.15). It is therefore with some complacency that he addresses the assembled lords, expressing the disingenuous hope that "the grac'd person of our Banquo" (3.4.40) is merely tardy rather than fallen upon "mischance" (42). But no sooner has he said these words than he turns to find the ghost of his old companion seated in the king's place. His shock is profound, and his language significant. In effect he is petrified, turned to stone.

Desperately he resolves to visit the weird sisters and compel them to show him the future. But when they do, it is only to present him with another Gorgon, one he will neither recognize nor interpret correctly. For the first apparition summoned by the witches is "an armed Head," prefiguring Macbeth's own ignoble decapitation. Had he read the apotropaic warning in the disembodied head, or in its words, his story might have ended differently. But his failure to "beware the Thane of Fife" (4.1.72), like his inability to comprehend the limits of his own power and knowledge, spell his doom. It remains for the Thane of Fife to transform him into yet another "new Gorgon," a warning sign to Scotland and to the audience of tragedy.

When Macduff confronts Macbeth on the field of battle, he offers, unwittingly, an explanation of the second apparition displayed by the witches, the bloody child. The apparition had proclaimed that "None of woman born/Shall harm Macbeth"

(4.1.80–1) so that Macbeth departed confident of his safety. But now Macduff reveals that he "was from his mother's womb/ Untimely ripp'd" (5.8.15–16). Macduff's Caesarean birth recalls the moment before the play began when, according to the sergeants' report, Macbeth "carv'd out his passage" (1.2.19) through the rebels and "unseam'd" Macdonwald "from the nave to th'chops" (22).[55] To be "not of woman born" is at least rhetorically to be exempt from the gender anxiety that so torments Macbeth – to be a man born only from a man. And the image of parthenogenesis suggested by this deliberately "paltering" phrase may also bring to mind the figure of Athena, the virgin war goddess, bearer of the Gorgon shield, who sprung full grown, armed and shouting from the head of her father, Zeus. Both of these births avoid the normal "passage" through the female body. Both avoid a disabling identification with the mother and with female weakness, empowering the figures thus begotten as appropriate emblems of retribution. Hearing this phrase – "from his mother's womb/Untimely ripp'd" – Macbeth's courage begins to fail. "I'll not fight with thee," he declares (22). "Then yield thee, coward," retorts Macduff,

> And live to be the show and gaze o' th' time!
> We'll have thee, as our rarer monsters are,
> Painted upon a pole, and underwrit,
> "Here may you see the tyrant." (5.8.23–7)

"Monster," a word which for the Renaissance carried the modern meaning of an unnatural being, also retained the force of its Latin root, monēre (to warn), and hence meant a divine portent or sign. In Macduff's scenario the picture of Macbeth is to become an object lesson, a spectacle, a warning against tyranny, a figure for theater and for art. Like the head of Medusa, this painted figure would serve a monitory role, much in the manner of the dead suitors whose severed heads were to adorn the walls of Antioch in *Pericles*. Ultimately, however, taunted by so inglorious a fate, Macbeth decides to fight – and it is at this point that the next "new Gorgon" appears. Macbeth is slain, and in the next scene we find the stage direction, "Enter Macduff with Macbeth's head."

On the stage this is, or should be, an extremely disturbing moment. The head is presented to the spectators, both the onstage Scottish troops and the audience in the theater, and it is reasonable to suppose that before Macduff's speech of homage to Duncan's son, Malcolm ("Hail, King! for so thou art" (5.9.19]) there should be a brief silence. Even though this is a bloody play, and the soldiers are engaged in bloody battle, the sudden appearance of a severed head – and a recognizable one, at that – might give one pause. The audience, if not turned to stone, is at least likely to be taken aback. Macduff the avenging Perseus, Macbeth the horrified Medusa head, are presented as if in allegorical tableau. And since there is no stage direction that indicates departure, the bloody head of the decapitated king must remain onstage throughout all of Malcolm's healing and mollifying remarks. In his final speech he refers to "this dead butcher" (5.9.35), presumably with some sort of gesture in the direction of the head. However complete Malcolm's victory, however bright the future for Scotland under his rule, the audience is confronted at the last with a double spectacle; the new king and the old tyrant, the promising future and the tainted past.

Yet just as the head of Medusa became a powerful talisman for good once affixed to the shield of Athena, so the head of Macbeth is in its final appearance transformed from an emblem of evil to a token of good, a sign at once minatory and monitory, threatening and warning. Not in the painted guise foreseen by Macduff, but in its full and appalling reality, the head of the monster that was Macbeth has now become an object lesson in tyranny, a demonstration of human venality and its overthrow – "the show and gaze o' th' time."

The severed head, the gory locks of Banquo, and the armed head that appears as the witches' first apparition – all these have an iconographic congruence to the "new Gorgon" Macduff announced. But there is yet one more episode in the play which, to me at least, suggests associations with the Gorgon story, and which is, in its way, the most remarkable version of that story in the play. I refer to the final apparition displayed for Macbeth on the heath, at his importunate insistence. You will recall that the witches had told him to "seek to know no more" and that he had nonetheless insisted on an answer to his final question, "shall Banquo's issue ever/Reign in this kingdom?" (4.1.102–3). As we have seen, he threatens to curse them if they do not reply, and is answered by a chorus that makes plain that the ensuing vision is taboo, not to be gazed upon: "Show!/Show!/Show!/Show his eyes, and grieve his heart;/Come like shadows, so depart" (4.1.107–11). Now there appear what the stage directions describe as "*A show of eight Kings, (the eighth) with a glass in his hand, and Banquo last.*" Macbeth's anguished response is worth quoting in full because of its relevance to our line of inquiry:

> Thou art too like the spirit of Banquo; down!
> Thy crown does sear mine eyeballs. And thy hair,
> Thou other gold-bound brow, is like the first.

> A third is like the former. Filthy hags,
> Why do you show me this? – A fourth? Start, eyes?
> What, will the line stretch out to th' crack of doom?
> Another yet? A seventh? I'll see no more.
> And yet the eighth appears, who bears a glass
> Which shows me many more; and some I see
> That twofold balls and treble sceptres carry.
> Horrible sight! Now I see 'tis true,
> For the blood-bolter'd Banquo smiles upon me,
> And points at them for this. [*Apparitions vanish.*]
> > What, is this so?
> *1 Witch.* Ay, sir, all this is so. But why
> Stands Macbeth thus amazedly? (112–26)

"Why stands Macbeth thus amazedly?" We could answer with the Doctor's words from the sleepwalking scene: "My mind she has mated, and amaz'd my sight." Notice Macbeth's words: "Sear mine eyelids"; "start, eyes"; "horrible sight." Once again Macbeth is a man transfixed by what he has seen, once again in effect turned to stone. His murders have been for nothing; Banquo's sons will inherit the kingdom. This is his personal Gorgon, the sign of his own futility and damnation.

But the form of this particular apparition has more to tell us. The eighth king appears with "a glass," which shows us many more kings to come. A glass is a mirror – in the context of the scene a magic mirror, predicting the future, but as a stage prop quite possibly an ordinary one, borne to the front of the audience where at the first performance King James would have been seated in state. James, of course, traced his ancestry to Banquo, a fact which – together with his interest in witchcraft – may have been the reason for Shakespeare's choice of subject. The "glass" is another transgression of the inside/outside boundary, crossing the barrier that separates the play and its spectators.

Moreover, the word "glass" in Shakespeare's time meant not only "mirror" but also "model" or "example." Thus Hamlet is described as "the glass of fashion and the mould of form" (*Hamlet* 3.1.153); Hotspur as "the glass/Wherein the noble youth did dress themselves" (*2 Henry IV* 2.3.21), and King Henry V, in a variant of the figure, as "the mirror of all Christian kings" (*Henry V* 2. Prologue. 6). For the apparition of the eighth king to reflect such a "glass" (in the person of James I) with the glass he bears would therefore approximate in metaphorical terms the optical phenomenon of infinite regress when two mirrors face one another. Banquo's line would indeed "stretch out to th' crack of doom." Implicitly this trope is already present, since the king reflects all his ancestors. In this sense as well he is "a glass/Which shows [Macbeth] many more." James himself would later explicate this figure of the king as mirror in a speech to Parliament on 21 March, 1609:

> Yee know that principally by three wayes yee may wrong a Mirrour.
>
> First, I pray you, look not vpon my Mirrour with a false light: which yee doe, if ye mistake, or mis-vunderstand my Speach, and so alter the sence thereof.
>
> But secondly, I pray you beware to soile it with a foule breath, and vncleane hands: I meane, that yee peruert not my words by any corrupt affections, turning them to an ill meaning, like one, who when hee hears the tolling of a Bell, fancies to himself, that it speakes those words which are most in his minde.
>
> And lastly (which is worst of all) beware to let it fall or breake: (for glass is brittle) which ye doe, if ye lightly esteeme it, and by contemning it, conforme not your selues to my perswasions.[56]

What I would like to suggest here is that the reflecting glass or mirror in this scene is the counterpart of Perseus's reflecting shield, another transgression of the boundary between stage and reality. Perseus, we are told, was able to gaze on the reflection of Medusa without harm, although had he looked at her directly he would have been turned to stone. But the reflection or deflection of the dreadful image made it bearable. When the head was presented to Athena, and its image fixed on her aegis, it became a positive force, allied with the goddess and the virtues for which she stood. In the context of *Macbeth* the reflecting glass is the binary opposite of Macbeth's severed head: the glass is a happy spectacle demonstrating the long line of kings descended from Banquo, a line which James would doubtless hope to have "stretch out to th' crack of doom"; the head is a dismal spectacle signifying the end of a tyrant's solitary reign. Both are displaced versions of the Gorgon myth, "new Gorgons," since what horrifies Macbeth gratifies King James and the Jacobean audience. Indeed it may not be too extreme to suggest that James himself is the Athena figure here, to whom the head of the slain Macbeth is offered as a talisman and sign. The code of flattery which attended the theater of patronage would surely have allowed such a trope, and the apotropaic function of the severed head, warding off evil, would have been entirely consonant with the play's other compliment to English kings, the mention of the "healing benediction" (4.3.156) – the sovereign's ability to cure scrofula ("the evil") with the "king's touch," a custom which dated from the reign of Edward the Confessor, and was still in practice at the time of

James I. Yet the fact that the "glass" transgresses the boundary of representation implies once again that tranquil containment is not possible without opening a new rift.

"There's no art
To find the mind's construction in the face"

What is reflected in the mirror is thus, on the one hand, the king, and on the other hand, the sexually ambiguous head of the Medusa. There are in fact historical reasons why it should come as no surprise to find that gender undecidability in Shakespeare is profoundly implicated in power. England had recently been ruled by a Queen who called herself a Prince, used the male pronoun in all her state papers, and was widely rumored to possess some of the anatomical features of the male sex. In a famous passage in her speech to her troops at Tilbury – when she appeared in the costume of an androgynous martial maiden – she declared:

> I know that I have the body but of a weak and feeble woman, but I have the heart and stomach of a king, and a king of England, too.[57]

Louis Montrose puts the matter of the queen's two bodies clearly when he remarks that "As the female ruler of what was, at least in theory, a patriarchal society, Elizabeth incarnated a contradiction at the very center of the Elizabethan sex/gender system."[58] "More than a man, and, in troth, sometimes less than a woman," as Cecil wrote to Harington.[59]

As for King James, he was known to have not only a wife but also male favorites. A preacher at St Paul's Cross spoke openly in a sermon about the King and "his catamites." Sir Walter Raleigh, discussing the King's special friend, the Duke of Buckingham, is reported to have said that royal favorites "were frequently commanded to uncomely, and sometimes unnatural, employments,"[60] and James himself wrote longingly to Buckingham as his "sweet child and wife," while expressing in his poems and letters his desire for "sweete bedchamber boyes."[61] "The love the king shewed," wrote Francis Osborne, "was as amorously conveyed, as if he had mistaken their sex, and thought them ladies."[62] Historically as well as dramatically, then, one can ask: was the Queen a man? Was the King a queen?

Elizabeth and James, in other words, themselves encoded boundary transgression at precisely the point of maximum personal and political power. This play marks the gender undecidability of monarchs. But if the curtain rises too soon on the bearded witches, revealing a scene of gender undecidability, is the final scene a restoration of decidability? Does Macbeth's brandished head apotropaically dismiss uncertainty, or reinscribe it? *That* is what remains uncertain. The attempts of feminists and others to reassign gender and power in *Macbeth* merely replicate the fundamental resistance we have seen in Freud, the refusal to regard the enigma as such, to gaze upon the head of the Medusa, to recognize the undecidability that may lie just beneath the surface of power – and perhaps of sexuality itself.

The prevalence of the Medusa image and its own uncanny propensity for appearing at moments of aesthetic or representational crisis underscores the aptness of the figure's obsessive presence in *Macbeth*. Linked repeatedly to gender and to threatening sexual manifestations, it is also found again and again in the context of poetic anxiety and the anxiety of narrative completion. John Freccero has convincingly shown that the Medusa against which the furies warn Dante's pilgrim in *Inferno* (9.52–63) represents "a sensual fascination and potential entrapment, precluding all further progress,"[63] the danger of narcissistic fascination with the poet's own creation. "Petrification by the Medusa," Freccero argues, "is the real consequence of Pygmalion's folly"[64] This kind of self-conscious poetic idolatry, "a refusal to go beyond, a self-petrification"[65] is both the risk and the triumph of secular poetry, as exemplified in the appropriately named poet Petrarca, who acknowledges the risk of turning to stone in the idolatrous adoration of his own creation, *Laura/lauro*, the poetic subject and the poetic garland: "*Medusa e l'error mio m'han fatto un sasso.*"[66] Such a reification immortalizes the poet as much as it does his ostensible subject. Gender undecidability is here a figure for the anxiety of art. Dante's Virgil covers the pilgrim's eyes to protect him from the sight of the Medusa, and the poet turns, immediately to warn the reader:

> O voi ch'avete li 'ntelletti sani,
> Mirate la dottrina ch s'asconde
> Sotto 'l velame de lie versi strani. (9.61–3)

> [O you possessed of sturdy intellects,
> observe the teaching that is hidden here
> beneath the veil of verses so obscure.]

Here Dante substitutes his own apotropaic warning for the sight of the Medusa — a warning produced and engendered by the absence, refusal, or denial of that sight. The reader, in fact, is invited not to look away, but to look at, *mirate*, to observe that which is veiled or displaced by the Medusa. The text presents itself as a legible sight, a survivable alternative to the petrification of the Medusa gaze, which would prevent a return to the world above (*nulla sarebbe di tornar mai suso*).

The word "apotropaic," so frequently associated with the power of the severed Medusa head, means "turning away" or "warding off," and derives from the same root as "trope," and also as Atropos, the third of the Moirai or Fates – Atropos whose name means the Inflexible or the Inexorable, she who cannot be turned away. Like the Gorgons, the Fates were three in number; they are represented in myth as old women, and probably originated not as abstract powers or destiny but as birth-spirits, telling the story of a child's future. The thread they spin, the tale or plot they weave, is the individual's destiny, the life line or the plot line. Atropos is variously described as spinning or singing, both creative arts, then as cutting the thread of life short. The Latin word *Fata* itself is probably àn adaptation of the singular *fatum*, "that which is spoken." In fact, the Fates seem from the first to have been connected with narrative, and perhaps also with prophetic powers, as are Shakespeare's Weird Sisters. It is not entirely surprising, therefore, that an apotropaic object like the Medusa head, especially when represented in visual art or poetry, would have a doubled message to deliver, a message at once seductive and dangerous, enabling and disabling.

Not only in antiquity and the Middle Ages, but also in the Renaissance, the image of Medusa exercised a powerful fascination over visual artists. Cellini's famous statue of *Perseus* in the Bargello Museum in Florence holds aloft a rather romanticized head of Medusa with attractive classical features, and Rubens's Baroque version of the head (in the Picture Gallery in Vienna) wears an anguished expression and a plenitude of writhing snakes. But the two most provocative renderings of the subject in the period are probably a lost work by Leonardo da Vinci described in Vasari's *Life of Leonardo*, and Caravaggio's arresting painting now in the Uffizi Gallery. Both illustrate the transgressive representational powers of the Medusa, as well as the durability of the myth.

Vasari tells a remarkable and pertinent anecdote about the Leonardo Medusa. When the artist was still a very young man, his father, Ser Piero, gave him a round panel of wood (Vasari's word is *rotella* which, it is interesting to note, means a round shield) and asked him to paint something on it. Leonardo, says Vasari,

> resolved to do the Head of Medusa to terrify all beholders. To a room to which he alone had access, Leonardo took lizards,

newts, maggots, snakes, moths, locusts, bats, and other animals of the kind, out of which he composed a horrible and terrible monster . . . . When it was finished Leonardo told his father to send for it when he pleased, as he had done his part. Accordingly Ser Piero went to his rooms one morning to fetch it. When he knocked at the door Leonardo opened it and told him to wait a little, and, returning to his room, put the round panel in the light on his easel, which he turned with its back to the window to make the light dim; then he called his father in. Ser Piero, taken unaware, started back, not thinking of the round piece of wood, or that the face which he saw was painted, and was beating a retreat when Leonardo detained him and said, "This work is as I wanted it to be; take it away, then, as it is producing the effect intended."[67]

The disembodied head, placed as if on a shield, terrifies and repels, while its creator wields the power of his creation, which is also the (suspended) power of parricide.

The life of Leonardo da Vinci held a particular fascination for Freud, whose 1910 essay on the painter's development attempts to explore the "peculiarity of [his] emotional and sexual life . . . in connection with Leonardo's double nature as an artist and as a scientific investigator,"[68] and concludes that "after his curiosity had been activated in infancy in the service of sexual interests he succeeded in sublimating the greater part of his libido into an urge for research"[69] – an extension and displacement of the "intense desire to look, as an erotic instinctual activity" which occurs in infantile development "before the child comes under the dominance of the castration-complex."[70] In this early essay on "Leonardo da Vinci and a Memory of his Childhood" Freud explicitly connects Leonardo's homosexuality to his desire to see his mother's penis, and his "disgust" at the appalling discovery that she lacks one. The theories of narcissism, fetishism and castration which would be elaborated in later works are here directly applied to the "youthful investigator"[71] who deflected his sexual desires into artistic creation, but even more centrally, into scientific curiosity, into *looking*. That Leonardo was an illegitimate child suggests a further nuance in Vasari's anecdote. The apotropaic head, the disembodied emblem and threat of castration, the sign of the androgynous mother, is displayed to the artist's father and produces "the effect intended," the consternation and repulsion of the father. Thus the son asserts control over his disconcerted parent, sending him away with the painted Medusa head, the son's own repellent and fascinating "work." In this image of the independent youthful investigator it is perhaps possible to see a self-portrait of Freud the analyst as creator and scientist, exhibiting his own Medusa head, the concept of the castration-complex, to an audience simultaneously fascinated and horrified.

To portray the head of Medusa as if on a shield, round or oblong, was not uncommon in the fifteenth and sixteenth centuries. The head is directly conceived as an apotropaic object that will protect the shield-bearer from harm. This seems also to be the case in the striking Caravaggio *Medusa*, which is painted on canvas and stretched over a round convex shield.[72] Her mouth is open as if crying out, blood streams from her neck, and her head is wreathed in a profusion of lively snakes. Presumably this work, like other similar representations, is intended to depict the aegis of Athena (or Minerva). It is in essence the Renaissance equivalent of those Roman Medusa masks discovered by archaeologists.

However, one other factor in the rendering of the Caravaggio *Medusa* may be of some interest in the light of our discussion. We know that for the *Medusa* as well as for his *Bacchus* and the decapitated Goliath in *David with the Head of Goliath* (and possibly for *Judith Beheading Holofernes*) Caravaggio reproduced by reflection his own face in a mirror. It therefore seems possible to consider Caravaggio's painting as a representation not – or not only – as Athena's shield, but also as Perseus's. Instead of being mounted on the shield, the head would in that case be reflected in it, and the viewer would share the immunity of Perseus. Since he gazes not directly upon the head of Medusa – which would by convention turn him to stone – but rather on its reflection, he can contemplate horror in safety. As Lady Macbeth points out in chiding Macbeth for his fears, "'tis the eye of childhood/That fears a painted devil" (2.2.51–2).

Whether the Medusa of the Caravaggio painting is considered a deflected image (and the shield that of Perseus) or a displaced image (and the shield Athena's), the result for the spectator is largely the same. He beholds a terrifying spectacle which, if it were encountered in the flesh, would be devastating to him – but he beholds it, as it were, from a safe distance, insulated by art. It would be tempting to conclude that the same is true of the Gorgon's heads in Shakespeare's play, that Shakespeare permits us to gaze at the face that should turn us to stone. This is indeed the conclusion to which Joyce Carol Oates comes in an essay that clearly articulates the theory of displacement and vicarious purgation:

> Critics who chide me for dwelling on unpleasant and even
> bloody subjects miss the point: art shows us how to get through

and transcend pain, and a close reading of any tragic work (*Macbeth* comes immediately to mind) will allow the intelligent reader to see how and why the tragedy took place, and how we, personally, need not make these mistakes. The more violent the murder in *Macbeth*, the more relief one can feel at *not* having to perform them. Great art is cathartic; it is always moral.[73]

Yet in the very wording of this passage we find an uncanny doubleness that exposes the fragility of such a reassuring formulation. "The more violent the murders in *Macbeth*, the more relief one can feel at *not* having to perform them." Notice Oates's word, *perform*. Murders, she implies, must be *performed* – that is, both committed and theatrically acted. This instability in language, this double sense of performance, makes it impossible to know exactly where to locate the boundary between stage and reality. In order to work apotropaically, tragedy *must* cross that boundary. The action may be an imitation, but the purgation is real – the emotion must be felt. The curtain rises too soon, and will not fall on cue. The danger seemingly foreclosed by art may be unleashed by the shifting, transgressive status of representation itself. The voyeuristic act which is the role of the audience in the theater has us coming and going; the desire to look, which is itself transgressive, cannot be dismissed as merely the disinterested glance of a spectator, the "objective" view of the "scientific investigator," displacing our passion – and our danger – as Freud's Leonardo displaced his.

In its self-conception, in its stage history, in the doubleness of its final tableau, *Macbeth* seems almost paradigmatically to be a play that refuses to remain contained within the safe boundaries of fiction. It is a tragedy that demonstrates the refusal of tragedy to be so contained. As it replicates, it implicates. Things will not remain within their boundaries: sleepers and forests walk, the dead and the deeds return, the audience stares at forbidden sights. This is what the plot of *Macbeth* is about. Yet what is most uncanny about the play is perhaps that it is *both* apotropaic and atropic, *heimlich* and *unheimlich*, faltering with us constantly in a double sense. It is as though we too can in the end only cry, with Lady Macbeth's doctor, "A great perturbation in nature, to receive at once the benefit of sleep and do the effects of watching!"

6

Hamlet: giving up the ghost

But the calling back of the dead, or the desirability of calling them back, was a ticklish matter, after all. At bottom, and boldly confessed, the desire does not exist; it is a misapprehension precisely as impossible as the thing itself, as we should soon see if nature once let it happen. What we call mourning for our dead is perhaps not so much grief at not being able to call them back as it is grief at not being able to want to do so.

Thomas Mann, *The Magic Mountain*

The phantom which returns to haunt bears witness to the existence of the dead buried within the other.

Nicholas Abraham, "Notes on the Phantom"

For here the day unravels what the night has woven.

Walter Benjamin, "The Image of Proust"

A murder done in Vienna

In the fall of 1897 Sigmund Freud's mind was running on *Hamlet*. A letter he wrote to Wilhelm Fliess in October contained the first exposition of the Oedipus complex, later to be elaborated in *The Interpretation of Dreams* (1900) but here already fully articulated, both as it presents itself in Sophocles and, in a more repressed and hysterical fashion, in *Hamlet*:

> Everyone in the audience was once a budding Oedipus in fantasy, and each recoils in horror from the dream fulfillment here transplanted into reality, with the full quantity of repression which separates his infantile state from his present one.
> Fleetingly the thought passed through my head that the same thing might be at the bottom of *Hamlet* as well. I am not thinking of Shakespeare's conscious intentions, but believe, rather, that a real event stimulated the poet to his representation, in that his unconscious understood the unconscious of his hero.

How does Hamlet the hysteric justify his words, "Thus conscience does make cowards of us all?" How does he explain his irresolution in avenging his father by the murder of his uncle – the same man who sends his courtiers to their death without a scruple and who is positively precipitate in murdering Laertes? How better than through the torment roused in him by the obscure memory that he himself had contemplated the same deed against his father out of passion for his mother, and – "use every man after his desert, and who should 'scape whipping?" His conscience is his unconscious sense of guilt. And is not his sexual alienation in his conversation with Ophelia typically hysterical? And his rejection of the instinct that seeks to beget children? And, finally, his transferral of the deed from his own father to Ophelia's? And does he not in the end, in the same marvellous way as my hysterical patients do, bring down punishment on himself by suffering the same fate as his father of being poisoned by the same rival?[1]

Less than a month before, Freud had written to Fliess the famous letter in which he reveals his "great secret" – that he has abandoned the seduction theory: "I no longer believe in my *neurotica*."[2] Persuaded by the surprising frequency with which such seductions by fathers of children seemed to occur in his patients, and by the fact that the unconscious contains no "indications of reality," he had determined that such acts were plausibly to be considered as fantasies rather than as personal history: "surely such widespread perversions against children are not very probable"; "in all the cases, the *father*, not excluding my own, had to be accused of being perverse."[3]

Reversing himself on so crucial a point, and in effect dismantling the theory he had counted on to bring him wealth and fame, Freud addresses himself, in the letter to Fliess, to his own emotions. He had expected to be "depressed, confused, exhausted,"[4] but he feels just the opposite. "It is strange, too, that no feeling of shame appeared."[5] In fact, he feels impelled to take a journey, and now proposes to visit his friend in Berlin. "If during this lazy period I were to go to the Northwest Station on Saturday evening I could be with you by noon on Sunday,"[6] or, if this does not suit their schedules, "do the same conditions obtain if I go straight to the Northwest Station on Friday evening?"[7]

The proposal for a visit is treated as a digression, from which Freud now recalls himself:

Now to continue my letter. I vary Hamlet's saying, "To be in readiness": to be cheerful is everything! I could indeed feel quite discontent. The expectation of eternal fame was so beautiful, as was that of certain wealth, complete independence, travels, and lifting the children above the severe worries that robbed me of my youth. Everything depended on whether or not hysteria would come out right. Now I can once again remain quiet and modest, go on worrying and saving.[8]

Yet this apparent digression, this detour via the Northwest Station, in fact takes him directly back to the subject: *Hamlet*, and the way in which "a real event" might make the unconscious understand the intentions of the hero. For in this passage Freud twice proposes a journey to the Northwest Station, a locus that suggests what is literally a new train of thought. It is Hamlet, of course, who announces that he is "but mad north-north-west" (2.2.378),[9] feigning madness for a purpose. Freud's slip into the Northwest Station will likewise confirm that he is not "depressed, confused, exhausted, afflicted with shame," or "discontent," as he might be, but actually in control of his daydreams of fortune and independence, however he appears to the outside world. His letter to Fliess concludes with the hope that he will soon hear "How all of you are and whatever else is happening between heaven and earth."[10] "There are more things in heaven and earth, Horatio,/Than are dreamt of in your philosophy" (1.5.165-6), says Hamlet to his confidant, conceiving the plan to "put an antic disposition on" (172), to present himself as mad north-north-west. Fliess is an appropriate Horatio figure, idolized as a man of superior learning. But we may even hear a faint reminder of another passage from Shakespeare's play here, Hamlet's half-sardonic, half-serious self-accusation to Rosencrantz and Guildenstern: "I am very proud, revengeful, ambitious . . . What should such fellows as I do crawling, between earth and heaven?" (3.1.123-8).

Freud's projected journey to the Northwest Station has about it something of the same quality as the Italian walk he describes in his essay on "The Uncanny" in which time after time he arrived at the same place, "recognizable by some particular landmark"[11] – a "factor of involuntary repetition which surrounds with an uncanny atmosphere what would otherwise be innocent enough, and forces upon us the idea of something fateful and inescapable where otherwise we should have spoken of 'chance' only."[12] The recognizable landmark here is both the railway terminus and *Hamlet*. When he came to write up his ideas about Hamlet for *The Interpretation of Dreams* (1900), Freud himself made the same connection, bringing the quotation to the surface:

The prince in the play, who had to disguise himself as a madman, was behaving just as dreams do in reality; so that we can say of dreams what Hamlet says of himself, concealing the true circumstances under a cloak of wit and unintelligibility: "I am but mad north-north-west."[13]

Hamlet is a play not only informed *with* the uncanny but also informed *about* it. The Ghost is only the most explicit marker of uncanniness, the ultimate articulation of "uncertainty whether something is dead or alive."[14] In *Hamlet*, as we shall see, Shakespeare instates the uncanny as sharply as he does the Oedipus complex – or, to put the matter more precisely, Freud's concept of uncanniness finds as explicit an expression in the play as does his concept of the complicated sexual rivalry between father and son.

The essay on "The Uncanny," as we have already several times noted, goes out of its way to deny the status of Shakespearean ghosts *per se* as instances of this phenomenon. We have seen that *Hamlet* is the subtext for some of Freud's own self-analysis. It is also a powerful subtext for the essay on "The Uncanny," despite (or because of?) the explicit disavowals of the relevance of Shakespeare's ghosts. Thus the central literary work that provides Freud with his chief enabling example of uncanniness, Hoffman's story "The Sand-Man," is described in terms that closely resemble the plot of *Hamlet*.

> In the story from Nathaniel's childhood, the figures of his father and Coppelius represent the two opposites into which the father-image is split by the ambivalence of the child's feeling: whereas the one threatens to blind him, that is, to castrate him, the other, the loving father, intercedes for his sight. That part of the complex which is most strongly repressed, the death-wish against the father, finds expression in the death of the good father, and Coppelius is made answerable for it.[15]

This division of the father into loving and threatening figures, one castrating and the other protecting, is accompanied by the presence of an apparently desirable young woman who turns out to be a mechanical creation of the bad father (Coppola/Coppelius) working in collusion with *her* supposed father, Professor Spalanzani: "But Olympia was an automaton whose works Spalanzani had made, and whose eyes Coppola, the Sand-Man, had put in."[16] This would be an unfairly reductive description of Ophelia, to be sure, but there are striking similarities in the structures of the two situations. In both the young woman is used as a bait or lure for a transaction involving the young man, the threatening father, and the "Professor," his colleague or accomplice. As a consequence of these events (the death of his father, the threats of the Sand-Man, the discovery of the girl-doll's true nature, the betrayal of the old men in league against him) the young student goes mad and kills himself.

Thus in not talking about *Hamlet* Freud is in a sense talking about *Hamlet*, and Hamlet's relationships with Claudius, Polonius, Ophelia and the Ghost. Indeed the passage on the *non*applicability of the Shakespearean ghosts to the kind of uncertainty Freud calls "the uncanny" is introduced at precisely this point in his explication of "The Sand-Man," as a way of turning from the apparent but unimportant uncanniness of Olympia's status ("uncertainty whether an object is living or inanimate"[17]) to the centrality of the castration complex as figured in the Sand-Man's threat to put out Nathaniel's eyes.

Two kinds of things cause a sensation of uncanniness: beliefs that have been surmounted, and repressed complexes.

> An uncanny experience occurs either when repressed infantile complexes have been revived by some impression, or when the primitive beliefs we have surmounted seem once more to be confirmed . . . these two classes of uncanny experience are not always sharply distinguishable. When we consider that primitive beliefs are most intimately connected with infantile complexes, and are, in fact, based upon them, we shall not be greatly astonished to find the distinction often rather a hazy one.[18]

> The distinction between what has been repressed and what has been surmounted cannot be transposed onto the uncanny in fiction without profound modification; for the realm of phantasy depends for its very existence on the fact that its content is not submitted to the reality-testing faculty.[19]

Here we have returned to the distinction that Freud makes in his letter to Fliess rejecting the seduction theory, between what happened "in reality" and what happened in fantasy. In *Hamlet*, as I will want to suggest, such distinctions, insofar as they can be made, are presented in the guise of encapsulated artifacts, or what are often called "insets": the play within the play, the story of Old Hamlet's death ("sleeping within my orchard" – a dream? and if so, whose?), Ophelia's disturbingly knowledgeable ballads with their disconcerting sexual references, so ambiguously (and ambivalently) applicable to her father, brother, and lover.

But at the center of the question of uncanniness lies not only the castration complex but also the compulsion to repeat. "Whatever reminds us of this inner *repetition-compulsion* is perceived as uncanny."[20] Repetition, and the repetition compulsion, are figured throughout *Hamlet*: in the double play, dumbshow and dialogue, their double existence never satisfactorily explained despite the ingenuity of critics; in the Queen's two marriages, the twin husbands ("Look here upon this picture, and on this,/The counterfeit presentment of two brothers" [3.4.53–4]); in the double murder of fathers, Hamlet's father killed by Claudius, Laertes' father killed by Hamlet.

Every critical observation on doubling in the play, from the psychoanalytic ("the decomposing of the original villain into at least three father figures, the ghost, Polonius, and Claudius"; "The splitting of the hero into a number of brother figures: Fortinbras, Horatio, Laertes, and Rosencrantz-and-Guildenstern")[21] to the rhetorical ("the most pregnant and interesting of [the play's] linguistic doublings is undoubtedly hendiadys")[22] is an implicit commentary on the compulsion to repeat.

Moreover, *Hamlet* is a play that enacts the repetition compulsion even as it describes it. (1) The ghost of old Hamlet appears to young Hamlet and urges him to revenge; (2) the ghost of young Hamlet, "pale as his shirt," "with a look so piteous in purport/As if he had been loosed out of hell/To speak of horrors" (2.1.78–91) appears to Ophelia in her closet and, in dumbshow, raising a sigh both "piteous and profound," returns from whence he has come; (3) the ghost of Ophelia, mad, appears before her brother Laertes and incites him to revenge for the death of their father Polonius.

What, indeed, is revenge but the dramatization and acculturation of the repetition compulsion?

The anamorphic ghost

The agent of repetition here, clearly, is the ghost. And what is a ghost? It is a memory trace. It is the sign of something missing, something omitted, something undone. It is itself at once a question, and the sign of putting things in question. Thus Barnardo, one of the officers on guard duty, suggests that "this portentous figure/Comes armed through our watch so like the King/That was and is *the question* of these wars" (*Hamlet* 1.1.109–11). Onstage, as in the plot of a tale or story, a ghost is the concretization of a missing presence, the sign of what is there by not being there. " 'Tis here!" " 'Tis here!" " 'Tis gone!" cry the sentries (1.1.141–2).

Horatio's learned disquisition, reminding his onstage hearers and his offstage audience simultaneously of events in classical Rome and in Shakespeare's recent play *Julius Caesar*, offers an historical (and stage-historical) context for the ghost:

> In the most high and palmy state of Rome
> A little ere the mightiest Julius fell,
> The graves stood tenantless and the sheeted dead
> Did squeak and gibber in the Roman streets. (1.1.113–16)

Horatio associates the appearance of a ghost with the death of Julius Caesar. Jacques Lacan associates it with the castration complex, the "veiled phallus."

> The hole in the real that results from loss, sets the signifier in motion. This hole provides the place for the projection of the missing signifier, which is essential to the structure of the Other. This is the signifier whose absence leaves the Other incapable of responding to your question, the signifier that can be purchased only with your own flesh and blood, the signifier that is essentially the veiled phallus . . . swarms of images, from which the phenomena of mourning rise, assume the place of the phallus: not only the phenomena in which each individual instance of madness manifests itself, but also those which attest to one or another of the most remarkable collective nadnesses of the community of men, one example of which is brought to the fore in *Hamlet*, i.e., the ghost, that image which can catch the soul of one and all unawares when someone's departure from this life has not been accompanied by the rites that it calls for.[23]

What does it mean to say that the ghost takes the place of the missing signifier, the veiled phallus? The ghost – itself traditionally often veiled, sheeted, or shadowy in form – is a cultural marker of absence, a reminder of loss. Thus the very plot of *Hamlet* replicates the impossibility of the protagonist's quest: "the very source of what makes Hamlet's arm waver at every moment, is the narcissistic connection that Freud tells us about in his text on the decline of the Oedipus complex: one cannot strike the phallus, because the phallus, even the real phallus, is a *ghost*."[24]

Thus, not only is the ghost the veiled phallus, but the phallus is also a ghost. Lacan takes as his point of departure Freud's essay on "The Passing of the Oedipus Complex" (1925), which explores the dilemma of the child caught between his desires and his fear of castration. When the inevitable conflict arises between the child's narcissistic investment in his own body and the "libidinal cathexis of the parent-objects," writes Freud,

> the object-cathexes are given up and replaced by identification. The authority of the father or of the parents is introjected into the ego and there forms the kernel of the super-ego, which takes its severity

from the father, perpetuates his prohibition against incest, and so insures the ego against a recurrence of the libinal object-cathexis.[25]

We might think that Freud's "super-ego" and Lacan's "Name-of-the-Father" would both be names for the Ghost in *Hamlet*. Yet this Lacan seems explicitly to deny when, writing on the subject of certainty in "The Unconscious and Repetition," he remarks on "the weight of the sins of the Father, borne by the ghost in the myth of Hamlet, which Freud couples with the myth of Oedipus."

> The father, the Name-of-the-Father, sustains the structure of desire with the structure of the law – but the inheritance of the father is that which Kierkegaard designates for us, namely, his sin.
>   Where does Hamlet's ghosts come from, if not from the place from which he denounces his brother for surprising him and cutting him off in the full flower of his sins? And far from providing Hamlet with the prohibitions of the Law that would allow his desire to survive, this too ideal father is constantly being doubted.[26]

The Ghost is incompletely a representative of the Law, because both he and the tale he tells allow the son to doubt. He puts in question his own being as well as his message. Is he a spirit of health or goblin damn'd? Is this the real Law? Is this the truth? As long as the Law of the father is doubted or put in question, it cannot be (or is not) internalized, not assimilated into the symbolic, and therefore blocks rather than facilitates Hamlet's own passage into the symbolic, where he will find his desire. The finding of desire is the recognition of lack, the acceptance of castration. But the doubt Hamlet experiences gives him the idea that there is something left. "It is here," says Lacan, "that Freud lays all his stress – doubt is the support of his certainty."

He goes on to explain why: "this is precisely the sign," he says "that there is something to preserve. Doubt, then, is a sign of resistance."[27]

To put the matter in a slightly different way: the Name-of-the-Father is the dead father. *This* father – the Ghost – isn't dead enough. The injunction to "Remember me" suggests that he is not quite dead. Hamlet must renounce him, must internalize the Law by forgetting, not by remembering. This is the only way he can be put in touch with his own desires, and with the symbolic.

But Hamlet is the poet of doubt. Polonius reads aloud to the King and Queen Hamlet's love poem to Ophelia, a paean to negation:

> Doubt thou the stars are fire,
> Doubt that the sun doth move,
> Doubt truth to be a liar,
> But never doubt I love (2.2.116–19)

The meaning of "doubt" is itself in doubt as the phrase is repeated, shifting from something like "dispute" or "challenge" to "suspect" or "fear." The litany of doubt here is an invitation to put things in question, at the same time that it puts in question the whole procedure of putting something in question. When we consider, additionally, the very dubious "truth" value of the statement that "the stars are fire" and "the sun doth move" – both presumptions put in question by Renaissance science – we find that a verse that purports to assert certainty and closure in fact undermines that certainty in every gesture.

We should distinguish here between repression and foreclosure in the child's experience of the symbolic order. Repression (*Verdrängung*) submerges or covers over unconscious thoughts that foreclosure (*Verwerfung*) does not permit. In other words, foreclosure preempts the experiences that repression would conceal. For both Lacan and Freud, what makes the difference here is castration, or the acceptance of castration. If a child forecloses the idea of castration, he (or she) rejects the Name-of-the-Father in favor of the Desire-of-the-Mother. Rather than accepting the loss of the phallus, the child wishes to *be* the mother's phallus, the completion of her desire, thus rejecting the limits implied by castration: the Law of the Father, the network of social roles (language, kinship, prohibitions, gender roles) that make up what Lacan calls the symbolic order. Lacan calls this "the failure of the paternal metaphor,"[28] and predicts that the foreclosure of the Name-of-the-Father, of the constitution of the Law in the symbolic, can lead to psychosis, and to delusions.

> It is the lack of the Name-of-the-Father in that place which, by the hole that it opens up in the signified, sets off the cascade of reshapings of the signifier from which the increasing disaster of the imaginary proceeds, to the point at which the level is reached at which signifier and signified are stabilized in the delusional metaphor.
>
> But how can the Name-of-the-Father be called by the subject to the only place in which it could have reached him and in which it has never been? Simply by a real father, not necessarily by the subject's own father, but by A-father.[29]

The failure of the paternal metaphor. This is not unrelated to what might be called paternal undecidability, or the undecidability of paternity – the fact, so often commented on in Shakespeare's plays, that the father is always a suppositional father, a father by imputation, rather than by unimpeachable biological proof. "I think this is your daughter," says Don Pedro to Leonato at the beginning of *Much Ado About Nothing*, and Leonato replies, "Her mother hath many times told me so" (1.1.104–5). (As if to underscore the point, Benedick interposes with interest, "Were you in doubt, sir, that you ask'd her?") Prospero speaks to the same paternal obsession when he replies to Miranda's question, "Thy mother was a piece of virtue, and/She said thou wast my daughter" (*The Tempest* 1.2.56–7). This doubt, on which paternity, legitimacy, inheritance, primogeniture, and succession all depend, is the anxiety at the root of the *cultural* failure of the paternal metaphor – that is, its failure because of its status as metaphor, its nontranslatability into the realm of proof.

And when the failure of the paternal metaphor is regarded, not from the standpoint of the father contemplating the horror of bastardy, but from the point of view of the son, we have the dilemma of Hamlet, who simultaneously seeks and denies the authority of the law, the imprint of the father, what he calls "thy commandment" and "my word," (1.5.102;110) – the Ghost's word of command, "his speech, the word (*le mot*), let us say of his authority" the place reserved for "the Name-of-the-Father in the promulgation of the law."[30] The more the father is idealized, the more problematic is the presence of doubt, the gap in certainty that instates paternal undecidability:

> the ravaging effects of the paternal figure are to be observed with particular frequency in cases where the father really has the function of a legislator or, at least has the upper hand, whether in fact he is one of those fathers who make the laws or whether he poses as the pillar of the faith, as a paragon of integrity and devotion, as virtuous or as a virtuoso, by serving a work of salvation, of whatever object or lack of object, of nation or of birth, of safeguard or salubrity, of legacy or legality, of the pure, the impure or of empire, all ideals that provide him with all too many opportunities of being in a posture of undeserving, inadequacy, even of fraud, and, in short, of excluding the Name-of-the-Father from its position in the signifier.[31]

Confronted with an overplus, a superfluity of fathers (psycho-analytic readers all comment on the splitting of the father into Claudius, Polonius, even old Fortinbras and old Norway), Hamlet finds both too many fathers and too few – he is too much in the son, but where is paternity, where is the law? Displacing onto these easier targets complaints he is blocked from voicing to the Ghost (because the Ghost is his father? because the Ghost is a ghost? because the Ghost is dead? but he is not dead, otherwise he would not walk, and how can he be dead without ever really having been alive?) Hamlet encounters doubt. Indeed, as in the case of the Medusa, where a multiplicity of penises is imagined to cover the unimaginable horror of no penis, of castration, so here the multiplicity of fathers covers the fact of lack. Covers it, in *Hamlet*, by foreclosing rather than repressing it.

We have seen that Lacan, following Freud, sees doubt as the sign of resistance. The image that he chooses to describe this doubt in the case of dream narratives is that of the mark, spot, or stain: "that which marks, stains, spots the text of any dream communication – *I am not sure, I doubt.*"[32]

The stain is the sign of uncertainty – of the fact that one cannot be certain. And this too seems to be the function of the spot or stain in *Hamlet*. When Hamlet challenges his mother in her bedroom to turn her eyes, her gaze, inward, she sees "such black and grained spots/As will not leave their tinct" (3.4.90–1). These spots are not certainties but gaps, doubts – what did she do? and why? Most centrally, in his soliloquy in Act 4 on thinking and "dull revenge," Hamlet says of himself, "how stand I then,/That have a father kill'd, a mother stain'd" (4.4.56–7), and the ambiguity of the grammatical construction is telling. He has a father who has been killed, a mother who has been stained – but by whom? Does he not also by the terms of this utterance assert, or acknowledge, that he has killed a father, stained a mother?

In his essay on *Hamlet*, Lacan thus concerns himself with Shakespeare's play as a remarkable example of the topology of human desire, "the drama of Hamlet as the man who has lost the way of his desire."[33] This is not the only case in which Lacan finds the way of his own theoretical desire by turning to a Renaissance artifact. On another occasion he examines one of the most striking of Renaissance paintings, a painting which has lately excited a good deal of commentary among literary theorists, Holbein's portrait of 1533 called *The Ambassadors*. The famous work, which contains a preeminent example of the optical device known as the anamorphosis, discloses another ghost.

> Begin by walking out of the room, in which no doubt it has long held your attention. It is then that, turning round as you leave – as the author of the *Anamorphoses* describes it – you apprehend in this form . . . What? A skull.[34]

The object half obscured beneath the feet of the ambassadors in the depiction of *vanitas*, the skull, cannot fail to remind us of the skull in *Hamlet* – which is itself, in Act 5, followed by what Lacan, in fact identifies in the *Hamlet* essay as a *vanitas*: the objects wagered in the final duel scene, he writes, are "staked against death. This is what gives their presentation the character of what is called a *vanitas* in the religious tradition."[35] Holbein's skull, which is not seen as a skull except from an exceptional or eccentric angle, is called "the phallic symbol, the anamorphic ghost."[36] Yet, Lacan insists, what we see here is "not the phallic symbol, the anamorphic ghost, but the gaze as such, in its pulsatile, dazzling and spread out function, as it is in this picture."[37] "Look here upon this picture, and on this" (3.4.53). "The King is a thing . . . of nothing" (4.2.26–30). The anamorphic ghost, the embedded, embodied, and distorted figure of a ghostly skull beneath the apparently solid feet of the ambassadors – what is this but an anamorphism of the ghost and the Ghost, the Ghost (once again, uncannily, inevitably) of Hamlet's father?

Lacan goes on:

> This picture is simply what any picture is, a trap for the gaze. In any picture, it is precisely in seeking the gaze in each of its points that you will see it disappear.[38]

"This picture is simply what any picture is, a trap for the gaze." What is *this* but the play-within, the "Mouse-trap," "the image of a murther done in Vienna" (3.2.248–9). Long treated as a dramatic presentation that encodes misdirection, putting the real play in the audience, setting up Claudius and Gertrude as the real Player King and Player Queen, the "Mouse-trap," also known as "The Murder of Gonzago," appropriates the gaze and makes it the function of the play. Again Lacan's description (in *Four Concepts*) of *The Ambassadors* is apposite:

> In Holbein's picture I showed you at once – without hiding any more than usual – the singular object floating in the foreground, which is there to be looked at, in order to catch, I would almost say, *to catch in its trap*, the observer, that is to say us . . . . The secret of this picture is given at the moment when, moving slightly away, little by little, to the left, then turning around, we see what the magical floating object signifies. It reflects our own nothingness, in the figure of the death's head.[39]

That is not how it is presented at first . . . . At the very heart of the period in which the subject emerged and geometral optics was an object of research, Holbein makes visible for us here

something that is simply the subject as annihilated – annihilated
in the form that is, strictly speaking, the imaged embodiment . . .
of castration, which for us, centres the whole organization of the
desires through the framework of the fundamental drives.[40]

Holbein's portrait shows "the subject as annihilated" – which is the
subject of *Hamlet*, a play situated on the cusp of the emergence of
what has come to be known as the modern subject.[41] For there is a
way in which *Hamlet* performs the same operation as Holbein's
painting upon the gaze and the trope of *vanitas*. Its final tableau of
the death's head in the graveyard scene is another critique of the
subject. What then is being caught in the trap Hamlet sets for the
King, the King who is a thing of nothing? Is it Claudius who is
caught in the "Mouse-trap," or Hamlet as the signifier of the
modern subject, already marked by negation, already dressed in
black?
  Lacan's own theoretical fantasy of the distortion produced by an
anamorphism is determinedly phallic:

> How is it that nobody has ever thought of connecting this
> with . . . the effect of an erection? Imagine a tattoo traced on the
> sexual organ *ad hoc* in the state of repose and assuming its, if I
> may say so, developed form in another state.
>   How can we not see here . . . something symbolic of the
> function of the lack, of the appearance of the phallic ghost?[42]

"My father, in his habit as he lived!" (3.4.135) "My father's spirit –
in arms!" (1.2.254) "Thou, dead corse, again in complete steel"
(1.4.52). The anamorphic ghost of old Hamlet, erected to full form
by the gaze, contrasts sharply with the same figure in the "state of
repose," recumbent, passive, "sleeping within my orchard" (1.5.59),
who receives the poison in the ear, the incestuous rape of a brother.
The Ghost recounts the fantasy-nightmare of his own castration:
"Thus was I, sleeping, by a brother's hand/Of life, of crown, of
queen, at once dispatch'd,/Cut off even in the blossoms of my sin"
(1.5.74–6).
  This is what Hamlet has already fantasized, what he recalls in his
ejaculation, "O my prophetic soul!" (1.5.40) And as in the case of
Julius Caesar, the dead man turned ghost is more powerful than he
was when living, precisely because he crosses boundaries, is not
only transgressive but *in* transgression, a sign simultaneously of
limit and of the violation of that limit, the nutshell and the bad
dreams. Thus the murder empowers the Ghost and his ghostly
rhetoric, the language spoken in, by, and through the Name-of-the-
Father. The Hyperion-father who obsesses Hamlet in his soliloquies

and in his conversations with his mother is erected from this moment, from the moment of the father's absence and death, half-guiltily acknowledged as the son's desire. The castration fantasy of the sleeping father in the orchard enacts both Hamlet's desire and its repression, which are in this moment identical. Here again Lacan is suggestive, when he writes of the impossibility of not wanting to desire:

> what does *not wanting to desire* mean? The whole of analytic experience – which merely gives form to what is for each individual at the very root of his experience – shows us that not to want to desire and to desire are the same thing.
>
> To desire involves a defensive phase that makes it identical with not wanting to desire. Not wanting to desire is wanting not to desire.[43]

This is the condition in which we encounter Hamlet for much of the play, the condition of desiring not to desire. Look where his desires have gotten him – or not gotten him. He walks out of Ophelia's closet and into Gertrude's. Here again we have closet drama, and of a high order – plays not meant to be acted. Hamlet's accusation of his mother catches her in the trap set for the gaze: "O Hamlet, speak no more!/Thou turn'st mine eyes into my very soul,/And there I see such black and grained spots/As will not leave their tinct" (3.4.88–91). The black spot she sees is Hamlet, Hamlet as marker, Hamlet as floating signifier, as his blackness becomes metonymically a sign of mourning, of negation, of absence, of the impossible desire to tell the difference between desire and the repression of desire.

What would your gracious figure?

The ghostly phallus as anamorphosis – that is, as *form* – assumes a certain visibility, however veiled. The Name-of-the-Father, on the other hand, is a function of the signifier, of language as a system of signs rather than shapes. As we shall see, the ghost – in *Hamlet*, as well as in a number of other literary guises – presents itself not only as a trap for the gaze but also a trope for the voice.

In an influential essay on prosopopeia as the "fiction of the voice-from-beyond-the-grave," Paul de Man writes:

> It is the figure of prosopopeia, the fiction of an apostrophe to an absent, deceased, or voiceless entity, which posits the possibility of the latter's reply, and confers upon it the power of speech. Voice assumes mouth, eye, and finally face, a chain that is

manifest in the etymology of the trope's name, *prosopon poiein*, to confer a mask or a face (*prosopon*). Prosopopeia is the trope of autobiography, by which one's name, as in the Milton poem, is made as intelligible and memorable as a face. Our topic deals with the giving and taking away of faces, with face and deface, *figure*, figuration and disfiguration.[44]

The quotation from Milton with which de Man is here concerned is, perhaps inevitably, the sonnet "On Shakespeare" as cited and discussed in Wordsworth's *Essays Upon Epitaphs*. De Man singles out the thirteenth and fourteenth lines of this sixteen-line sonnet for special commentary.

> Then thou our fancy of itself bereaving
> Dost make us marble with too much conceiving.

Here de Man observes that the phrase "dost make us marble," in the *Essays Upon Epitaphs*, "cannot fail to evoke the latent threat that inhabits prosopopeia, namely that by making the dead speak, the symmetrical structure of the trope implies, by the same token, that the living are struck dumb, frozen in their own death."[45]

Milton's sonnet "On Shakespeare" is dated 1630, and was published in the Second Folio of Shakespeare's Plays in 1632. Merritt Y. Hughes speculates that "Milton's questionable date, 1630, suggests that the poem was written some time before its publication, possibly with the expectation that the Stratford monument instead of the Droeshout portrait would be represented as the frontispiece of the Folio."[46] Thus the reference to "Marble," as well as the "piled Stones" of line 2, the "Monument" of line 8 and the "Tomb" of line 16 would be pertinent to the memorial occasion, and to the illustration accompanying the memorial verses. "Dost make us Marble," as Hughes also points out in a note, closely resembles the apostrophe to Melancholy in *Il Penseroso*, who is urged to "Forget thyself to Marble" (1.42). In the sonnet, however – and this is part of de Man's point – it is the spectator, the reader, the mourner who becomes marble. As Michael Riffaterre comments, paraphrasing de Man's argument:

> Chiasmus, the symmetrical structure of prosopopeia, entails that, by making the dead speak, the living are struck dumb – they too become the monument. Prosopopeia thus stakes out a figural space for the chiasmic interpretation: either the subject will take over the object, or it will be penetrated by the object."[47]

But in the case of the Stratford monument (or indeed, though less neatly, the Droeshout portrait), this exchange of properties has already taken place. The voice of the dead Shakespeare pictured on the tomb (and in the sonnet) speaks through the plays that succeed them in the Folio.

Moreover, the same exchange has been prefigured and depicted in Shakespeare's plays themselves, most straightforwardly – if such a figuration is ever straightforward – in *The Winter's Tale*, where a statue comes to life and speaks. The awakening of Hermione, a true animation of the uncanny, is prepared for by a moment in the scene that precedes it, when an anonymous Third Gentleman reports the wonderment of the court at the reunion of King Leontes and his lost daughter Perdita. "At the relation of the Queen's death," he reports, Perdita was so moved that "Who was most marble there chang'd color." (5.2.89–80) The intimation is the more pointed because of the specific moment at which it occurs in the narrative – "the relation of the Queen's death" – and it sets up, in dramatic terms, the mysterious finale, the revelation of a truth not known to the audience: that Hermione is alive.

The awakening of the Queen itself takes the form of apostrophe, as Leontes, Perdita, and Paulina all address the "dear stone" and offer to join her in her inanimate fate: "does not the stone rebuke me/For being more stone than it? O royal piece,/There's magic in thy majesty, which has/My evils conjr'd to remembrance, and/ From thy admiring daughter took the spirits,/Standing like stone with thee" (5.3.38–42). Here a trope familiar from lyric "comes to life," as it were, in drama, and there occurs a double uncanniness. As the statue of Hermione moves and speaks, the figure of prosopopeia likewise comes alive.

The trope of the living and speaking statue, posing the question of "whether an object is living or inanimate"[48] as does the "statue of Hermione" is certainly not unique to Shakespeare. To broaden the context of this discussion of uncanny authority, I will here briefly wander through a larger sculpture garden of ghostly animation.

Molière's *Dom Juan, ou Le Festin de Pierre*, first acted in 1665,[49] includes a particularly "scandalous" (in Shoshana Felman's sense) example of the trope of the talking stone. Molière's subtitle depends on a punning doubleness in "Pierre," which means both "stone" and "Peter," the name of the Commander whose statue walks and talks in *El burlador de Sevilla y Convidado de Piedra* – a play by the Spaniard Tirso de Molina published in 1632, which was the principal source for *Dom Juan*. Molière's statue has no name – it is described as "the Statue of the Commander" in the list of *dramatis personae*, and is addressed formally by both Dom Juan and Sganarelle as "Your Excellency the Commander." In Molière's play the statue first "comes to life" in Act 3 when it nods in response to an invitation to dine with Dom Juan, then returns the compliment in Act 4, inviting Dom Juan to dinner, to the "stone feast" of the subtitle.

When it appears in Mozart's *Don Giovanni*, and especially in Peter Shaffer's recent drama on the life of Mozart, *Amadeus*, the statue becomes a reproving father, a revenger of his own death, a superego looming enormous over the philandering Dom Juan and bearing him off to hell. In Mozart's opera, with libretto by Lorenzo da Ponte, the Commendatore is killed by Don Giovanni when he discovers Giovanni attempting to seduce his daughter.[50] In Act 2 of the opera, the statue speaks, predicting Giovanni's death. The servant Leporello thinks its voice comes from another world, but Giovanni assumes it to be that of a mortal antagonist, and strikes out with his sword. The inscription on the statue proclaims its purpose of vengeance. When the statue nods, twice, in response to the invitation to supper tended by Leporello, Giovanni demands that it speak: "Speak if you can! Shall I see you at supper?" The statue answers affirmatively, and duly appears – accompanied by the portentous music of the Overture – in Giovanni's house, inviting Giovanni to sup with him in turn, and no longer seeking revenge, but rather repentance. Giovanni accepts the dinner invitation, but refuses to repent, and is engulfed in flames.

The statue is referred to several times in this act as "the stone man," and Leporello seems to draw attention to its stoniness and that of Giovanni when he remarks to Donna Elvira that his master "has a heart of stone." When it disappears, the statue of the Commendatore is also, interestingly, described as a ghost, as Donna Elvira concludes that "It is surely the ghost I met," when she left Giovanni's house, having failed – like the statue – to persuade him to repent.

In this version, the Commendatore is a punishing father figure, but specifically the father of a woman betrayed by the hero. Killed by inadvertence (as is Polonius, who occupies a similar paternal role), he reappears in the plot as an undecidable apparition who is read differently by the two spectators, Giovanni and Leporello. For all his differences from them, Leporello is in something of the place of Horatio and the sentries, crediting the other-worldly origin of the spectre, and eliciting only gesture – not language – from his invitation. Giovanni demands speech, responds to his intercourse with the statue with bravado, and is then disconcerted by a second visit.

The transferential mention of the "heart of stone," which is attributed not to the Commendatore, who is literally a stone man, but to Don Giovanni, who behaves like one, may remind us of Hermione and Leontes ("does not the stone rebuke me/For being more stone than it?" [*Winter's Tale* 5.3.37–8]) and also of the language of *Othello* as characterized by Stanley Cavell.

> As he is the one who gives out lies about her, so he is the one who will give her a stone heart for her stone body, as if in his words of stone which confound the figurative and literal there is the confounding of the incantátions of poetry and magic. He makes of her the thing he feels ("my heart is turned to stone" [4.1.178])[51]

An analogous transference is arguably taking place in *Hamlet*, as the son imputes to the Ghost commands and wishes he would like to receive from the father, and which have the dual authority of concurring with (because they personate) his own desires, and presenting themselves as externally (and paternally) motivated instructions, imposed *upon* rather than *by* the ambivalently situated son. Hamlet's word for this stony instruction is the appropriately chosen "commandment" ("thy commandment all alone shall live/ Within the book and volume of my brain" [1.5.102–3]). As Moses received the stone tablets of the law, so Hamlet sets down in his tables the words he hears from – or the words he gives to – the Ghost.

There are some grounds for arguing a connection between Mozart and *Hamlet*. Mozart attended a production of *Hamlet* staged by a touring company in Salzburg in 1780, and subsequently wrote to his father, "If the speech of the Ghost in *Hamlet* were not so long, it would be far more effective." In calculating the effect of a subterranean ghostly voice in the theater – in this case for *Idomeneo* – he was concerned that the dramatic intervention be unearthly:

> Picture to yourself the theatre, and remember that the voice must be terrifying – must penetrate – that the audience must believe that it really exists. Well, how can this effect be produced if the speech is too long, for in this case the listeners will become more and more convinced that it means nothing. If the speech of the Ghost in *Hamlet* were not so long, it would be far more effective.[52]

In 1789 a German newspaper, reviewing a performance of *Don Giovanni*, commented that "Mozart seems to have learned the language of ghosts from Shakespeare – a hollow, sepulchral tone seemed to rise from the earth; it was as though the shades of the departed were seen to issue from their resting-places."[53] The comparison has also appealed to the imagination of modern Mozart scholars. William Gresser compares *Don Giovanni* Act 2 scene 7 explicitly to *Hamlet*, remarking on the problem of temporality in

Mozart's second act, and on the belief that a ghost could only walk between midnight and dawn.[54]

Peter Shaffer's *Amadeus* points the parallel. News of the death of Mozart's stern father Leopold is brought to him by two "venticelli," two "little winds," purveyors of gossip and rumor. Salieri, who is with Mozart at the time, consoles him with words that closely resemble Claudius's to Hamlet ("Do not despair. Death is inevitable, my friend")[55] and promptly transforms himself into a father substitute, opening his arms "in a wide gesture of paternal benevolence," as Mozart, eluding this embrace, falls on his knees and cries "Papa!" "So rose the Ghost Father in *Don Giovanni!*" comments Salieri, as the scene closes. The next scene (2.9) begins with "the two grim chords which open the overture to *Don Giovanni,*" and which also accompany on the stage "the silhouette of a giant black figure, in cloak and tricorne hat. It extends its arms menacingly and engulfingly, toward its begetter" – that is, toward Mozart. And Salieri comments to the audience, as if completing his previous thought, "A father more accusing than any in opera."[56]

Mozart reports to Salieri that his wife thinks he's mad, and that he thinks so too. He has seen a "Figure in [his] dreams" (2.13) gray and masked, who instructed him "Take up your pen and write a Requiem" (2.17). And Salieri costumes himself, deliberately, in a cloak and mask of gray, "as – the Messenger of God!" "as the Figure of his dreams! [*Urging*] 'Come! – Come! – Come! . . .' " (2.15):

Salieri.	He stood swaying, as if he would faint off into death. But suddenly – incredibly – he realized all his little strength, and in a clear voice called down to me their words out of his opera *Don Giovanni,* inviting the statue to dinner.
Mozart.	[*Pushing open the "window"*] O statua gentillisima, venite a cena! [*He beckons in his turn*]
Salieri.	For a moment one terrified man looked at another. Then – unbelievably – I found myself nodding, just as in the opera. Starting to move across the street! [*The rising and falling scale passage from the Overture to Don Giovanni sounds darkly, looped in sinister repetition. To this hollow music Salieri marches slowly upstage.*] Pushing down the latch of his door – stamping up the stairs with stone feet. There was no stopping it. *I was in his dreams!*[57]

Shaffer, in describing the masked apparition, writes that "he was not a crudely melodramatic figure – a spooky, improbable Messenger of Death – but a more poetic and dangerous apparition, a messenger from God stepping out of Mozart's confessed dreams."[58]

From this father-son encounter, with its reminder of the way the father can personate both Death and the Law, we are led back to *Hamlet*, as Freud's walk through the provincial town in Italy led unerringly, and uncannily, back to the quarter inhabited by prostitutes. In his discussion of the Oedipus complex Freud stresses the fact that *Hamlet* was "written immediately after the death of Shakespeare's father (in 1601), that is, under the immediate impact of his bereavement and, we may well assume, while his childhood feelings about his father had been freshly revived."[59] Freud adds that Shakespeare had lost his own son, Hamnet, at an early age, and thus was in a double position of bereavement, a son mourning a father and a father mourning a son. (This, of course, is the doubled situation Joyce describes in *Ulysses*, and the ocassion for the remarkable discussion of *Hamlet* in that novel: "Gravediggers bury Hamlet *père* and Hamlet *fils*. A king and a prince at last in death, with incidental music.")[60]

Hermione and the Commander – two stony "statues," both taken as monuments to (and representations of) the dead, the dead parent. One "statue" actually made of stone that nods and speaks, inviting a friend to supper, the other "statue" deservedly enrobed in its quotation marks, since it is actually the queen herself, Hermione masquerading as a statue, condemned to the "fate of stone" by her husband's skepticism. As Stanley Cavell remarks, "One can see this as the projection of his own sense of numbness, of living death . . . the man's refusal of knowledge of his other is an imagination of stone."[61] The Ghost in *Hamlet* resembles both of these monumental figures. Like them, he is specifically associated with the "fate of stone," with the marble sepulchre. "Tell," pleads Hamlet,

> Why thy canoniz'd bones, hearsed in death,
> Have burst their cerements; why the sepulchre,
> Wherein we saw thee quietly inurn'd,
> Hath op'd his ponderous and marble jaws
> To cast thee up again. (1.4.46–51)

The sudden animation of the monument, opening "his ponderous and marble jaws," underscores the uncanniness of the apparition which is not itself a statue but is, nonetheless, a similarly idealizing representation. And the key question about this apparition, as about the others, is whether it will speak.

The statue of the Commander in Molière first nods, startling the servant Sagnarelle, and subsequently speaks to Dom Juan, inviting him to supper. The final test for Hermione is articulated by Camillo: "If she pertain to life let her speak too" (*Winter's Tale* 5.3.113). The question of whether the Ghost will speak is a central preoccupation of the whole first Act of *Hamlet*, and has a great deal to do with the way it is described and addressed. "It would be spoke to," says Barnardo. Horatio, as a "scholar," is asked to do the job. Popular belief had it that "A ghost has not the power to speak till it has been first spoken to; so that, notwithstanding the urgency of the business on which it may come, everything must stand still till the person visited can find sufficient courage to speak to it."[62] Horatio valiantly tries to interview it on two occasions in scene 1, urged on by Marcellus's apt invitation, "Question it, Horatio":

Horatio.	What art thou that usurp'st this time of night,
	Together with that fair and warlike form
	In which the majesty of buried Denmark
	Did sometimes march? By heaven I charge thee speak!
Marcellus.	It is offended.
Barnardo.	See, it stalks away!
Horatio.	Stay! Speak, speak, I charge thee speak!
	Exit Ghost (1.1.46–51)
Horatio.	Stay, illusion!
	If thou hast any sound or use of voice,
	Speak to me.
	If there be any good thing to be done
	That may to thee do ease, and grace to me,
	Speak to me.
	If thou art privy to thy country's fate,
	Which happily foreknowing may avoid,
	O speak!
	Or if thou hast uphoarded in thy life
	Extorted treasure in the womb of earth,
	For which, they say, your spirits oft walk in death,
	Speak of it, stay and speak! (1.1.127–39)

The cock crows, and though Barnardo thinks "it was about to speak," it starts away. We may notice that the constant pronoun here is *it*, not *he*, and that the "apparition" is carefully described as "*like* the King," as one who "usurp'st" the time of the night (a loaded word in the circumstances) and the "fair and warlike form" of the dead King, "buried Denmark," was wont to appear. "It" =

King Hamlet. "It" is a space of conjecture, to be questioned. But the proof is to come, with the imparting of this tale to "young Hamlet." "For, upon my life," says Horatio, "this spirit, dumb to us, will speak to him" (171–2).

Cautiously, we may return to de Man's definition of prosopopeia, the master trope, the trope of tropes: "the fiction of the voice-from-beyond-the-grave,"[63] "the fiction of an apostrophe to an absent, deceased, or voiceless entity, which posits the possibility of the latter's reply, and confers upon it the power of speech."[64] This description not only coincides with the dramatic circumstances of the first scene of *Hamlet*, it exemplifies it. "Our topic deals with the giving and taking away of faces, with face and deface, *figure*, figuration and disfiguration."[65]

When Hamlet is informed by Horatio of the appearance of "a figure like your father" (1.2.199) he asks, inevitably, "Did you not speak to it?" But the other question, on which he is curiously insistent, is whether the sentries saw the apparition's *face*: "saw you not his face?" "look'd he frowningly?" "Pale or red?" "And fix'd his eyes upon you?" (229–33). We know that the Elizabethans often used *its* and *his* interchangeably but still there is something striking about Hamlet's recurrent use of *he* and *his* after all the *its* of scene 1. Hamlet himself will return to the neuter pronoun after this exchange ("Perchance 'twill walk again" [242]; "If it assume my noble father's person/I'll speak to it" [243–4]) so that the brief gendering of the figure comes as a moment of achieved personating or animation, to be followed by a return to the objectification of *it*, which, as the *OED* tells us, is used "now only of things without life." Is the Ghost animate or inanimate? Certainly it is animated – but the he/it distinction marks an act of naming that is an act of choice, confirmed when Hamlet sees the Ghost face to face:

Horatio.	Look, my lord, it comes!
Hamlet.	Angels and ministers of grace defend us!
	Be thou a spirit of health, or goblin damn'd,
	Bring with thee airs from heaven, or blasts from hell,
	Be thy intents wicked, or charitable,
	Thou com'st in such a questionable shape
	That I will speak to thee. I'll call thee Hamlet,
	King, father, royal Dane. O, answer me!
	(1.4.38–45)

Critical attention has usually been focused on the spirit/goblin, heaven/hell problem here – is this a false ghost or a true ghost, a delusion or a sign? But what seems equally central is the structure of address. Hamlet *chooses* to name the Ghost with those na᠁᠁s which are for him most problematical: King, father, royal Dane.[66]

Hamlet addresses the "questionable shape" and brings it to speech, and therefore to a kind of life. Does he, in doing so, fulfill de Man's dire prophecy: "the latent threat that inhabits prosopopeia, namely that by making the dead speak, the symmetrical structure of the trope implies, by the same token, that the living are struck dumb, frozen in their own death?"[67]

In the fiction of address, what Jonathan Culler suggestively terms "this sinister reciprocity"[68] is always present *as* a threat. But if it is latent in lyric, it may become manifest in drama, and in *Hamlet* it does. *This* is the nature of revenge in *Hamlet*, the unremitting demand of the Ghost, leading to Hamlet's final paradoxical declaration, "I am dead." De Man elsewhere points out that "the object of the apostrophe is only addressed in terms of the activity that it provokes in the addressing subject."[69] Our attention is focused on the *speaker*. Culler interestingly comments on this argument that "apostrophe involves a drama of 'the one mind's modifications,' "[70] and I would like to take his metaphor here seriously – for it is precisely a *dramatic* situation that is produced by this structure of address, which is why it is plausible to say that Hamlet constructs his own Ghost, makes use of the "gracious figure" of his father by utilizing the equally gracious figure of prosopopeia. Since apostrophe and prosopopeia so often involve a sensation of loss (not only in the post-Enlightenment lyric as observed by commentators like de Man, Culler, and Hartman, but in the elegiac tradition and the epitaphic texts of the Renaissance), the fiction of address itself performs a paradoxical function, not unlike that performed by Hamlet's "I am dead": it instates that which it mourns, makes present that which it declares absent and lost. "The poem," says Culler, "denies temporality in the very phrases – recollections – that acknowledge its claims," the narrator can "find, in his poetic ability to invoke [the mourned object] as a transcendent presence, a sense of his own transcendent continuity."[71] This is the transaction that takes place in *Hamlet*. "I am dead" And "I am alive to contemplate and mourn – and avenge – the dead" coexist in the same sensibility, in the same moment of naming. And this capacity, on the part of apostrophe and prosopopeia, is, exactly, *dramatic*: "Apostrophe is not the representation of an event; if it works, it produces a fictive, discursive event."[72] In *Hamlet* (as in *The Winter's Tale*) the effect of the dramatic mode is to dis-figure the trope of address to a dead or inanimate object, and ventriloquize its response as part of the ongoing dramatic action. "Marry, how? tropically?" (*Hamlet* 3.2.237–8) The Ghost is not – or not only – an instance of the unmetaphoring[73] of prosopopeia. It is also the *manifestation* of that "latent threat" implicit in the trope itself. The rhetorical figure ("a figure like your father", 1.2.199), under the operation of the uncanny, comes to life, is dis- or un-figured ("then saw you not his face", 1.2.229), and exacts its sinister reciprocity: "that the living are . . . frozen in their own death."[74]

Begging the question

Uncanny reciprocity is thus created by the transference of death to the living and voice to the dead. But what does the dead voice say? What kind of commandment does the ghostly father in *Hamlet* hand down?

The Ghost's commandment comes in the form of a double imperative: "Remember me!" and "revenge!" What I will attempt to demonstrate here is that this double imperative is in fact a double bind. But first, a look at the first part of the commandment, the imperative to remember.

Hamlet is indeed a play obsessively concerned with remembering and forgetting. Not only does the Ghost in his first appearance call upon Hamlet to "Remember me," and provoke his son to take that "commandment" as his "word" (1.5.95–111); when he appears again in the Queen's closet he makes the same demand, this time in the negative: "Do not forget!" (3.4.110). Claudius, the new King, acknowledges that "Though yet of Hamlet our dear brother's death/The memory be green" (1.2.1–2) and a fit circumstance for grief, yet insists that "we with wisest sorrow think on him/Together with remembrance of ourselves" (6–7). Hamlet, in soliloquy, is pained by the memory of his mother's passionate attachment to his father: "Heaven and earth,/Must I remember? Why, she would hang on him/As if increase of appetite had grown/By what it fed on" (1.2.142–5). And "O God, a beast that wants discourse of reason/Would have mourn'd longer" (151–2). In a sardonic mood he laments the frailty of memory two months after his father's death (and his mother's remarriage):

> O heavens, died two months ago and not forgotten yet! Then there's hope a great man's memory may outlive his life half a year, but, by'r lady, 'a man must build churches then, or else shall 'a suffer not thinking on, with the hobby-horse, whose epitaph is, "For O, for O, the hobby-horse is forgot" (3.2.130–5)[75]

When he comes to her closet, Gertrude, chiding him for his flippancy, asks "Have you forgot me?" and receives a stinging

reply: "No, by the rood, not so;/You are the Queen, your
husband's brother's wife,/And would it were not so, you are my
mother" (3.4.14–16). When in the same scene, after the Ghost's
injunction: "Do not forget!" Hamlet reminds her that he must go to
England, she answers, "Alack,/I had forgot" (201).

Ophelia herself is constantly associated with the need to
remember. Laertes urges her to "remember well" (1.3.84) his
cautions about Hamlet's untrustworthiness as a suitor, and she
answers that " 'Tis in my memory lock'd" (85). In the scene where
she is "loosed" to Hamlet in the lobby he says to her, "Nymph, in
thy orisons/Be all my sins remember'd" (3.1.88–9) and she offers
him "remembrances of yours/That I have longed long to re-deliver"
(92–3). Her next offerings of remembrance will be the flower-
giving, when she gives her brother "rosemary, that's for
remembrance, pray you, love, remember. And there is pansies, that
for thoughts" (4.5.175). "A document in madness, thoughts and
remembrance fitted," he concludes (4.5.175–9).

Forgetting, and especially forgetting oneself, is closely connected
to manners, but also to something more. Hamlet greets Horatio,
whom he has not seen since Wittenberg, with "Horatio – or I do
forget myself" (1.2.161). Much later in the play he apologizes for
grappling with Laertes: "I am very sorry, good Horatio,/That to
Laertes I forgot myself,/For by the image of my cause I see/The
portraiture of his" (5.2.75–8). At the beginning of Act 5 scene 2 he
takes up his tale of the voyage to England, checking to see if
Horatio "remember[s] all the circumstance" (1–2). "Remember it,
my lord!" Horatio exclaims (3). Hamlet describes the moment on
shipboard when he opened Claudius's death-warrant, "Making so
bold,/My fears forgetting manners, to unseal/Their grand commission" (5.2.16–18), and comments on his pretense of aristocratic
carelessness: "I once did hold it, as our statists do,/A baseness to
write fair, and labor'd much/How to forget that learning, but, sir,
now/It did me yeman's service" (5.2.33–6). "Antiquity forgot,
custom not known" (4.5.105), the rabble call for Laertes to be king.
Hamlet presses Osric to forego courtesy and to put his hat back on
his head: "I beseech you to remember" (5.2.104). Hamlet's dying
request is for Horatio to tell his story, and in the final moments
Fortinbras asserts that he has "some rights of memory in this
kingdom" (399) which, with the support of Hamlet's "dying voice,"
he is now prepared to claim.

Recent critical discussions of the two Hegelian terms for
memory, *Erinnerung* and *Gedächtnis*, can shed light on the problem
we are considering, the relationship between memory and revenge.
Initiated by Paul de Man in an essay on "Sign and Symbol in

Hegel's *Aesthetics*,"[76] the discourse on memory has since developed in a number of provocative directions.[77]

Erinnerung, ("recollection") as de Man defines it, after Hegel, is "the inner gathering and preserving of experience,"[78] while *Gedächtnis* ("memory") is "the learning by rote of *names*, or of words considered as names, and it can therefore not be separated from the notation, the inscription, or the writing down of these names. In order to remember, one is forced to write down what one is likely to forget."[79]

How can this distinction help us to understand the complexity of Hamlet's mandate to turn his mourning into revenge?

When Hamlet first appears on stage, he is beset by *Erinnerung*, interiorizing recollection, the consciousness of loss. Loss is what he thinks he *has* – not just "the trappings and the suits of woe," but "that within which passes show" (1.2.85–6). He will not relinquish this memory, which he hugs to himself. Claudius has a number of motives for calling his "obstinate condolement" "a course/Of impious stubbornness" (1.2.93–4), but he is not altogether wrong. Loss is what Hamlet has instead of both mother and father – and loss is what he must lose, or learn to live with.

Freud describes such immersion, when it reaches the state of melancholia, as a kind of fetishization, a privatizing and husbanding of grief, a refusal to let go.[80] In Hamlet this condition is exemplified by the first soliloquy, "O that this too too sallied flesh would melt" (1.2.129–50), with its longing for dissolution, its flirtation with self-slaughter, and its fragmented and particularized memory of both his father and his mother.

The encounter with the Ghost disrupts his absorption in the past as recollection. Abruptly Hamlet is wrenched from *Erinnerung* to *Gedächtnis*, from symbol to sign, or, to use de Man's terms, from symbol to allegory. From this point forward he is compelled to constitute the past by memorization, by inscription, by writing down.

> Remember thee!
> Ay, thou poor ghost, whiles memory holds a seat
> In this distracted globe. Remember thee!
> Yea, from the table of my memory
> I'll wipe away all trivial fond records,
> All saws of books, all forms, all pressures past
> That youth and observation copied there,
> And thy commandment all alone shall live
> Within the book and volume of my brain,
> Unmix'd with baser matter. Yes, by heaven!
> O most pernicious woman!

O villain, villain, smiling, damned villain!
My tables – meet it is I set it down
That one may smile, and smile, and be a villain!
At least I am sure it may be so in Denmark!
[*He writes.*]
So, uncle, there you are. Now to my word:
It is, 'Adieu, adieu! remember me.'
I have sworn't. (1.5.95–112)

The "tables" of Act 1 scene 5 are writing tables, somewhat like Freud's "Mystic Writing-Pad,"[81] which is, in turn, somewhat like the operations of memory as inscription of memory, *Gedächtnis*. Polonius alludes to a similar kind of table when he repudiates the role of "desk or table-book" (2.2.36) in his conversation with the Queen, announcing that he could not, like such inanimate objects, merely remain "mute and dumb" (137) when he learned of Hamlet's overmastering love for ·Ophelia. Polonius's choice of mute and dumb objects is suggestive, since both desk and table-book are surfaces for writing. His refusal to "play" the desk or table-book denies the possibility of prosopopeia, of a speaking record. Thus while Polonius declines to be such a table, Hamlet takes dictation from the Ghost so as to carry about with him the transcribed and inscribed "word," whether his "tables" are tables of wax, of paper, or of memory.[82]

The writing tables, then, must take the place of another kind of "table" in *Hamlet*, the table at which one eats and drinks, the kind of table associated not with *Gedächtnis* but with *Erinnerung*. For the language of *Erinnerung*, of interiorization, in this play is the language of digestion, of eating: "the funeral bak'd-meats/Did coldly furnish forth the marriage tables" (1.2.180–1); "Heaven and earth,/Must I remember? Why, she would hang on him/As if increase of appetite had grown/By what it fed on" (142–5). Even the famous soliloquy on the sullied-sallied-solid flesh, the wish that the flesh would "melt, thaw, and resolve itself into a dew" (1.2.129–30) reflects this burden of interiorization. Hamlet, unable either to escape or to complete the desired *Erinnerung*, is caught between cannibalism and anorexia, spewing forth in language what he cannot swallow,[83] taunting Claudius with a reminder of "how a king may go a progress through the guts of a beggar" (4.3.30–1). Caught, that is, until he is catapulted into an even more difficult trap by the double pull of the paternal imperative, an imperative so indigestible that it must be written down. The feast, like the one to which the Commander invites Dom Juan, is a feast of stone.[84]

Jacques Derrida, writing on memory and mourning, writing in

memory of and in mourning for Paul de Man, suggests that
Gedächtnis and *Erinnerung* are central to "the possibility of
mourning," and that "the inscription of memory" is "an effacement
of interiorizing recollection."[85] In the "tables" speech, Hamlet
limns precisely the effacement of *Erinnerung* by *Gedächtnis*. By
writing down the Ghost's "commandment" he both inscribes and
constitutes the paternal story of a past which, in its pastness, is
necessarily fictive, since it is only experienced *as* past, as tale, as
narrative. Thus Derrida writes,

> for Paul de Man, great thinker and theorist of memory, there is
> only memory but, strictly speaking, the past does not exist. It
> will never have existed in the present, never been present, as
> Mallarmé says of the present itself: *"un présent n'existe pas."* The
> allegation of its supposed "anterior" presence *is* memory, and is
> the origin of all allegories. If a past does not literally exist, no
> more does death, only mourning, and that other allegory,
> including all the figures of death with which we people the
> "present," which we inscribe (among ourselves, the living) in
> every trace (otherwise called "survivals"): those figures strained
> toward the future across a fabled present, figures we inscribe
> because they can outlast us, beyond the present of their
> inscription: signs, words, names, letters, this whole text whose
> legacy-value, as we know "in the present," is trying its luck and
> advancing, *in advance* "in memory of . . ."[86]

Derrida's allusion to Mallarmé is pertinent, for Mallarmé was a
great admirer of Shakespeare's *Hamlet*, describing it as *la pièce que
je crois celle par excellence*, "what I consider to be *the* play."[87] And
for Mallarmé Hamlet is already a ghost.

> *L'adolescent évanoui de nous aux commencements de la vie et qui
> hantera les esprits hauts ou pensifs par le deuil qu'il se plaît à
> porter, je le reconnais, qui se débat sous le mal d'apparaître.*

> [That adolescent who vanished from us at the beginning of life
> and who will always haunt lofty, pensive minds with his
> mourning, I recognize him struggling against the curse of having
> to appear.[88]]

We may notice not only his word *hantera*, "will haunt," but also the
verb tenses in this passage: Hamlet "vanished" "will always haunt,"
"I recognize him," "struggling to appear." In this sentence, too,
Hamlet himself is never present, is always a trace or an anticipation,

haunting Mallarmé and other readers, other audiences.[89] He struggles not only against the curse of having to appear, but also with the very difficulty of appearing (*le mal d'apparaître*); in this too he is like a ghost, like the Ghost. Mallarmé's Hamlet is thus just what Derrida describes: "a figure strained toward the future across a fabled present." What makes Mallarmé's mind pensive is mourning – mourning *for* the vanished Hamlet as well as in appreciation of Hamlet's own loss.

But what, exactly, does Hamlet write? (Or does he write at all? Critics and editors divide on this question, as to whether he whips out a table or mimes the taking of dictation.)[90] What he claims to record is "thy commandment," and the conjunction of "table" and "commandment" is suggestive. Implicit in the scene, but not always explicitly noted, is its relationship to the moment in Exodus when God gives to Moses "two tables of testimony, tables of stone, written with the finger of God" (Exod. 31:18). In the Mosaic case, *God* writes, and Moses, angry with the idolatrous Israelites dancing about the golden calf, casts the tables out of his hands and breaks them. Moses then returns to God and pleads with Him to show him His glory. And God says to him, "Thou canst not see my face: for there shall no man see me, and live" (Exod. 33:20). Contrary to the case of prosopopeia, there must here be voice without face, speech without face. And God commands Moses to hew "two tables of stone like unto the first: and I will write upon *these* tables the words that were in the first tables, which thou brakest" (34:1). The tables that Moses brings to the Israelites, the foundations of the Law, are thus themselves copies, the second version written by God in substitution for the first, the originals, which were broken, which were lost. Moses breaks the tablets because the people were breaking the commandments they did not yet have. Even this law, the great original, is a copy and a substitution.

When we turn our attention once again to Hamlet's tables, we can see the operation of substitution here through erasure, the inscription on the tables of "thy commandment," which is – to revenge? to remember? to do the one through the agency of the other? We may notice that the same word, "commandment," is used to denote Hamlet's other act of inscription as substitution, the "new commission" that sends Rosencrantz and Guildenstern, instead of Hamlet, to be executed in England. The Ambassador from England arrives upon the bloody scene at the close of the play, and comments – in a figure that recalls the murder of King Hamlet – "The ears are senseless that should give us hearing,/To tell him his commandment is fulfill'd,/That Rosencrantz and Guildenstern are dead" (5.2.368–70), and Horatio, taking "his commandment" to

refer to Claudius' original intent, replies, "He never gave commandment for their death" (374).

Hamlet's writing is thus already a copy, a substitution, a revision
of an original that does not show its face in the text. Whether it be
the revisionary "tables," the interpolated "dozen or sixteen lines,"
or the redirected "new commission" signed with a usurped
signature, Hamlet's writing is always, in fact, ghost writing.

Forgetting the hobbyhorse

As we have seen (above, Chapters 2 and 3), Nietzsche's theory of
historical repetition suggests that the world is itself a constructed
fiction, so that what is "remembered" is in fact invented as a
memorial object, and put in place in the past – put, perhaps, in the
place of the past. J. Hillis Miller, describing "two kinds of
repetition," the Platonic model based upon resemblance, and the
Nietzschean model based upon difference, observes that "this lack
of ground in some paradigm or archetype means that *there is
something ghostly about the effects of this second type of repetition*"[91]
and, again, that, "the second is not the negation or opposite of the
first, but its 'counterpart' in a strange relation whereby *the second is
the subversive ghost of the first, always already present within it as a
possibility which hollows it out.*"[92] If my understanding of *Hamlet* is
correct, the Ghost is itself a figuration of that "subversive ghost,"
that "something ghostly." Just as Shakespeare's *Richard III* figures
the deformation of history through his own physical deformity and
the deformations detectable in language and plot throughout the
play, so the Ghost in *Hamlet* marks the text of that play as a belated
harbinger of repetition as difference. The command to "Remember
me!" encodes the necessity of forgetting.

Miller cites a very suggestive passage from Walter Benjamin's
essay on Proust, in which Benjamin mulls the same relationship I
have been exploring – that between memory and forgetting:

> the important thing for the remembering author is not what he
> experienced, but the weaving of his memory, the Penelope work
> of recollection. Or should one call it, rather, a Penelope work of
> forgetting? Is not the involuntary recollection, Proust's *mémoire
> involontaire*, much closer to forgetting than what is usually
> called memory? And is not this work of spontaneous recollection,
> in which remembrance is the woof and forgetting the warp, a
> counterpart to Penelope's work rather than its likeness? For here
> the day unravels what the night has woven.[93]

What, then, are we to make of the reminders of remembering, the cautions against forgetting, of which the Ghost's two visitations are the benchmarks? It might seem natural to assume that remembering would facilitate reparation, restitution, and recuperation – that the way to rectify an error, or expiate a crime, is through a memory of the act, and even of the historical circumstances that produced, provoked, or surrounded the act. Yet this is precisely what the play of *Hamlet* does *not* tell us. Rather than facilitating action, remembering seems to block it, by becoming itself an obsessive concern, in effect fetishizing the remembered persons, events, or commands so that they become virtually impossible to renounce or relinquish. Our contemporary sense of "hobbyhorse" as a constant preoccupation sums up this fetishizing instinct fairly well: the hobbyhorse must *be* forgot in order for action to follow.

Consider the Ghost's two visitations and his reiterated command. The Ghost asks Hamlet to do two things: to remember and to revenge. Repeatedly on the first occasion he urges revenge. "If thou didst ever thy dear father love . . . Revenge his foul and most unnnatural murther" (1.5.23–5). "Bear it not" (81). "Let not the royal bed of Denmark be/A couch for luxury and damned incest" (82–3). Hamlet is to "[pursue] this act" (84) to revenge his father's murder, while sparing his mother any punishment: "Taint not thy mind, nor let thy soul contrive/Against thy mother aught" (85–6). But he is *to act*, he is *to revenge*. "Adieu, adieu, adieu, remember me" (91). Remember and revenge. But these two injunctions are not only different from one another, they are functionally at odds. For the more Hamlet remembers, the more he meditates the "word" that he takes as the Ghost's "commandment" and inscribes on his tables, the more he is trapped in a round of obsessive speculation. Far from goading him to action, the Ghost's twice iterated instruction, "Remember me," "do not forget," impedes that action, impedes revenge. What Hamlet needs to do is not to remember, but to *forget*.

> Imagine the extremest possible case of a man who did not possess the power of forgetting at all and who was thus condemned to see everywhere a state of becoming: such a man would no longer believe in his own being, would no longer believe in himself, would see everything flowing asunder in moving points and would lose himself in this stream of becoming . . . . Forgetting is essential to action of any kind . . . it is altogether impossible to love at all without forgetting. Or, to express my theme even more simply: there is a degree of sleeplessness, or of rumination, of the historical sense, which is harmful and ultimately fatal to

the living thing, whether this living thing be a man or a people or a culture.

> To determine . . . the boundary at which *the past has to be forgotten if it is not to become the gravedigger of the present*, one would have to know exactly how great the *plastic* power of a man, a people, or a culture is: I mean by plastic power the capacity to develop out of oneself in one's own way, to transform and incorporate into oneself what is past and foreign, to heal wounds, to replace what has been lost, to recreate broken moulds.[94]

The "boundary at which the past has to be forgotten if it is not to become the gravedigger of the present." This is Nietzsche, again in "The Use and Abuse of History." Nietzsche's gravedigger is also Hamlet's, a talismanic figure who digs up the pate of a politician, the skull of a lawyer, the bones of a great buyer of land, and jowls them indifferently to the ground (5.1.75–112). It is Hamlet, on this occasion, who "consider[s] too curiously" (205), who speculates about the noble dust of Alexander stopping a bunghole, and "Imperious Caesar, dead and turn'd to clay" who "Might stop a hole to keep the wind away" (213–14). Hamlet, who is still prey to the "rumination, of the historical sense, which is harmful and ultimately fatal to the living thing, whether this living thing be a man or a people or a culture."[95] The gravedigger himself marks Hamlet's boundaries. He came to his trade "that day that our last king Hamlet overcame Fortinbras" (143–4), "the very day that young Hamlet was born" (147). Harold Jenkins in the Arden edition of *Hamlet* remarks

> What matters is that when Hamlet came into the world a man began to dig graves and has now been at it for a lifetime . . . . As Hamlet's talk with the grave-digger thus links the grave-digger's occupation with the terms of Hamlet's life, will it not seem to us that the hero has come face to face with his own destiny?[96]

Yet the gravedigger has the same uncanny valence as the Mower in Marlowe's *Edward II*;[97] he is the figuration of Hamlet's mortality, as the skull of Yorick is the fragmented emblem of that mortality. Re-membering is here reconstituted through a process of dis-membering, of disarticulation of parts, of dislocation of bones and members.

But there is more that is uncanny in this passage of Nietzsche, for it seems throughout to be haunted by the ghost of *Hamlet*. "I have striven," he writes in the foreword to "The Use and Abuse of History," "to depict a feeling by which I am constantly tormented;

I *revenge myself upon it* by handing it over to the public."[98] "It" is
the abuse of history, the preoccupation with the past that can inhibit
life, making it "stunted and degenerate."[99] Nietzsche's *revenge* is to
be a "meditation" he describes as "untimely" – but then it must *be*
untimely in order to be effective: "for I do not know what meaning
classical studies could have for our time if they were not untimely –
that is to say, acting counter to our time and thereby acting on our
time and, let us hope, for the benefit of a time to come."[100] It is not,
I think, entirely fanciful to wish to juxtapose these remarks to
Hamlet's famous *cri de coeur*, "The time is out of joint – O cursed
spite,/That ever I was born to set it right!" (1.5.188–9). And we may
perhaps go further and suggest that Nietzsche in this exclamation,
this profession of revenge – like Hamlet in his own professions of
belatedness and determination – is himself a revenant, a ghost, a
figure dislocated in and from history ("classical studies"; "earlier
times") and constituted (or self-constituted) as not only critic but
critique.

This is Hamlet's use of the classical past as well as Nietzsche's; the
Pyrrhus play ("Aeneas's Tale to Dido") the constant reminders that
his father was Hyperion to Claudius's satyr, that he himself is
confronted with a choice of Hercules – these too are uses of history
that verge upon the abusive because they place Hamlet rhetorically
on the margins of history rather than in the midst of historical
process. It is only when he writes himself back into that process,
with the agency of his father's signet ring, later claiming his place in
history ("This is I,/Hamlet the Dane!" [5.1.257–8]) by an act of self-
naming, that he moves beyond untimely meditation, the belatedness
of soliloquy, toward action. For action is inextricably bound with
forgetting.

> Consider the cattle, grazing as they pass you by: they do not
> know what is meant by yesterday or today, they leap about, eat,
> rest, digest, leap about again, and so from morn till night and
> from day to day, fettered to the moment and its pleasure or
> displeasure, and thus neither melancholy nor bored. This is a
> hard sight for a man to see.... A human being may well ask an
> animal: "Why do you not speak to me of your happiness but
> only stand and gaze at me?" The animal would like to answer,
> and say: "The reason is I always forget what I was going to say"
> – but then he forgot this answer, too, and stayed silent: so that
> the human being was left wondering.
> But he also wonders at himself, that he cannot learn to forget
> but clings relentlessly to the past: however far and fast he may
> run, this chain runs with him. And it is a matter for wonder: a

moment, *now here and then gone*, nothing before it came, again nothing after it has gone, nonetheless *returns as a ghost* and disturbs the peace of a later moment.[101]

" 'Tis here." " 'Tis here." " 'Tis gone." Nietzsche's meditation, Nietzsche's revenge, incorporates (or "incorpses")[102] *Hamlet* as a manifestation of the haunting presentness of the past. Hamlet remembers; Polonius forgets. "What was I about to say?/By the mass, I was about to say something./Where did I leave?" Reynaldo: "At 'closes in the consequence' " (2.1.49–51). What Polonius forgets is precisely what closes in the consequence: causality, history. " 'The reason is I always forget what I was going to say' – but then he forgot this answer, too." Polonius forgets: Hamlet remembers. Hamlet's own meditation on revenge and bestial oblivion is so close to Nietzsche's that we may wonder whether Nietzsche's complex of ideas, from revenge to the ghost to the beast to the gravedigger, does not derive in some way from Shakespeare's great untimely meditation, and in particular, from the soliloquy in Act 4 scene 4:

> How all occasions do inform against me,
> And spur my dull revenge! What is a man,
> If his chief good and market of his time
> Be but to sleep and feed? a beast, no more.
> Sure He that made us with such large discourse,
> Looking before and after, gave us not
> That capability and godlike reason
> To fust in us unus'd. Now whether it be
> Bestial oblivion, or some craven scruple
> Of thinking too precisely on th' event –
> A thought which quarter'd hath but one part wisdom
> And ever three parts coward – I do not know
> Why yet I live to say, "This thing's to do,"
> Sith I have cause, and will, and strength, and means
> To do't. (4.4.32–46)

Now, what does it mean to say that Nietzsche's meditation on revenge and forgetting situates itself as a rewriting of *Hamlet*? Is this merely a way of repositioning Shakespeare as the great authority, the great original, in whose work all ideas, all controversies, all contestations are already present? Is Shakespeare the *locus classicus* (or the *locus renascens*) of the move to place subversion within containment? And/or is *Hamlet* – as I have suggested above – the play that articulates, or represents, the construction of the modern subject?

I think that the last of these questions can be answered,

tentatively, in the affirmative, and that this accounts at least in part for the befuddlement and irritation some contemporary critics demonstrate when they are asked to come face to face with this play. It is too close to us. What look like critiques, analyses, implementations of *Hamlet* to make some *other* point (philosophical, political, psychoanalytic) dissolve to bring us back to the play itself, not as referent, but as origin – or marker of the unknowability of origins, what Freud called the navel of the dream: "There is at least one spot in every dream at which it is unplumbable – a navel, as it were, that is its point of contact with the unknown";[103]

> There is often a passage in even the most thoroughly interpreted dream which has to be left obscure; this is because we become aware during the work of interpretation that at this point there is a tangle of dream-thoughts which cannot be unravelled and which moreover adds nothing to our knowledge of the content of the dream. This is the dream's navel, the spot where it reaches down into the unknown.[104]

When Terry Eagleton complains that "Hamlet has no 'essence' of being whatsoever, no inner sanctum to be safeguarded: he is pure deferral and diffusion, a hollow void which offers nothing determinate to be known" and that "Hamlet's jealous sense of unique selfhood is no more than the negation of anything in particular. How could it be otherwise, when he rejects the signifiers by which alone the self, as signified, comes into its determinacy?"[105] he is registering a protest (though a postmodern and somewhat satisfied protest) against this Alice's-rabbit-hole quality in the play's text. Likewise when Jonathan Goldberg, in a characteristically rich and compressed three pages on Hamlet, suggests that "Hamlet's divided identity – and with it his delays and deferrals, his resistance to the ghostly plot, his inability to act and his compulsions to repeat – are the result of his *identification* with his father's words," and that "The depth of his interiority is his foldedness within a text that enfolds him and which cannot be unfolded,"[106] he is at once finding within Shakespeare's play the reflection of his own critical and theoretical moment, Derridean and Lacanian, and – at the same time, and through the same process – locating the play's power precisely in its capacity to assume the guise of contemporaneity and timely contestation. That critics write their own Hamlets, as, for example, Coleridge, Goethe, and T.S. Eliot, have done, is something of a commonplace for us. That they are *compelled* to do so – that this is *their* compulsion to repeat – because the play limns a preconscious moment that can only be retrieved *through* repetition and not through memory, reinscribes the paradox of the play as itself a *mise en abyme* without (exactly, precisely, without) the primal scene at which it is constantly hinting, and which we are constantly on the brink of remembering, falsely, fictively. The ghost of *Hamlet* - the ghost *in Hamlet* - is this illusion of the articulation of our own perception of desire and its denial, our own conviction that "the spot where it reaches down to the unknown" *can* be plumbed, even if it is found to be a hollow void. *Hamlet* is the play of undecidability. But/and it is the play of the uncanny, the play in which the *Heimlich* and the *Unheimlich* are opposite and identical, the play that demonstrates that you can't go home again. Why? Because you *are* home - and home is not what you have always and belatedly (from *un*home) fantasized it to be. Hence, once again, forgetting and remembering. And revenge. In other words, *transference*.

Freud is quite clear about the dynamic that links remembering, forgetting, and action. The patient forgets something because he/she represses it, and in order to retrieve that which has been repressed, he or she *acts*. The repetition-compulsion becomes a way of remembering, as well as a substitution for unretrievable or unretrieved memories. Consider this passage from the 1914 essay, "Recollection, Repetition, and Working Through":

> We may say that here the patient *remembers* nothing of what is forgotten and repressed, but that he expresses it in *action*. He reproduces it not in his memory but in his behaviour; he *repeats* it, without of course knowing that he is repeating it . . . .
>
> As long as he is under treatment he never escapes from this compulsion to repeat; at last one understands that it is his way of remembering.
>
> The relation between this compulsion to repeat and the transference and resistance is naturally what will interest us most of all. We soon perceive that the transference is itself only a bit of repetition, and that the repetition is the transference of the forgotten past not only on to the physician, but also on to all the other aspects of the current situation. We must be prepared to find, therefore, that the patient abandons himself to the compulsion to repeat, which is now replacing the impulse to remember, not only in his relation with the analyst but also in all other matters occupying and interesting him at the time, for instance, when he falls in love or sets about any project during the treatment.[107]

Furthermore, the degree of resistance to the analyst and to quiescent remembering determines the degree to which acting out takes place.

The greater the resistance the more extensively will expressing in action (repetition) be substituted for recollecting . . . if, then, as the analysis proceeds, this transference becomes hostile or unduly intense, consequently necessitating repression, remembering immediately gives way to expression in action. From then onward the resistances determine the succession of the various repetitions. The past is the patient's armoury out of which he fetches his weapons for defending himself against the progress of the analysis, weapons which we must wrest from him one by one.[108]

This last analogy sounds disquietingly like the end of *Othello* ("Take you this weapon/Which I have here recover'd from the Moor" [5.2.239–40]: "I have another weapon in this chamber" [252]), but the pattern of resistance and repetition is uncannily like the plot of *Hamlet*. Indeed, it is not surprising to think of *Hamlet* as the story of an analysis, for what is analysis but a contemporary restaging of the pattern of deferral and substitution that we recognize in *Hamlet*? If our question, or one of our questions, concerns the relationship of memory and revenge, it is here answered, at least in part, by the compulsion to repeat. "As long as he is under treatment he never escapes from this compulsion to repeat; at last one understands that it is his way of remembering." This compulsion to repeat, "which is now replacing the impulse to remember," encompasses the killing (and not killing) of fathers, the accusation of women, the plays within the play, dumb show, and talking cure. The transference-neurosis is induced as a kind of therapeutic substitution, which *can* be cured or worked on because it is present rather than lost, and because it is, in some sense, play. "We admit it into the transference as to a playground."[109]

The transference thus forms a kind of intermediary realm between illness and real life, through which the journey from the one to the other must be made. The new state of mind has absorbed all the features of the illness; it represents, however, an artificial illness which is at every point accessible to our interventions. It is at the same time a piece of real life, but adapted to our purposes by specially favourable conditions, and it is of a provisional character. From the repetition-reactions which are exhibited in the transference the familiar paths lead back to the awakening of the memories, which yield themselves without difficulty after the resistances have been overcome.[110]

This is a reasonably appropriate description of the role played by the play within the play in *Hamlet*, and also by Hamlet's role as chorus (analyst) of the "Mouse-trap" (or even of the first Player's Pyrrhus speech). Real and provisional, "adapted to our purposes" with or without the addition of a dozen or sixteen lines, close enough to the original or originary situation (at least as it is fantasized or retold) yet safely "artificial" and thus able to be discounted or bounded, the play within the play does exhibit many of the symptoms of transference-neurosis, as in fact do the soliloquies that problematize the *activity* of others (Fortinbras, the First Player, Pyrrhus, even Laertes) as contrasted with the ruminative passivity of Hamlet.

The connection between repressed thoughts and memories and the compulsion to repeat is also strongly argued in *Beyond the Pleasure Principle* (1920), and it is not surprising that both of these Freudian texts have been used by narratologists to develop strategies of narrative displacement, substitution, and delay. In *Beyond the Pleasure Principle* Freud again states that "the compulsion to repeat must be ascribed to the unconscious repressed"[111] and comments on the odd but undeniable fact that people often compulsively repeat things that are not, and seem never to have been, pleasurable. How then is the compulsion to repeat related to the pleasure principle?

> The artistic play and artistic imitation carried out by adults, which, unlike children's, are aimed at an audience, do not spare the spectators (for instance, in tragedy) the most painful experiences and yet can be felt by them as highly enjoyable. This is convincing proof that, even under the dominance of the pleasure principle, there are ways and means enough of making what is in itself unpleasurable into a subject to be recollected and worked over in the mind."[112]

Tragedy – whether exemplified by *Hamlet* or by "The Murder of Gonzago" – thus can produce pleasure when it is received as a repetition. But if the illusion represented by the players conduces to pleasure when categorized as play, what of the kind of compulsion to repeat that results in a different sort of illusion – the terrifying spectacle of the ghost? "Stay, illusion!" (1.1.127) Three times in *Beyond the Pleasure Principle* Freud evokes the image of some "daemonic" power produced by the repetition-compulsion.

> What psycho-analysis reveals in the transference phenomena of neurotics can also be observed in the lives of some normal people. The impression they give is of being pursued by a malignant fate or possessed by some "daemonic" power; but

psycho-analysis has always taken the view that their fate is for
the most part arranged by themselves and determined by early
infantile influences.[113]

The manifestations of a compulsion to repeat (which we have described as occurring in the early activities of infantile mental life
as well as among the events of psycho-analytic treatment) exhibit
to a high degree an instinctual character and, when they act in
opposition to the pleasure principle, give the appearance of some
"daemonic" force at work.[114]

It may be presumed, too, that when people unfamiliar with
analysis feel an obscure fear – a dread of rousing something that,
so they feel, is better left sleeping – what they are afraid of at
bottom is the emergence of this compulsion with its hint of possession by some "daemonic" power.[115]

In the terms of *Hamlet*, this "daemonic" force or power, if it is to
be ascribed to or even personified by the Ghost, is the compulsion
to repeat which repression substitutes for remembering. Confronted
with the Ghost's command, "Remember me!" Hamlet remembers
that he is commanded to remember, but displaces that which he is
unable to remember into compulsive behavior of a kind that translates *him* into a daemon, into a ghost. Thus he appears as a silent
spectacle in Ophelia's closet, pale, sighing, as if "loosed out of hell"
(2.1.80). The passivity of Hamlet, his apparent position of being
acted on rather than acting, is also commensurate with the impres-
sion of being possessed, while in fact giving the name of "possession" to the repetition compulsion.

We may note that in both of these texts Freud represents the patient as male. Interestingly, however, when he comes to speak more
closely of "transference-love" he shifts genders, to describe the circumstances of a female patient – and therefore, by implication, of a
male analyst. And here again there is a ghost come from the grave –
or from the unconscious. But from whose?

To urge the patient to suppress, to renounce and to sublimate the
promptings of her instincts, as soon as she had confessed her
love-transference, would not be an analytic way of dealing with
them, but a senseless way. It would be the same thing *as to conjure up a spirit from the underworld by means of a crafty spell
and then to dispatch him back again without a question.* One
would have brought the repressed impulses out into consciousness only in terror to send them back into repression once more.

Nor should one deceive oneself about the success of any such proceeding. When levelled at the passions, lofty language achieves very little, as we all know. The patient will only feel the humiliation, and *will not fail to revenge herself for it.*[116]

The passion evoked by the analyst should rather be put in the service of the analysis, as the same kind of "playground" (or *playground*) occupied by the transference-neurosis described above. The "spirit from the underworld" is the patient's desire, and the denial or repression of that desire will send the ghost tunneling underground again, and prompt the analysand to *revenge*. But revenge upon what?

Turning the tables

For Hamlet himself, who or what is the Ghost? We could say that for Hamlet the Ghost is – or at least, is supposed to be – what Lacan calls the *sujet supposé savoir*, the subject who is supposed to know. "As soon as the subject who is supposed to know exists somewhere," says Lacan, "there is transference."[117] Who is, who *can* be, invested with such authority, such being-in-knowledge? For Lacan, "If there is someone to whom one can apply there can be only one such person. This *one* was Freud, while he was alive."[118] What a muted accolade is this – "This *one was* Freud, while he was alive." And now that he is dead? Lacan does not say, or does not say directly, who is the new *one*, the new *sujet supposé savoir*. But does he need to? The King is dead, long live . . . And so in *Hamlet*, also, the investment of authority is not without a sense of question and cost. Can the Ghost be the subject who is supposed to know only *because* he is dead? "O my prophetic soul," cries Hamlet (1.5.40). The Ghost is supposed to know – that is, to confirm – what Hamlet did not know he knew.

"The analyst," says Lacan, "occupies this place in as much as he is the object of the transference. Experience shows us that when the subject enters analysis, he is far from giving the analyst this place."[119] Then when does Hamlet enter into a transferential relationship with the Ghost? When, precisely, he is given to think that his own authority is confirmed. Notice how much like an analytic situation is Hamlet's own response to this uncanny consultant.

Given that analysis may, on the part of certain subjects, be put in question at its very outset, and suspected of being a lure – how is it that around this *being mistaken* something stops? Even the psycho-analyst put in question is credited at some point with a certain infallibility, which means that certain intentions, betrayed, perhaps, by some chance gesture, will sometimes be attributed even to the analyst put in question, "*You did that to test me!*"[120]

For Hamlet's testing of the Ghost ("The spirit that I have seen/May be a dev'l, and the dev'l hath power/T'assume a pleasing shape ... yea, and perhaps,/Out of my weakness and my melancholy,/As he is very potent with such spirits,/Abuses me to damn me. I'll have grounds/More relative than this" [2.2.598–604]) is really in many ways the provision of a test for himself. Does he believe the Ghost, or not? Does the Ghost have authority?

The Ghost that comes "in such a questionable shape" (1.4.43) is immediately put in question, is in fact, as we have begun to see, the shape or sign of putting things in question. We could almost designate him as is done in Spanish with an inverted question mark before each appearance, before each utterance, and with another question mark following each. Plain as the Ghost's utterances may seem, Hamlet *wants* them to be a riddle, a problem, a question.

> Be thy intents wicked, or charitable,
> Thou com'st in such a questionable shape
> That I will speak to thee. I'll call thee Hamlet,
> King, father, royal Dane. (1.4.42–5)

"Certain intentions, betrayed, perhaps, by some chance gesture" seem to provoke in Hamlet a wish to name, to pin upon his *sujet supposé savoir* the signifier Lacan has called "*le nom-du-père*" [the Name-of-the-Father]. Lacan's term derives in part from a critique of the traditional Christian invocation all too appropriate to *Hamlet*: "In the name of the Father, the Son, and the Holy Ghost." Coupling this formula with the biological indeterminacy of paternity, Lacan notes that

> the attribution of procreation to the father can only be the effect of a pure signifier, of a recognition, not of a real father, but of what religion has taught us to refer to as the Name-of-the-Father.
>
> Of course, there is no need of a signifier to be a father, any more than to be dead, but without a signifier, no one would ever know anything about either state of being.
>
> ... insistently Freud stresses the affinity of the two signifying relations that I have just referred to, whenever the neurotic subject (especially the obsessional) manifests this affinity through the conjunction of the themes of the father and death.
>
> How, indeed, could Freud fail to recognize such an affinity, when the necessity of his reflexion led him to link the appearance

of the signifier of the Father, as author of the Law, with death, even to the murder of the Father – thus showing that if this murder is the fruitful moment of debt through which the subject binds himself for life to the Law, the symbolic Father is, in so far as he signifies this Law, the dead Father.[121]

Lacan extends this view further by underscoring the homonymic double meaning of *"nom-du-père,"* which in French sounds identical to the expression *"non-du-père"* – *"no"* of the father. The father – the dead father, the symbolic father – is the Law. For Freud, of course, this symbolic father is not the Christian father but the father of Jewish law. And the law commands, "thou shalt *not*": "If thou hast nature in thee, bear it *not,*/Let *not* the royal bed of Denmark be/A couch for luxury and damned incest/But howsomever thou pursuest this act,/Taint *not* thy mind, *nor* let thy soul contrive/Against thy mother aught" (Ghost to Hamlet, 1.5.81–6); "Do *not* forget" (Ghost to Hamlet, 3.4.110, in Gertrude's closet).

Freud, it will be recalled, made much of the connection between the writing of *Hamlet* and the death of Shakespeare's father. In *The Interpretation of Dreams*, he cites the Shakespearean scholar Georg Brandes[122] to demonstrate that

> *Hamlet* was written immediately after the death of Shakespeare's father (in 1601), that is, under the immediate impact of the bereavement and, as we may well assume, while his childhood feelings about his father had been freshly revived. It is known, too, that Shakespeare's own son who died at an early age bore the name of "Hamnet," which is identical with "Hamlet."[123]

Yet there is another father involved here, as Freud's preface to the second edition of *The Interpretation of Dreams* (1908) makes clear. For that masterpiece of analytic invention was itself written right after the death of Freud's *own* father. In his preface, Freud writes:

> this book has a further subjective significance for me personally – a significance which I only grasped after I had completed it. It was, I found, a portion of my own self-analysis, my reaction to my father's death – that is to say, to the most important event, the most poignant loss, of a man's life.

There may therefore be a connection between Freud's interpretation of Hamlet and the death not only of *Shakespeare*'s father but also of *Freud*'s father.

Similarities between Freud's story and Hamlet's have been noticed by recent revisionist biographers, often in connection with

his recantation of (or "suppression of")[12] the seduction theory,
which held that neuroses originated in actual sexual encounters –
with adults, often parents, servants, or older children – experienced
in childhood. Marianne Krüll, for example, argues that Hamlet's
situation – "a son dwelling with impotent rage on the ruthlessness
of his mother and his uncle – had parallels with Freud's own
family."[126] The "uncle" in the Freud story was his half-brother
Philip, called "Uncle" by Freud's niece and nephew, and represented
in Freud's own dream associations in such a way as to suggest some
real or imagined sexual relationship between Philip and his (Freud's)
mother.[127] Krüll's book argues that Freud received from his father,
Jacob, an ambivalent mandate: he was commanded to show filial
piety, to honor his father as instructed by the Fifth Commandment,
and above all not to inquire into his father's secrets, or his past; at
the same time, he was commanded to seek success in the secular
world, to become a great man. The son's resentment at this
impossible double task was identical, says Krüll, to that felt by
Jacob Freud toward *his* father, Schlomo (Sigmund's Hebrew name).
"Neither of them rebelled against his father, and both shouldered
the contradictory mandate of making his own way, even while
remaining dutiful sons."[128] "To complete its hold over him" writes
John Gross, "the mandate forbade him to acknowledge the feelings
of resentment that it inspired, his rage against Jacob for saddling him
with an insoluble problem."[129] This "mandate," we may notice, is
very like the "word" Hamlet receives from the Ghost in the "tables"
scene, together with the troublesomely ambivalent command,
"Remember me!"

A dream mentioned by Freud in slightly different versions in the
letters to Fliess and *The Interpretation of Dreams*[130] concerns the
arrangements he made for his father's funeral, and the criticism he
incurred from relatives for choosing "the simplest possible ritual"[131]
though he did so in accordance with his understanding of his
father's wishes. It is this dream that Krüll has in mind when she
writes that like Hamlet,

> Freud too has been given orders by his late father in a dream
> which, though the subject was not revenge, as in Hamlet's case,
> nevertheless caused the son comparable qualms of conscience.
> Another reason for Freud, in my view, to feel so drawn to the
> Hamlet theme.[132]

Not only the funeral of old Hamlet, swiftly followed by Gertrude's
remarriage, but even more particularly the "hugger-mugger"
interment (4.5.84) of Polonius and the "maimed rites" accompanying
Ophelia's obsequies (5.1.219) – so disturbingly punctuated by

Laertes's twice iterated demand, "What ceremony else?" (5.1.233; 225) – correspond to Freud's own anxieties about performing his duty to the dead.

In the dream – which he tells Fliess took place *after* his father's funeral, and which in *The Interpretation of Dreams* he describes as taking place *before* – he sees a notice-board inscribed with the phrase, "You are requested to close the eyes," which he interprets as an ambivalent statement; in *The Interpretation of Dreams* the ambivalence has made its way onto the notice-board itself, so that the sign reads "*either*

> "You are requested to close the eyes"
> or, "You are requested to close an eye."

I usually write this [says Freud] in the form:

"You are requested to close $\frac{the}{an}$ eye(s)."[133]

Closing the eyes is a funerary rite, a service performed on the eyes of the dead; closing *an* eye is winking at (overlooking) an offense or slight. As Freud writes to Fliess, "The sentence on the sign has a double meaning: One should do one's duty toward the dead (an apology, as though I had not done it and were in need of leniency) and the actual duty itself. The dream thus stems from the inclination to self-reproach that regularly sets in among the survivors."[134]

The generalization at the end denies any *particular* ambivalence occasioned by this specific bereavement, but the whole letter, like the ones preceding it during his father's illness, speaks openly of Freud's own feeling. Jacob Freud died on 23 November 1896. A little less than a year later, with affirmations of relief and release rather than "disgrace," Freud abandoned the seduction theory. Whatever else his motivations were for making this crucial change, the seduction theory came dangerously close to an accusation of the father, as is pointed out in the famous letter to Fliess of September, 1897. Jeffrey Mason, whose controversial book, *The Assault on Truth: Freud's Suppression of the Seduction Theory*, has occasioned much disputation among psychoanalysts, notes that the original English edition of the letters (itself provocatively entitled *The Origins of Psychoanalysis*)[135] omitted the reference to Freud's own father, by using an ellipsis: "in every case . . . blame was laid on perverse acts by the father." The three dots appear in the letter in place of the phrase Masson translates as "the father, not excluding my own." The editors, Marie Bonaparte, Ernst Kris, and Freud's daughter Anna, comment that their editorial principle was one of "omitting or abbreviating everything publication of which would be inconsistent with professional or personal confidence . . . Omissions have been indicated by dots."[136] Even translation, here, acts out the story of suppression. Thus the discarding of the seduction theory, and the substitution of the Oedipus complex, not only opened the way for the discovery of the inner life of the child and the foundations of modern psychoanalysis, but also paid a kind of filial duty, honoring the memory of the father, and of fathers. The child's (Freud's own) fantasies, not the parent's actions, were to blame. Or if no blame was to be attached, at least there was no accusation against the parent. Are we – and were Freud's fellow analysts – being requested to close an/the eye(s)?

The story by means of which Freud substitutes infantile fantasy for child abuse is the story of Oedipus, who, by killing his father and marrying his mother, acts out in reality what every man is said to live in fantasy. Oedipus, then, becomes a paradigm for every man. Or does he? In the course of a discussion of the differences between *Oedipus* and *Hamlet*, Freud indicates that the later play represents a cultural advance: "the changed treatment of the same material reveals the whole difference in the mental life of these two widely separated epochs of civilization: the secular advance of repression in the emotional life of mankind."[137] What Oedipus *does* (kills his father, marries his mother), Hamlet *fantasizes* but *represses*, so that "we only learn of [this fantasy's] existence from its inhibiting consequences."[138] And yet this, to Freud, is very much more interesting than the straightforward enactment of the desire. Oedipus gives his name to the complex Freud discovered in every child's fantasy life, but it is Hamlet rather than Oedipus who engages Freud's own fascination, and his most extended discussion on the subject.

It is therefore not entirely clear which of the two dramas is "closer to home." *Hamlet* looks like a repressed version of the Oedipus story but in being a story *of* repression, it may in fact be closer to the story of "modern" man. There may, in other words, be *two* originary stories in Freud's mind, *both* of which are too close for comfort, and between which the story of Oedipus emerges as a compromise formation: the story of the father's sins, to which Freud dutifully closes his eyes by abandoning the seduction theory; and the story of repressed filial ambivalence, hesitation, and resentment towards an impossible paternal mandate, which Freud relegates to the status of secondary revision. The story of killing the father, which would seem to express Freud's filial ambivalence, in fact represses it: the murdered father can forever remain innocent while the son shoulders the guilt. The Oedipus story does not account for filial love.

While Freud thus confers upon Oedipus a primacy he denies to Hamlet, Hamlet remains a half-hidden centre of preoccupation throughout Freud's work. *Hamlet* is of course the Shakespearean text that has most intrigued psychoanalysts and psychoanalytic critics after Freud. But the writings of Freud himself seem uncannily to circle back upon the subject – and subjects – of *Hamlet*. Consider some of these titles: *The Interpretation of Dreams* (1900); "On Narcissism" (1914); "Mourning and Melancholia" (1917); "Negation" (1925); "A Note Upon the 'Mystic Writing-Pad' " (1925).

In "Mourning and Melancholia" (1917), for example, we find a fascinating treatment of the relationship between narcissism and mourning, and the need for the relinquishment of mourning to free the ego. Here Freud comments on "the mental faculty called *conscience*"[139] on the way in which "the self-reproaches are reproaches against a loved object which have been shifted onto the patient's own ego,"[140] especially the kind of self-reproach in which "the mourner himself is to blame for the loss of the loved one, *i.e.*, desired it."[141] Freud explicitly makes a connection in this essay between mourning and revenge, suggesting that both melancholics and obsessional neurotics "usually succeed in the end *in taking revenge*, by the circuitous path of self-punishment, on the original objects and in tormenting them by means of the illness."[142]

"The tendency to *suicide* which makes melancholia so interesting – and so dangerous"[143] is, according to Freud's argument, occasioned by the element of sadism intrinsic to such object loss. "In the two contrasting situations of intense love and suicide," Freud writes (still ostensibly on the general case of melancholia), "the ego is overwhelmed by the object, though in totally different ways . . . The most remarkable peculiarity of melancholia, and one most in need of explanation, is the tendency it displays to turn into mania accompanied by a completely opposite symptomology."[144] And here both the "antic disposition" (1.5.172) and Hamlet's disconcertingly "merry" tone in the "Mouse-trap" scene can be located. Hamlet, in short, is a textbook melancholic. Or is he the textbook itself, disclosing in the "book and volume of [his] brain" (1.5.103) the very symptomology Freud describes, the "three conditioning factors in melancholia – loss of the object, ambivalence, and regression of libido into the ego," of which, as Freud points out, "the first two are found also in the obsessional reproaches arising after the death of loved persons"?[145] Is this to commit the naive error of early psychoanalytic criticism, to diagnose a literary character as if he were a person? or is it, rather, to diagnose the symptomology of the *play*, and to see that symptomology informing the book and volume of *Freud's* brain?

The essay on "Mourning and Melancholia" itself contains a ghost that points the way, if not to the answers to such questions, at least to the questions themselves. For the case of Hamlet is cited, here, in an essay otherwise devoid of concrete examples – but cited in an oblique way, as a glancing analogue rather than an animation of the condition being described. Here is Freud's text, again, on the general case of the melancholic:

> When in his exacerbation of self-criticism he describes himself as petty, egoistic, dishonest, lacking in independence, one whose sole aim has been to hide the weaknesses in his own nature, for all we know it may be that he has come very near to self-knowledge; we only wonder why a man must become ill before he can discover truth of this kind. For there can be no doubt that whoever holds and expresses to others such an opinion of himself – one that Hamlet harboured of himself and all men – that man is ill, whether he speaks the truth or is more or less unfair to himself.[146]

Hamlet's cameo appearance in this passage, where he is evoked (and quoted in a footnote – "Use every man after his desert, and who shall 'scape whipping") comes in connection with one of the least particularized "symptoms" the essay will discuss. In effect he is used as a marker of typical melancholia. *His* repressions and ambivalences are nowhere cited, nor is the extraordinary aptness of his situation for a discussion of the *difference* between mourning and melancholia.

It begins to become clear that for Freud, the text of *Hamlet* occupies the place both of the patient (the entity to be analyzed) and of the *sujet supposé savoir* (the storehouse of psychoanalytic knowledge). The axis of authority from analyst to patient or analyst to text is commutative and reversible, as Shoshana Felman has shown in the case of literature and psychoanalysis: "With respect to the text, the literary critic occupies thus at once the place of the psychoanalyst (in the relation of interpretation) *and* the place of the patient (in the relation of transference)."[147] Lacan, in a celebrated axiom, declared that "the unconscious is structured like a language."[148] Felman adds that "*literature, in its turn, is the unconscious of psychoanalysis,* that the unthought-out shadow in psychoanalytic theory is precisely its own involvement with literature; that literature *in* psychoanalysis functions precisely as its 'unthought'; as the condition of possibility *and* the self-subversive blind spot of psychoanalytical *thought*."[149]

For Freud, *Hamlet* – the play, not the Prince – becomes not the analyzed but the analyst, the *sujet supposé savoir*, the ur-text of the Oedipus complex and not the other way around. *Hamlet* is, we might say, the navel of Freud's dream – the place of origination that marks the undiscoverable fact of origin, the "one spot in every dream that is unplumbable," "its point of contact with the unknown."

Later in life, Freud found an ingenious way of taking revenge on the authority both of his father and of Shakespeare. In *Moses and Monotheism* (1927–39), he wrote a family romance for the entire Jewish tradition, in which he claimed that Moses was not a Jew but a noble Egyptian – a text that Marianne Krüll describes as "Freud's last will and testament, in which he both accounts to his father and also settles accounts with him."[150] It was in those same years that Freud decided that Shakespeare was not, after all, the author of the Shakespeare plays. "The man of Stratford . . . seems to have nothing at all to justify his claim."[151]

But the ghost of *Hamlet* was not to be laid to rest so easily. Witness the following letter from one of Freud's own ambivalent "sons," C. G. Jung:

Dear Professor Freud,
    I accede to your wish that we abandon our personal relations, for I never thrust my friendship on anyone. You yourself are the best judge of what this moment means to you. "The rest is silence."[152]

Post Ghost

Ghosts always pass quickly, with the infinite speed of a furtive apparition, in an instant without duration, presence without present of a present which, coming back, only *haunts*. The ghost, *le re-venant*, the survivor, appears only by means of figure or fiction, but its appearance is not nothing, nor is it a mere semblance.

Derrida, "The Art of Mémoires"

– What is a ghost? Stephen said with tingling energy. One who has faded into impalpability through death, through absence, through change of manners. Elizabethan London lay as far from Stratford as corrupt Paris lies from virgin Dublin. Who is the ghost from *limbo patrum*, returning to the world that has forgotten him? Who is king Hamlet?

James Joyce, *Ulysses*

I

Whatever else it is, the *Hamlet* Ghost is an animation of the earlier theatrical genre known as revenge tragedy, come to summon protagonist and play to a genre already beginning to fade. Ghosts always come back, but they are always already belated when they come – it is only when they return, *re-venant*, that they *are* ghosts, and carry the authority of their own belatedness. The Ghost comes to summon Hamlet – and *Hamlet* – to a dramatic world which is no longer present. If Hamlet as a character is located in the place of the emergence of the modern subject, so *Hamlet* as a play is located on another, and equally indeterminate and undeterminable boundary. Between Hamlet and the Ghost, there is not only a conflict of generations but also a conflict of genres. The *Ur-Hamlet*, Belleforest, the *Spanish Tragedy*, *A Warning for Fair Women*, *Der bestrafte Brudermord* – all these precursors and schoolfellows, themselves interrogated by the scholar and critic of *Hamlet* for clues as to Shakespeare's sources, Shakespeare's authority – such texts are the Rosencrantzes and Guildensterns of this quest for an understanding of how the present text came to be as it is. The diagnosis of *madness* so earnestly alleged by Polonius, so gratefully received by Claudius, is a diagnosis of the play's dislocation from its origins, or rather, the play's repudiation of the obligations and possibilities of origin or origination, of paternity, of knowing one's father. As Shoshana Felman writes,

In the play of forces underlying the relationship between philosophy and fiction, literature and madness, the crucial problem is that of the subject's *place*, of his *position* with respect to the delusion. And the position of the subject is not defined by *what* he says, nor by what he talks *about*, but by the place – unknown to him – *from which* he speaks.[153]

"A little more than kin, and less than kind" (1.2.64–5) is a statement about genre and its conceptual limitations akin to, and of a more radical kind than, Polonius's canonical remarks on "tragical-comical-historical-pastoral" (2.2.398–9). By the time the actors arrive the genre of revenge tragedy has already been put in question by the questionable shape of the Ghost, of whose injunctions neither Hamlet nor the play are ever entirely free, but whose iterated command to revenge prompts a revenge upon revenge tragedy rather than a compliance with all its "forms . . . and pressures past" (1.5.100). It is no accident that Hamlet speaks to the players of "form and pressure" (3.2.24), as he has spoken of them to the Ghost:

> Suit the action to the word, the word to the action, with this special observance, that you o'erstep not the modesty of nature: for any thing so o'erdone is from the purpose of playing, whose end, both at the first and now, was and is, to hold as 'twere the mirror up to nature: to show virtue her own feature, scorn her own image, and the very age and body of the time his form and pressure. . . . O there be players that I have seen play – and heard others praise, and that highly – not to speak it profanely, that, neither having th'accent of Christians nor the gait of Christian, pagan, nor man, have so strutted and bellow'd that I have thought some of Nature's journeymen had made men, and not made them well, they imitated humanity so abominably. (3.2.16–35)

"Neither having th'accent of Christians nor the gait of Christian, pagan, nor man" – "[having] so strutted and bellow'd" – "imitated humanity so abominably" – this reads curiously like a critique of the older forms of revenge tragedy – and even of the Ghost. Thomas Lodge's 1596 report of the "ghost which cried so miserably at the theatre, like an oyster-wife, *Hamlet, revenge*"[154] in a performance of what scholars usually call the *Ur-Hamlet*, and Hamlet's own comment on the "Mouse-trap" play, "Come, the croaking raven doth bellow for revenge" (a conflation of two lines from *The True Tragedy of Richard III*: "The screeking Raven sits croking for revenge./Whole heads of beasts come bellowing for revenge") both situate the cry for revenge in the realm of the melodramatic, and accord with Hamlet's apparent views about bad theater.

Whether the *Hamlet* Ghost is Christian, pagan, or man is a question that has much vexed the academic community – prompting studies like Eleanor Prosser's influential *Hamlet and Revenge*[155] – and, indeed, the question troubled scholars, readers and audiences even before there was an academic community. Prosser notes that "throughout the Restoration and most of the eighteenth century, the Ghost was treated as a terrifying figure,"[156] that in the nineteenth century, "the questionable spirit that had so terrified Betterton and Garrick became transmuted by sentimentalism into an unquestioned spirit of health who aroused not horror but reverence," and that "as a result the Ghost became a pompous bore."[157] "The traditional view that the Ghost's command is to be obeyed," Prosser concludes, "has, indeed, held the stage since the Restoration, but this view has been made possible only by changing stage business, by modifying the interpretation of the Ghost, and, above all, by cutting contradictory lines and scenes."[158] Prosser, who believes that the play is Christian and that the Ghost is not to be obeyed – that revenge is un-Christian – tries to exorcize these changes, cuts and modifications by restoring the play to its original meaning, maintaining that "our attitude toward revenge is almost the same as the Elizabethan attitude, and it is doubtful that human nature has changed,"[159] and that "we find the tragic issue to be rooted in an ethical dilemma [revenge] that is universal."[160]

The difficulty of holding an essentialist view of the Ghost, or of *a* ghost, is implicit in and intrinsic to the nature (if that is the word) of ghosts themselves. To instate a meaning, or a dramatic effect, is to divest it of some of its power, the power that inheres in the sequence " 'Tis here!" " 'Tis here!" " 'Tis gone!". It is the nature of ghosts to be gone, so that they can return. When they are predictable, when they are no longer uncanny, they are no longer ghosts, but characters, capable of being inscribed in stage history.

Prosser's long and learned book is put to the service of one central purpose: to prove that the Ghost is an evil spirit that should not be trusted or obeyed. In this she goes counter to the received wisdom of critics like Bradley, who assume that the Ghost is trustworthy, or at least assume that Hamlet – and the Elizabethans – thought so. To write *against* the Ghost, as Prosser does, seems a curious thing to do, especially when the ranks of apologists *for* it go out of their way to rationalize revenge, discounting any hints of the daemonic. Prosser is not alone in this contention, as she herself points out.[161] Nonetheless, the project is interesting as a gesture of demystification, and even of defiance. Prosser denies the authority of the Ghost, and summons alternative authorities to bolster her denial. This is very like the project of scholars (and others) who write books demonstrating conclusively that Shakespeare is not the author of the plays. In both cases authority is flouted and rejected, under the comfortable visor of scholarship. The undecidability of paternity is here decided in the negative, allowing an unconflicted, authorized rebellion against authority. But to do this *requires* an essentialist reading of the Ghost, since if it behaves like a ghost, only in traces and belatedly, taking on "meanings" in a demonstrably delusive and subjective way, it can neither support the energy of rebellion, nor gratify the survivor.

II

Why do we still maintain the centrality of Shakespeare? Why in a time of canon expansion and critique of canonical literature does Shakespeare not only remain unchallenged, but in fact emerge newly canonized, as the proliferation of new critical anthologies – *Alternative Shakespeares, Political Shakespeare, Shakespeare and the Question of Theory*[162] – attests? Why does Harold Bloom exempt Shakespeare from the anxiety of influence, Geoffrey Hartman coedit with Patricia Parker an anthology of Shakespeare criticism, J. Hillis Miller bolster his argument about narrative theory with a reference to *Troilus and Cressida*?[163] Why does Terry Eagleton, who usually writes metacriticism, devote a book to William Shakespeare? Why does Elaine Showalter, who usually writes on nineteenth- and twentieth-century feminist topics, select Ophelia as the focus of a recent study?[164] Why with the current renaissance in Renaissance studies, is Shakespeare still the touchstone for new historicists, feminists, deconstructors? Why, in other words, do those who criticize canonical authority so often turn to Shakespeare to ratify the authority of their critique?

If anything is clear, it is that the Ghost is not – or not merely – Shakespeare *père* or Shakespeare *fils*, the son of John Shakespeare or the father of Hamnet – but rather "Shakespeare" itself. The ambiguous and ambivalent pronoun of Act 1 is appropriately used here, because Shakespeare is a concept – and a construct – rather than an author. We thus hear of the Shakespeare establishment, and of "Shakespeare" as a corpus of plays – a corpus "incorpsed" in innumerable authoritative editions, yet one that breaks the bounds – the margins – set to contain it, stalking the battlements of theory:

>   tell
> Why thy canoniz'd bones, hearsed in death,
> Have burst their cerements; why the sepulchre

> Wherein we saw thee quietly inurn'd,
> Hath op'd his ponderous and marble jaws
> To cast thee up again.

The Ghost is Shakespeare. He is the one who comes as a revenant, belatedly instated, regarded as originally authoritative, rather than retrospectively and retroactively canonized, and deriving increased authority from this very instatement of authority backward, over time. "The ghost, *le re-venant*, the survivor, appears only as a means of figure or fiction, but its appearance is not nothing, nor is it a mere semblance." This "presence without present of a present which, coming back, only *haunts*" haunts Freud, haunts Nietzsche, haunts Lacan, haunts postmodern England and postmodern America. The Ghost's command, his word, is "Remember me!" and we have done so, to the letter, *avant la lettre*, moving our remembrance further and further back until it becomes an originary remembrance, a remembrance of remembrance itself. "Remember me!" cries the Ghost, and Shakespeare is for us the superego of literature, that which calls us back to ourselves, to an imposed, undecidable, but self-chosen attribution of paternity. "Remember me!" The canon has been fixed against self-slaughter.

"A little more than kin and less than kind." Hamlet's bitter phrase inflects not only the problem of a ghostly genre, the unwriting and rewriting of revenge tragedy, but also the continuous attempt to render Shakespeare both kind and kin, of our time, our contemporary, always already postmodern, decentered. "Yet his modernity too, like Nietzsche's, is a forgetting or a suppression of anteriority."[165] This is de Man on Baudelaire. But it could be said of Hamlet – and of Shakespeare. This Baudelairization is not Bowdlerization, but transference, con-texting. We know that Shakespeare played the part of the Ghost in *Hamlet*. What could not be foreseen, except through anamorphic reading, was that he would *become* that Ghost. "Remember me!" the Ghost cries. "Do not forget." And, indeed, we do not yet seem quite able to give up that ghost.

Notes

Preface: Ghostlier demarcations

1 Sigmund Freud, "The Uncanny" in *Studies in Parapsychology*, ed. Philip Rieff, trans. Alix Strachey (New York: Collier Books, 1963), p. 42.
2 James Joyce, *Ulysses* (New York: Random House, 1986), p. 175.
3 Sigmund Freud, "Further Recommendations in the Technique of Psychoanalysis: Observations on Transference–Love," in *Therapy and Technique*, ed. Philip Rieff, trans. Joan Riviere (New York: Collier Books, 1963), p. 172.
4 John Keats, "This Living Hand" in *Keats: Poems and Selected Letters*, ed. Carlos Baker (New York: Charles Scribner's Sons, 1962) p. 367.
5 "The Uncanny," pp. 49–50.

1 Shakespeare's ghost writers

1 See *The Riverside Shakespeare*, ed. G. Blakemore Evans (Boston: Houghton Mifflin, 1974), p. 1684. Unless noted, all citations from the plays are to this edition.
2 James G. McManaway, *The Authorship of Shakespeare* (Washington, DC: Folger Shakespeare Library, 1962), p. 12.
3 ibid., pp. 12–13.
4 ibid., p. 29.
5 ibid., p. 19.
6 Charlton Ogburn, Jr., *The Mysterious William Shakespeare: The Myth and the Reality* (New York: Dodd, Mead, 1984), p. 145.
7 William F. and Elizabeth S. Friedman, *The Shakespearean Ciphers Examined* (Cambridge: Cambridge University Press, 1957), pp. 7; 181.
8 ibid., p. 1.
9 ibid., p. 5.
10 Michel Foucault, *Language, Counter-Memory, Practice*, ed. and trans. Donald F. Bouchard (Ithaca: Cornell University Press, 1977), p. 125.
11 Frank W. Wadsworth, *The Poacher from Stratford* (Berkeley and Los Angeles: University of California Press, 1958), p. 52. Wadsworth's book gives a good overview of the controversy.
12 ibid., p. 45.
13 *Harvard Magazine*, 77 (January 1975).
14 ibid., 77 (April 1975).
15 ibid.

16 John H. Stotsenburg, *An Impartial Study of the Shakespeare Title* (Louisville, Kentucky: J.P. Morton, 1904), p. 174.

17 S. Schoenbaum, *Shakespeare's Lives* (Oxford: Clarendon Press, 1970), p. 612.

18 Georg Brandes, *William Shakespeare: A Critical Study* (New York: Macmillan, 1909), p. 87. Cited in Ogburn, p. 153.

19 Wadsworth, p. 89.

20 Mark Twain, "Is Shakespeare Dead?" in *What is Man? And Other Essays* (New York and London: Harper Brothers, 1917), p. 324.

21 Ralph Waldo Emerson to William Emerson, 29 May 1849, in *The Letters of Ralph Waldo Emerson*, ed. Ralph L. Rusk (New York: Columbia University Press, 1939), 4, p. 149.

22 Horace Traubel, *Walt Whitman in Camden* (Boston: Small, Maynard, 1906), p. 136.

23 Walt Whitman, "November Boughs," in *Complete Poetry and Prose of Walt Whitman, as Prepared by Him for the Death Bed Edition* (New York: Pelligrini & Cudahy, 1948), 2, p. 404.

24 Sir Charles Spencer Chaplin, *My Autobiography* (New York: Simon & Schuster, 1964), p. 364. Ogburn, p. 260.

25 Ralph Waldo Emerson, "Shakespeare, or, The Poet," *Representative Men* in *Ralph Waldo Emerson: Essays and Lectures* (New York: Library of America, 1983) p. 720.

26 Henry James, Letter to Violet Hunt, 26 August 1903, in *The Letters of Henry James*, ed. Percy Lubbock (New York: Scribner, 1920), 1, p. 424.

27 Henry James, "The Birthplace," in *Selected Short Stories* (New York: Rinehart, 1955), pp. 246–47.

28 ibid., p. 238.

29 ibid., p. 256.

30 Twain, p. 372.

31 Ralph Waldo Emerson, *The Journals and Miscellaneous Notebooks of Ralph Waldo Emerson*, ed. Ralph H. Orth and Alfred R. Ferguson (Cambridge, Mass.: Harvard University Press, 1971), 9, p. 184.

32 Charles Dickens, Letter to William Sandys, 13 June 1847, in *Complete Writings of Charles Dickens*, ed. "by his sister-in-law" (Boston, Mass.: Charles E. Lauriat, 1923), 37, p. 206.

33 Samuel Taylor Coleridge, *Biographia Literaria* (1817), Chapter 15.

34 John Keats to George and Thomas Keats, 21 December 1817, in *The Selected Letters of John Keats*, ed. Lionel Trilling (Garden City, NJ: Doubleday Anchor Books, 1956), p. 103.

35 Keats to George and Georgiana Keats, 14 February–3 May 1819, *Selected Letters*, p. 229.

36 John Dryden, "An Essay on Dramatic Poesy," *The Works of John Dryden*, Notes and Life by Sir Walter Scott; revised by George Saintsbury. (Edinburgh: William Patterson, 1882–83), 15, p. 344.

37 Foucault, p. 130.

38 Matthew Arnold, "Shakespeare," in *The Poems of Matthew Arnold*,

ed. Kenneth Allott (London: Longmans, Green & Co., 1965), pp. 48–50, ll. 1–3.

39 Foucault, p. 166.

40 ibid., p. 117.

41 Nicholas Rowe, "Some Account of the Life, & c., of Mr. William Shakespeare," in *The Works of Mr. William Shakespeare, in Six Volumes* (London: Jacob Tonson, 1709), 1; p. vi.

42 William Oldys (ca.1743–61), quoted by E.K. Chambers, *William Shakespeare: A Study of Facts and Problems* (Oxford: Clarendon Press, 1930), 3, p. 278.

43 Sigmund Freud, *Beyond the Pleasure Principle*, 1; italics Freud's.

44 ibid., p. 37.

45 ibid., p. 45.

46 See Jacques Derrida, *Of Grammatology*, trans. G. C. Spivak (Baltimore: Johns Hopkins University Press, 1974), pp. 141–64.

47 Barbara Johnson, unpublished manuscript.

48 See J. H. Pafford, ed., *The Winters Tale*, The Arden Shakespeare (London: Methuen, 1963), p. 139n. Pafford cites Harold Brooks's observation that "with this clue one can see that Paulina's comparison of the first wife with any second has resemblance with Hamlet's indignant comparison of Gertrude's first husband with her second." For Gertrude's ears, see *Hamlet* 3.4.95.

49 Sigmund Freud, "The Uncanny," in *Studies in Parapsychology*, ed. Philip Rieff (New York: Macmillan, 1963), p. 40.

50 See Walter Benjamin, *Illuminations*, ed. Hannah Arendt, trans. Harry Zohn (New York: Schocken Books, 1969), p. 76.

51 ibid., p. 71.

52 ibid., p. 220.

53 ibid., p. 221.

54 ibid., p. 224.

55 Robert Lowell, "Epilogue," in *Day by Day* (New York: Farrar, Strauss & Giroux, 1977), p. 127.

56 Abel Gance, "Le Temps de l'image est venu," *l'Art cinématographique* (Paris: Gance, 1927) 2: 94F. Cited in Benjamin, "The Work of Art in the Age," *Illuminations*, pp. 221–2.

57 A concept is said to be "under erasure" when it is put in question or under critique. This signifying practice, employed by Martin Heidegger and, after him, by Jacques Derrida and other deconstructive critics, is described by Gayatri Spivak as "to write a word, cross it out, and then print both word and deletion. (Since the word is inaccurate, it is crossed out. Since it is necessary, it remains legible.)" (in Jacques Derrida, *Of Grammatology* (Baltimore: Johns Hopkins University Press, 1974), translator's preface, p. xiv.) Thus Heidegger, in *The Question of Being*, writes that "Man in his essence is the memory [or memorial, *Gedächtnis*] not of Being, but of B̶e̶i̶n̶g̶. This means that the essence of man is a part of that which in the crossed intersected lines of Being puts thinking under the claim of a more originary command [*anfänglichere Geheiss*]." (*The Question of Being*, tr. William Kluback

and Jean T. Wilde, bilingual edition (New York: Twayne Publishers 1958), cited by Spivak, p. xv). Spivak comments that "Heidegger is working with the resources of the old language, the language we already possess. To make a new word is to run the risk of forgetting the problem or believing it solved" (Spivak, p. xv). But, she remarks, it is important to distinguish between what Heidegger puts under erasure and what Derrida does. Heidegger critiques the master-word, "Being," a transcendental signifier. Derrida, while he does not reject this idea, is concerned with the "trace," "a word that cannot be a master-word, that presents itself as the mark of an anterior presence, origin, master" (*Of Grammatology*, p. xv). Spivak's example from Derrida is this: ". . . the sign ̶i̶s̶ that ill-named ̶t̶h̶i̶n̶g̶ . . . which escapes the instituting question of philosophy . . ." (*Of Grammatology*, p. 19). The nostalgia for a lost presence, a lost originary moment, that animates the writings of Heidegger is specifically absent from Derrida. "Derrida's ̶t̶r̶a̶c̶e̶ is the mark of the absence of a presence, an always already absent present, of the lack at the origin that is the condition of thought and experience" (Spivak, xvii). It is this specifically Derridean inflection of "under erasure," "*sous rature*," that so uncannily resembles a ghost – resembles, in fact, the ̶B̶e̶i̶n̶g̶ of a ghost. "There are more ̶t̶h̶i̶n̶g̶s̶ in heaven and earth, Horatio,/than are dreamt of in your philosophy" (*Hamlet* 1.5.166–67).

58 Jacques Derrida, "Signature, Event, Context," in *Margins of Philosophy*, trans. Alan Bass (Chicago: University of Chicago Press, 1982), p. 328.

59 T.S. Eliot, "Shakespeare and the Stoicism of Seneca," *Selected Essays* (New York: Harcourt, Brace & World, 1960), p. 67; M.C. Bradbrook, *Shakespeare and Elizabethan Poetry* (Harmondsworth: Penguin, 1964), p. 96; E. M. W. Tillyard, *Shakespeare's History Plays* (New York: Collier Books, 1962), p. 160. In a lecture on *Titus Andronicus* delivered at the Stratford (Ontario) Shakespeare Festival some years ago, Richard Wheeler alluded to this peculiar tendency in *Titus* criticism.

60 J. C. Maxwell, ed., *Titus Andronicus*, The Arden Shakespeare (London: Methuen, 1968), p. xxiv.

61 John Bulwer, *Chironomia* (London, 1644), p. 16. Cited in B. L. Joseph, *Elizabethan Acting* (London: 1951), p. 39. See Maxwell, ed., pp. 109–10.

62 Elaine Showalter, "Representing Ophelia: Women, Madness, and the Responsibilities of Feminist Criticism," in Patricia Parker and Geoffrey Hartman, eds., *Shakespeare and the Question of Theory* (New York: Methuen, 1985), p. 80.

2 Descanting on deformity: Richard III and the shape of history

1 See *The Riverside Shakespeare*, ed. G. Blakemore Evans (Boston: Houghton Mifflin, 1974). All citations from the plays are to this edition unless noted in the text.

2 Charles Ross, *Richard III* (Berkeley: University of California Press, 1981).

3 ibid., p. li.

4 ibid., p. 229.

5 ibid., p. li.

6 René Girard, "Hamlet's Dull Revenge," *Stanford Literary Review*. 1 (Fall 1984): 159.

7 Geoffrey Bullough, ed., *Narrative and Dramatic Sources of Shakespeare* (London: Routledge & Kegan Paul, 1975), 3, p. 223.

8 *The Yale Edition of the Complete Works of Sir Thomas More*, Vol. 2, *The History of King Richard III*, ed. Richard Sylvester (New Haven and London: Yale University Press, 1963), p. 7. Sir Horace Walpole, one of the earliest defenders of Richard's reputation, characterized More as "an historian who is capable of employing truth only as cement in a fabric of fiction," (Walpole, *Historic Doubts on the Life and Reign of Richard III* (London: J. Dodsley, 1768; [1965 ed.]), p. 116 and recent scholars have explicitly identified the kind of "fiction" More is writing as *drama*. Thus A. R. Myers asserts that "his history is much more like a drama, unfolded in magnificent prose, for which fidelity to historical fact is scarcely relevant," (Myers, "The Character of Richard III," originally published in *History Today*, 4 (1954), reprinted in *English Society and Government in the Fifteenth Century*, ed. C.M.D. Crowder, (Edinburgh and London: 1967), p. 119; cited in Ross. *Richard III*; and Alison Hanham argues that the *History* is really a "satirical drama" meant to display More's own cleverness rather than his command of fact. (Hanham, *Richard III and His Early Historians* [Oxford: Clarendon Press 1975], pp. 152–90.)

9 I am indebted to Richard Strier for this observation.

10 Sigmund Freud, "Some Character-Types Met With in Psychoanalytic Work," in *Character and Culture*, ed. Philip Rieff (New York: Collier Books, 1961), p. 159.

11 ibid., p. 160.

12 ibid., p. 161.

13 ibid.

14 ibid., p. 160.

15 Fritz Stern, *Gold and Iron* (New York: Vintage Books, 1979), p. 437.

16 Jacques Lacan, "The Mirror Stage as Formative of the Function of the I," in *Écrits*, trans. Alan Sheridan (New York: W.W. Norton 1977), p. 4.

17 Peter Saccio, *Shakespeare's English Kings* (New York: Oxford University Press, rpt 1978), pp. 158–9. In a recent study of biography and fiction in Tudor–Stuart history writing (*Biographical Truth: The Representation of Historical Persons in Tudor-Stuart Writing* [New Haven: Yale University Press, 1984]). Judith H. Anderson notes that historians regularly impeach Shakespeare's play for its lack of fidelity to historical fact, and points out accurately that the play would lose its power if it did not convince the audience that it was "somehow real history" (p. 111) – "Despite ourselves, we believe it" (p. 123). Yet

Anderson's view of Richard's deformity is a relatively conventional one. Citing Freud, and reasserting the humanistic commonplace that suffering creates art, she describes Richard as "the misshapen product of his nature and time and also, as we watch him in the play, the product of his own making" (p. 117). Whether self-fashioned or twisted by his own deformity, Richard is seen as compensating for a disability, rather than seizing that disability as the occasion for a theoretical exploration of the nature of deformation.

18 Pamela Tudor-Craig, *Richard III* (1973); cited in Ross, *Richard III*, pp. 80, 92–3.

19 Jonathan Culler, "Presupposition and Intertextuality," in *The Pursuit of Signs* (Ithaca: Cornell University Press, 1981), p. 177.

20 Antony Hammond, ed., *King Richard III*, The Arden Shakespeare (London and New York: Methuen, 1981), p. 338.

21 Edward Hall, *The Union of the Two Noble . . . Families of Lancaster and York* (1548) cited in Hammond, ed., p. 353.

22 See Sigmund Freud, "The Uncanny" (1919), in *Studies in Parapsychology*, ed. Philip Rieff (New York: Macmillan, 1963), pp. 19–60, especially pp. 38–42 on "the double" and the repetition-compulsion.

23 Hall, cited in Hammond, ed. p. 354.

24 More, p. 68.

25 Bullough, ed., p. 232.

26 Hammond, ed., p. 87.

27 E.M.W. Tillyard, *Shakespeare's History Plays* (New York: Collier Books, 1962), p. 72. Emphasis added.

28 Francis Bacon, *Essays Civil and Moral* (London: Ward, Lock, 1910), pp. 69–70.

29 Arthur Sherbo, ed., *Johnson on Shakespeare* (New Haven and London: Yale University Press, 1968), 7, p. 605.

30 Walter Jackson Bate, *Samuel Johnson* (New York: Harcourt Brace Jovanovich, 1979), p. 7. See Bate's sensitive treatment of these physical deformities and Johnson's apparent repression of their origins, esp. p. 9. My thanks to Joseph Bartolomeo for reminding me of the relevance of Johnson's own physical disabilities.

31 Bate, p. 7.

32 Samuel Johnson, "Preface to Shakespeare," in Sherbo, ed., 7, p. 91.

33 Houston A. Baker, Jr., "Caliban's Triple Play," in *"Race," Writing, and Difference*, ed. Henry Louis Gates, Jr., (Chicago: University of Chicago Press, 1986), p. 390.

34 ibid., p. 392.

35 ibid., p. 382.

36 Paul Howe, personal communication, January 1987.

37 Friedrich Nietzsche, "The Use and Abuse of History," in *Untimely Meditations*, trans. R. J. Hollingdale (Cambridge: Cambridge University Press, 1983), p. 61. Hollingdale translates this famous essay as "On the Uses and Disadvantages of History for Life." I use his translation, as being the most accurate modern version, but take the liberty of retaining the title by which the piece is best known to

English readers – and, I think, most suggestively rendered for argumentation.
38 ibid., p. 70–1. Emphasis added.
39 ibid., p. 61.
40 ibid., p. 70.
41 Robert N. Watson, *Shakespeare and the Hazards of Ambition* (Cambridge, Mass: Harvard University Press, 1984), p. 20. Janet Adelman, "Born of Woman, Fantasies of Maternal Power in *Macbeth*," in *Cannibals, Witches, and Divorce: Estranging the Renaissance*, ed. Marjorie Garber (Baltimore: Johns Hopkins University Press, 1986), pp. 91–3.
42 See Watson, p. 26.
43 Marjorie Garber, "What's Past is Prologue: Temporality and Prophecy in Shakespeare's History Plays," in *Renaissance Literary Genres: Essays on Theory, History and Interpretation*, ed. Barbara Lewalski, Harvard English Studies 14, (Cambridge, Mass: Harvard University Press, 1986), pp. 301–31.
44 "An Apology for Poetry," in *Sir Philip Sidney, Selected Poetry and Prose*, ed. David Kalstone (New York: Signet Classic, 1970), p. 227.
45 ibid., p. 233.
46 ibid., p. 249.
47 Nietzsche, p. 91.
48 "An Apology," p. 234.
49 Nietzsche, p. 106.
50 ibid., p. 95.
51 ibid.
52 Hayden White, *Metahistory: The Historical Imagination in Nineteenth-Century Europe* (Baltimore and London: Johns Hopkins University Press, 1973), p. 356.
53 ibid., p. 81.
54 ibid., pp. 85–6. Emphasis added.
55 ibid., p. 115.
56 ibid., p. 108.
57 ibid.

3 A Rome of one's own

1 Walter Benjamin, *Schriften*, I, p. 57. Cited in *Illuminations*, ed. Hannah Arendt, trans. Harry Zohn (New York: Schocken Books, 1969), p. 38.
2 Benjamin, *Schriften*, II, p. 192. Cited in *Illuminations*, p. 39.
3 Sigmund Freud, *Civilization and Its Discontents*, ed. and trans. James Strachey (New York: W.W. Norton, 1961), p. 16.
4 ibid., p. 17.
5 ibid., p. 17.
6 ibid.
7 ibid., p. 18.
8 ibid.

9 Sigmund Freud, *The Interpretation of Dreams*, trans. James Strachey (New York: Avon Books, 1965), p. 460.

10 See *The Riverside Shakespeare*, ed. G. Blakemore Evans (Boston: Houghton Mifflin, 1974). Unless noted, all citations from the plays are to this edition.

11 On the origins of this line, see T.S. Dorsch, ed., *Julius Caesar*, The Arden Shakespeare (London: Methuen, 1965), p. 67.

12 ed. L. B. Campbell, l. 383.

13 Jonathan Goldberg, *James I and the Politics of Literature* (Baltimore: Johns Hopkins University Press, 1983), pp. 166–7.

14 Walter Benjamin, "Theses on the Philosophy of History," in *Illuminations*, trans. Harry Zohn (New York: Schocken Books, 1969), p. 261.

15 Karl Marx, *The Eighteenth Brumaire of Louis Bonaparte*, in Karl Marx and Friedrich Engels, *Selected Works* (New York: International Publishers, 1968).

16 ibid., p. 15.

17 ibid., p. 17.

18 ibid., pp. 16–17.

19 ibid., p. 17.

20 Alexander Nehamas, *Nietzsche, Life as Literature* (Cambridge, Mass.: Harvard University Press, 1985), p. 227. Citations: *The Will to Power*, trans. Walter Kaufmann and R.J. Hollingdale (New York: Vintage Press, 1968); *Twilight of the Idols*, trans. Walter Kaufmann, in *The Portable Nietzsche*, ed. Walter Kaufmann (New York: Viking Press, 1954); *Ecce Homo*, trans. Walter Kaufmann (New York: Vintage Press, 1968).

21 Friedrich Nietzsche, "The Use and Abuse of History," in *Untimely Meditations*, trans. R. J. Hollingdale (Cambridge: Cambridge University Press, 1983), pp. 85–6.

22 Plutarch, *Life of Caesar*, trans. Sir Thomas North, in Walter W. Skeat, ed., *Shakespeare's Plutarch* (New York: Macmillan, 1875), pp. 103–4.

23 Plutarch, *Life of Brutus*, in Skeat, ed., p. 136.

24 Sigmund Freud, "The Uncanny," in *Studies in Parapsychology*, ed. Philip Rieff (New York: Collier Books, 1963), p. 47.

25 ibid., p. 57.

26 ibid.

27 ibid., p. 59.

28 Sigmund Freud, *The Interpretation of Dreams*, trans. James Strachey (New York: Avon Books, 1965), p. 456.

29 ibid., p. 460. Emphasis added.

30 ibid., p. 523.

31 ibid., p. 524.

32 Dorsch, ed., p. 16n.; cf. the same pun in *King John* 3.1.180.

33 Freud, "The Uncanny," pp. 49–50.

34 *Harper's Dictionary of Classical Literature and Antiquities*, ed. Harry Thurston Peck (New York: Cooper Square Publishers, 1965), p. 271.

35 Janet Adelman, *The Common Liar* (New Haven: Yale University Press, 1973), p. 132.

4 Freud's choice: "The Theme of the Three Caskets"

1 Sigmund Freud, "The Theme of the Three Caskets," in Philip Rieff, ed., *Character and Culture* (New York: Collier Books, 1963), pp. 67– 79.
2 ibid., p. 67.
3 Letter 4 July 1912, in Ludwig Binswanger, *Sigmund Freud: Reminiscences of a Friendship* (New York and London: Grune & Stratton, 1957), p. 45.
4 Freud, "Three Caskets," p. 68.
5 ibid., p. 69.
6 ibid.
7 ibid.
8 ibid., p. 70.
9 ibid.
10 ibid., p. 71.
11 ibid., p. 72.
12 ibid., p. 75.
13 ibid.
14 ibid.
15 ib

, trans. Arnold J. Pomerans (New

2.
22
23 Kr
24 ibid.,
25 On Re   Jacob Freud's second wife (and Amalie, therefore, as his third), see Josef Sajner, "Sigmund Freuds Beziehungen zu seinem Geburtsort Freiberg (Příbor) and zu Mähren," *Clio Medica*, 3, 1968, 170; Max Schur, *Freud, Living and Dying* (New York: 1972), p. 20; Henry F. Ellenberger, *The Discovery of the Unconscious. The History and Evolution of Dynamic Psychiatry* (New York: 1970), p. 425.
26 District Archives, photocopy by J. Sajner, reprinted by Krüll, table 4.
27 Schur, p. 191.
28 See *The Complete Letters of Sigmund Freud to Wilhelm Flies, 1887–1904*, ed. and trans. Jeffrey Moussaieff Masson (Cambridge, Mass.: Harvard University Press, 1985), p. 266n, and Krüll, pp. 55, 135–6.
29 Schur, p. 19.
30 Krüll, p. 137.
31 Masson, ed., 15 July 1896, pp. 194, 195; 9 October 1896, p. 201; 26 October 1896, p. 200; 2 November 1896, p. 202.
32 Sigmund Freud, *The Interpretation of Dreams*, trans. James Strachey (New York: Avon Books, 1965), p. xxvi.

33 Masson, ed., 12 August 1896, p. 195.
34 Freud, "Three Caskets," p. 78.
35 ibid., p. 78.
36 Letter 13 July 1883, in *Letters of Sigmund Freud*, selected and edited by Ernst L. Freud, trans. Tania and James Stern (New York: Basic Books, 1960), pp. 40–1.
37 Norman Holland, *Psychoanalysis and Shakespeare* (New York: Octagon Books, 1976), p. 65.
38 *Letters of Sigmund Freud*, 13 July 1883, p. 41.
39 Freud, "Three Caskets," p. 69.
40 ibid., p. 71.
41 Freud, *Interpretation of Dreams*, pp. 138–54.
42 ibid., p. 143.
43 ibid., p. 151.
44 ibid., p. 151.
45 ibid., p. 139.
46 ibid., p. 139. I am grateful to Michael Goldman for this suggestion.
47 Krüll, p. 248n.
48 Peter Swales, "Freud, Minna Bernays and the Conquest of Rome," *New American Review*, I, 1982.
49 Krüll, p. 9; Schur, p. 97, letter of 16 April 1896 to Fliess; Masson, ed., pp. 68, 69, 85, 181, 442.
50 *Letters of Sigmund Freud*, 9 July 1913, p. 301.
51 Freud's six children were: Mathilde, born 16 October 1887; Jean Martin, born 7 December 1889; Oliver, born 19 February 1891; Ernst, born 6 April 1892; Sophie, born 12 April 1893; and Anna, born 3 December 1895.
52 Krüll, p. 31.
53 *The Letters of Sigmund Freud and Arnold Zweig*, ed. Ernst L. Freud, trans. Professor and Mrs W. D. Robson-Scott (London: Hogarth Press/Institute of Psychoanalysis, 1970), letter of 26 February 1934, p. 66.
54 *Letters of Freud/Zweig*, 2 May 1935, p. 106.
55 ibid., p. 65.
56 ibid., p. 106.
57 Freud, "Three Caskets," pp. 67–8.
58 Norman Holland, *Psychoanalysis and Shakespeare* (New York: Octagon Books, 1976), p. 69.
59 Sigmund Freud, *Moses and Monotheism*, trans. Katherine Jones (New York: Vintage Books, 1939), pp. 55, 79, 143–4, 158, 175.
60 ibid., pp. 54–5.
61 ibid., p. 156.
62 ibid., p. 112.
63 Much has been written about castration, circumcision, and the courtroom scene. Several years ago Theodore Reik – noting that he was surely not the first psychoanalyst to do so – suggested that Shylock's bond as read out in court, demanding "a pound of flesh, be by him cut off/Nearest the merchant's heart" (4.1.232–3) was a

displacement upward of his earlier request to cut off the flesh "in what part of your body pleaseth me" (1.3.151) – that is, a displacement of a castration threat, itself derived from an unconscious Christian fear of the Jewish practice of circumcision: Theodore Reik, *The Search Within* (New York: Farrar, Strauss & Cudahy, 1956), p. 359.

Stanley Cavell offers a similar interpretation of this episode, based in part upon his reading of the "hath not a Jew eyes" speech in Act 3, scene 1. "I will force you to be the perfect narcissist," he hears Shylock as saying to Antonio in that speech: "I will perfect the analogy of my image with yours, I will take upon myself your sentence": Stanley Cavell, *The Claim of Reason: Wittgenstein, Skepticism, Morality and Tragedy* (New York: Oxford University Press, 1979), pp. 479–81.

> I do not insist, [explains Cavell in his own voice] that Shylock's proof – his better instruction – that Antonio is his *semblable* was (and psychically remains) to carve Antonio into a Jew, i.e., to do to him what circumcision, in certain frames of mind, is imagined to do, i.e., to castrate. I insist here only that the question rouses our horrified wonder that a pound, wherever it may be cut from, would result in so complete a disfigurement, amounting to metamorphosis ... We need not assume that any such change has been agreed upon if we allow that a confusion of identities persists. For *which* merchant (of Venice) is picked out by the phrase 'nearest the merchant's heart'? If this can be read as picking out Shylock, then it is equivalent to Shylock's original demand for the part that 'pleases' him.

Both Reik and Cavell predicate their insights upon an assumption of doubling or twinship, a moment of perceptual equipoise that enforces the disconcerting confusion of identities. Reik, writing shortly after the defeat of Hitler in Germany, is concerned with certain persistent Christian fantasies about Jews, Cavell with "skepticism with respect to other minds" and the epistemological uncertainty of identity. Each reader appropriates Shylock's scene, persuasively, to his own theoretical project, and finds the twinship of Shylock and Antonio in the courtroom a theatrical hypostasis, an onstage crux that reifies his own perceptions. See also Marc Shell, *Money, Language and Thought* (Berkeley: University of California Press, 1982), pp. 47–83.

5 *Macbeth*: the male Medusa

1 See *The Riverside Shakespeare*, ed. G. Blakemore Evans (Boston: Houghton Mifflin, 1974). Unless noted, all citations from the plays are to this edition.

2 For this and subsequent information about *Macbeth* and theatrical superstition I am indebted to Richard Huggett, *Supernatural On Stage: Ghosts and Superstitions of the Theater* (New York: Taplinger Publishing Company, 1975), pp. 153–211. I was witness to the Stratford, Ontario incident (July 1980).

3 Huggett, pp. 162–3.
4 Sigmund Freud, "The Uncanny," in *Studies in Parapsychology*, ed. Philip Rieff, trans. Alix Strachey (New York: Macmillan, 1963), p. 57.
5 Stéphane Mallarmé, *La Fausse Entrée Des Sorcières dans Macbeth*, in *Crayonné Au Théâtre, Oeuvres Completes* (Paris: Pléiade, 1945), p. 348. I am indebted to Barbara Johnson for calling this essay to my attention, and for the translation.
6 Huston Diehl, in "Horrid Image, Sorry Sight, Fatal Vision: The Visual Rhetoric of *Macbeth*," *Shakespeare Studies* 16 (1983): 191–203, comments on the problematics of reading the play, contrasting Macduff's ethical reading of the dead body of Duncan with Macbeth's rejection of the spiritual and ethical, and noting the audience's participation in the act of seeing and interpreting.
7 H.J. Rose, *A Handbook of Greek Mythology* (New York: E.P. Dutton, 1959), pp. 29–30.
8 What is the relationship between anxiety of gender and the anxiety generated by an application of Freud's theory? Is the Medusa head like a King Charles head for modern critical theory, a whimsical obsession, always turning up where least wanted and expected? Or is it, in fact, a radical of this play's dramatic subtext, everywhere present because everywhere absent, something we fall in love with because we fear to look on it? Medusa, after all, was a figure of surpassing beauty – it is for this reason, according to some versions of the story, that Athena had her killed, and annexed (while disabling) her beauty by depicting the head on her shield.
9 Jane Ellen Harrison, *Prolegomena to the Study of Greek Religion* (Cambridge: Cambridge University Press, 1922; rpt New York: Meridian Books, 1955), p. 187.
10 Caesare Ripa, *Iconologia* (Florence, 1613), p. 182.
11 Walter Friedländer, *Carvaggio Studies* (Princeton, N.J.: Princeton University Press, 1955), p. 88.
12 Francis Bacon, *The Wisedome of the Ancients*, trans. Arthur Gorges (London, 1619), p. 41.
13 ibid., p. 43.
14 ibid., p. 44.
15 Richard Hosley, ed., *Shakespeare's Holinshed* (New York: G.P. Putnam, 1968), p. 17. An excerpt from Holinshed's *Chronicles of Scotland* appears in Kenneth Muir, ed., *Macbeth*, The Arden Shakespeare (London: Methuen, 1962), pp. 170–88.
16 Alexander Ross, *Mystogogus Poeticus* (London, 1647), p. 103.
17 ibid., p. 213.
18 *The Political Works of James I, reprinted from the Edition of 1616*, ed. Charles Howard McHwain (Cambridge, Mass. Harvard University Press, 1918) p. 29.
19 ibid., p. 272.
20 ibid., p. 65.
21 ibid., p. 43.
22 ibid., p. 6.

23 ibid., p. 21.
24 ibid., p. xxviii.
25 ibid., pp. 18ff.
26 J.M.C. Toynbee, *Art in Britain Under the Romans* (Oxford: Clarendon Press, 1964), *passim*.
27 ibid., p. 136.
28 ibid., p. 32.
29 J.M.C. Toynbee, *Art in Roman Britain* (London: Phaidon Press, 1962), p. 163.
30 Nelson Glueck, *Deities and Dolphins: The Story of the Nabataeans* (New York: Farrar, Straus & Giroux, 1965), pp. 80–4.
31 Kathleen Basford, *The Green Man* (Ipswich, Suffolk: D.S. Brewer, 1978), pp. 9–22.
32 Karl Otfried Müller, *Introduction to a Scientific Study of Mythology*, trans. Leitch (London, 1844). Cited in Burton Feldman and Robert D. Richardson, Jr., *The Rise of Modern Mythology* (Bloomington: Indiana University Press, 1972), p. 420.
33 Freud, "The Uncanny," p. 47.
34 The "omnipotence of thoughts" ascribed to witches could be a self-elected characteristic, concomitant to certain modern mental disorders like schizophrenia – or a more ordinary outgrowth of loneliness and superstition. Thus Reginald Scot in his *Discovery of Witchcraft* (1584) describes them: "One sort of such as are said to be witches are women which be commonly old, lame, blear-eyed, pale, foul, and full of wrinkles; poor, sullen, superstitious, and papists; or such as know no religion: in whose drowsy minds the Devil hath gotten a fine seat; so as, what mischief, mischance, calamity, or slaughter is brought to pass, they are easily persuaded the same is done by themselves, imprinting in their minds an earnest and constant imagination thereof . . . .
   The witch . . . expecting her neighbors' mischances, and seeing things sometimes come to pass according to her wishes, curses, and incantations . . . being called before a Justice, by due examination of the circumstances is driven to see her imprecations and desires and her neighbors' harms and losses to concur, and as it were to take effect: and so confesseth that she (as a goddess) hath brought such things to pass." Cited in G.B. Harrison, ed., *Shakespeare: The Complete Works* (New York: Harcourt, Brace & World, 1952), pp. 1644–5.
35 Freud, "The Uncanny," p. 46.
36 ibid., p. 397.
37 ibid., p. 40.
38 ibid., p. 51.
39 Sigmund Freud, "Medusa's Head," in *Sexuality and the Psychology of Love*, ed. Philip Rieff (New York: Macmillan, 1963), p. 212.
40 See Neil Hertz, *The End of the Line* (New York: Columbia University Press, 1985), pp. 161–215.
41 Freud, "Medusa's Head," pp. 212–13.
42 ibid., p. 20.
43 ibid., pp. 31–2.

44 ibid., p. 35.
45 ibid., p. 57.
46 ibid., p. 47.
47 ibid.
48 ibid., p. 49.
49 For a useful and persuasive discussion of the consanguinities of Shakespearean and Freudian models of psychic representation in *Macbeth*, see David Willbern, "Phantasmagoric *Macbeth*" *ELR* 16 (1986): 520–49. Willbern deals succinctly with the problem of Shakespeare's uncanny prefiguration of Freud: "In brief," he writes, "Shakespeare dramatizes what psychoanalysis theorizes" (p. 544), and again, "Shakespeare prefigures Freud: drama enacts what theory affirms" (p. 545).
50 For another discussion of *Macbeth*, gender anxiety, and androgyny, see Robert Kimbrough, "Macbeth: The Prisoner of Gender," *Shakespeare Studies* 16 (1983): 175–90.
51 For a strong and appealing presentation of this case, see Janet Adelman, " 'Born of Woman': Fantasies of Maternal Power in *Macbeth*." in *Cannibals, Witches, and Divorce: Estranging the Renaissance*, ed. Marjorie Garber (Baltimore: Johns Hopkins University Press, 1986), pp. 90–121. Though I admire Adelman's essay, I differ with her conclusion, which maintains that "Macbeth is a recuperative consolidation of male power" (p. 111). Another thoughtful recent reading of the play is offered by Jonathan Goldberg in "Speculations: *Macbeth* and Source," *Post-Structuralist Readings of English Poetry*, ed. Richard Machin and Christopher Norris (Cambridge: Cambridge University Press, 1987). "The hypermasculine world of *Macbeth* is haunted," writes Goldberg, "by the power represented by the witches; masculinity in the play is directed as an assaultive attempt to secure power, to maintain success and succession, at the expense of women" (p. 52). Yet Goldberg too reads the witches, and Mary Queen of Scots, "the figure that haunts the patriarchal claims of the *Basilikon Doron*" (p. 53), as woman, as female, rather than as the emblems of a disquieting gender undecidability (bearded women; woman as head of state).
52 Muir, ed., p. 12.
53 In his notes on Shakespeare's sonnet 116, coincidentally another poetic narrative of marriage, a tempest, and a "wandering bark," Stephen Booth remarks that "many of the metaphors and ideas of this sonnet seem just on the point of veering off toward puerile joking about temporary abatement of female sexual desire." Booth situates the "puerile joking" and "preposterous teasing" (392) in the confident tone of the lover-poet; in *Macbeth* the tone is of course malevolent rather than dismissive, vengeful and vituperative rather than indulgent and affectionate – but the trope is a similar one. See also Booth's note on the word *bark* in Sonnet 80, line 7. *Shakespeare's Sonnets* (New Haven: Yale University Press, 1977), pp. 391–2.
54 Quoted in Frank Kermode, ed., *Four Centuries of Shakespearean*

Criticism. (New York: Avon Books, 1965), p. 537. From a report of a lecture given in Bristol in 1813.

55 Robert Watson describes the actions of several Shakespearean protagonists, Macbeth among them, as "enforcing their own rebirths by a sort of Caesarean section, carving out the opening through which the ambitious new identity appears" (*Shakespeare and the Hazards of Ambition*, p. 19). If recognized as a Caesarean operation, however, Macbeth's offstage action before the play begins encodes his own dramatic teleology, and thus insures the uncanny appropriateness of Macduff as the man who beheads him, also offstage, at the play's close.

56 *Political Works*, p. 325.

57 Paul Johnson, *Elizabeth I: A Study in Power and Intellect* (London: Weidenfeld & Nicolson, 1974), p. 320.

58 Louis Montrose, "Shaping Fantasies: Figurations of Gender and Power in Elizabethan Culture," *Representations* 1 (Spring, 1983): 77.

Queen Elizabeth was a cultural anomaly; and this anomalousness – at once divine and monstrous – made her powerful, and dangerous. By the skillful deployment of images that were at once awesome and familiar, this perplexing creature tried to mollify her subjects while enhancing her authority over them (p. 78).

59 Sir Robert Cecil to Sir John Harington, 29 May 1603, printed in John Harington, *Nugae Antiquae*, 3 vols (1779, rpt Hildesheim, 1968), 3, p. 264, quoted in Montrose, p. 78. Elizabeth, who had costumed herself as an Amazon queen, might well be represented as a Medusa, "at once divine and monstrous," by the generation after her death.

60 Lawrence Stone, *The Causes of the English Revolution, 1529–1642* (London: Routledge & Kegan Paul. New York: Harper and Row, 1972), p. 89. Stone cites a number of further references, and remarks about "the widespread gossip about James's sexual tastes" that "the importance of these stories lies in the fact of their existence, not in their truth" (p. 158, n.112).

61 Jonathan Goldberg, *James I and the Politics of Literature* (Baltimore: Johns Hopkins University Press, 1983), pp. 142–6; 269, n. 29.

62 Francis Osborne, *Some Traditional Memorialls on the Raigne of King James I*, in *Secret History of the Court of James I*, ed. W. Scott (Edinburgh, 1811), I, pp. 274–6.

63 John Freccero, "Medusa: The Letter and the Spirit," in *Dante: The Poetics of Conversion*, ed. and intro. by Rachel Jacoff (Cambridge, Mass.: Harvard University Press, 1986), p. 126.

64 ibid., p. 130.

65 ibid., p. 131.

66 Francesco Petrarca, *Rime Sparse*, 366.

67 Ludwig Goldscheider, *Leonardo da Vinci, Life and Work, Paintings and Drawings, with the Leonardo Biography by Vasari 1568* (London: Phaidon Press, 1964), pp. 13–14.

68 Sigmund Freud, *Leonardo da Vinci and a Memory of His Childhood*, trans. Alan Tyson (New York: W.W. Norton, 1964), p. 23.

69 ibid., p. 30.
70 ibid., p. 46.
71 ibid., p. 45.
72 Friedländer, pp. 87–9.
73 Joyce Carol Oates, "The Unique Universal in Fiction," in *Woman as Writer*, ed. Jeannette L. Webber and Joan Grumman (Boston: Houghton Mifflin, 1978), p. 174.

6 *Hamlet*: giving up the ghost

1 Sigmund Freud letter, 15 October 1897, in *The Complete Letters of Sigmund Freud to Wilhelm Fliess, 1887–1904*, ed. and trans. Jeffrey Moussaieff Masson (Cambridge, Mass.: Harvard University Press, 1985), pp. 272–3.
2 ibid., 21 September 1897, p. 264.
3 ibid.
4 ibid., p. 265.
5 ibid.
6 ibid.
7 ibid.
8 ibid., pp. 265–6.
9 See *The Riverside Shakespeare*, ed. G. Blakemore Evans (Boston, Mass.: Houghton Mifflin, 1974). Unless noted, all citations from the plays are to this edition.
10 Masson, ed., p. 266.
11 Sigmund Freud, "The Uncanny," in *Studies in Parapsychology*, ed. Philip Rieff (New York: Collier Books, 1963), p. 43.
12 ibid.
13 Sigmund Freud, *The Interpretation of Dreams*, ed. and trans. James Strachey (New York: Avon Books, 1965), pp. 480–1.
14 Freud, "The Uncanny," p. 30.
15 ibid., p. 37.
16 ibid., p. 33.
17 ibid., p. 35.
18 ibid., p. 55.
19 ibid., p. 56.
20 ibid., p. 44.
21 Norman N. Holland, *Psychoanalysis and Shakespeare* (New York: Octagon Books, rpt 1976), p. 165.
22 Frank Kermode, *Forms of Attention* (Chicago: University of Chicago Press, 1985), p. 49. See his whole argument, "Cornelius and Voltimand: Doubles in *Hamlet*," pp. 35–63.
23 Jacques Lacan, *The Four Fundamental Concepts of Psycho-Analysis*, ed. Jacques-Alain Miller, trans. Alan Sheridan (New York: W.W. Norton, 1981), p. 38.
24 Jacques Lacan, "Desire and the Interpretation of Desire in *Hamlet*," ed. Jacques-Alain Miller, trans. James Hulbert, in *Literature and Psychoanalysis*, ed. Shoshana Felman (Baltimore: Johns Hopkins

University Press, 1982), p. 50.

25 Sigmund Freud, "The Passing of the Oedipus Complex," in *Sexuality and the Psychology of Love*, ed. Philip Rieff (New York: Macmillan, 1963), p. 179.

26 Lacan, *The Four Fundamental Concepts*, pp. 34–5.

27 ibid., p. 35.

28 Jacques Lacan, *Écrits: A Selection*, trans. Alan Sheridan (New York: W.W. Norton, 1977), p. 215.

29 ibid., p. 219.

30 ibid., p. 218.

31 ibid., pp. 218–19.

32 Lacan, *The Four Fundamental Concepts*, p. 35.

33 Lacan, "Desire," p. 12.

34 Lacan, *The Four Fundamental Concepts*, p. 88.

35 Lacan, "Desire," p. 30.

36 Lacan, *The Four Fundamental Concepts*, p. 89.

37 ibid.

38 ibid.

39 ibid., p. 92.

40 ibid., pp. 88–9.

41 See Francis Barker, *The Tremulous Private Body: Essays on Subjection* (London: Methuen, 1984), pp. 25–40, for a compelling treatment of this question. The "modern subject" constituted here, of course, is male. Indeed, the centrality of *Hamlet* to the emergence of the "modern subject" seems connected to its *lack* of a powerful (or rather, an empowered) female presence. The play takes place entirely within the male unconscious, and its battleground is the conflict, quite specifically, of fathers and sons. Women are protected (the Ghost repeatedly tells Hamlet not to punish his mother) or dismissed ("get thee to a nunnery"; "Marry, I will teach you"). Yet the play uncannily includes the two female figures that have most preoccupied the modern feminist imagination – the Madwoman and the Mother.

42 Lacan, *The Four Fundamental Concepts*, pp. 87–8.

43 ibid., p. 235.

44 Paul de Man, "Autobiography as De-Facement," in *The Rhetoric of Romanticism* (New York: Columbia University Press, 1984), pp. 75–6.

45 ibid., p. 78.

46 Merritt Y. Hughes, ed., *John Milton, Complete Poems and Major Prose* (New York: Odyssey Press, 1957), p. 63.

47 Michael Riffaterre, "Prosopopeia," in *The Lesson of Paul de Man*, Yale French Studies 69 (1985): 112.

48 Freud, "The Uncanny," p. 35.

49 Molière, *The Miser and Other Plays*, trans. John Wood (Harmondsworth: Penguin, 1953).

50 Julian Rushton, *W.A. Mozart, Don Giovanni* (Cambridge: Cambridge University Press, 1981).

51 Stanley Cavell, *The Claim of Reason* (Oxford: Oxford University Press, 1979), p. 492.

52 Letter to Leopold Mozart, 29 November 1780. In Emily Anderson, ed., *The Letters of Mozart and His Family* (New York: W.W. Norton, 1985), p. 674.

53 "Dramaturgische Blätter," Frankfurt am Main, 1789, cited in Otto Erich Deutsch, *Mozart, A Documentary Biography*, trans. Eric Blom, Peter Branscome, and Jeremy Noble (Stanford: Stanford University Press, 1965), p. 341.

54 William Gresser, "The Meaning of 'due della notte' in *Don Giovanni*," *Mozart Jahrbuch* (1971–2): 244.

55 Peter Shaffer, *Amadeus* (New York: Signet, 1984), p. 108.

56 ibid., p. 110.

57 ibid., p. 137.

58 ibid., pp. xi–xii.

59 Freud, *Interpretation of Dreams*, p. 299.

60 James Joyce, *Ulysses* (New York: Random House, 1986), p. 175.

61 Cavell, pp. 481–2.

62 Francis Grose, *A Provincial Glossary*; Brand, *Popular Antiquities*, ed. Hazlitt; cited in Harold Jenkins, ed., *Hamlet*, The Arden Shakespeare (New York: Methuen, 1982), p. 424.

63 de Man, p. 77.

64 ibid., pp. 75–6.

65 ibid., p. 76.

66 For a full discussion of these distinctions, and of the history of the controversy, see Eleanor Prosser, *Hamlet and Revenge*, 2nd edn (Stanford: Stanford University Press, 1971).

67 de Man, p. 78.

68 Jonathan Culler, "Apostrophe," in *The Pursuit of Signs* (Ithaca: Cornell University Press, 1981), p. 148.

69 Paul de Man, *Allegories of Reading* (New Haven: Yale University Press, 1979), p. 29. See also Cynthia Chase, *Decomposing Figures* (Baltimore: Johns Hopkins University Press, 1986), pp. 82–112.

70 Culler, p. 148.

71 ibid., p. 152.

72 ibid., p. 153.

73 Rosalie Colie, *Shakespeare's Living Art* (Princeton: Princeton University Press, 1974), p. 11.

74 de Man, "Autobiography," p. 78.

75 " 'For O, for O, the hobby-horse is forgot' was the refrain of a popular song. . . . From its frequent use we seem to have an instance of a catch-phrase continuing in popularity after the original point of it had been lost. What is certain is that the hobby-horse, while very much remembered, became a byword for being forgotten and as such the occasion for numerous jokes in Elizabethan plays" (Jenkins, ed., 1982), pp. 500–1.

76 Paul de Man, "Sign and Symbol in Hegel's *Aesthetics*," *Critical Inquiry* 8 (Summer 1982): 761–75.

77 See Chase, pp. 113–26.

78 de Man, "Sign and Symbol," p. 771.

79 ibid., p. 772.
80 Sigmund Freud, "Mourning and Melancholia" (1917), in *General Psychological Theory*, ed. Philip Rieff (New York: Macmillan, 1963), pp. 164–79.
81 See Freud, "A Note upon the 'Mystic Writing-Pad' " (1925), in Philip Rieff, ed., *General Psychological Theory* (New York: Macmillan, 1963), pp. 207–12; Jacques Derrida, "Freud and the Scene of Writing," in *Writing and Difference*, trans. Alan Bass (Chicago: University of Chicago Press, 1978), pp. 196–231.
82 See Jonathan Goldberg, *Voice Terminal Echo* (New York: Methuen, 1986), p. 99.
83 Janet Adelman's fine essay, " 'Anger's My Meat': Feeding, Dependency, and Aggression in *Coriolanus*," in *Representing Shakespeare*, ed. Murray M. Schwartz and Coppelia Kahn (Baltimore: Johns Hopkins University Press, 1981), pp. 129–49, while it does not mention *Hamlet*, is in many ways relevant to Hamlet's situation as son and speaker, and to Gertrude's lack of nurturing qualities.
84 Shoshana Felman, *The Literary Speech Act*, trans. Catherine Porter (Ithaca: Cornell University Press, 1983), p. 55.
85 Jacques Derrida, *Mémoires: for Paul de Man*, trans. Cecile Lindsay, Jonathan Culler, and Eduardo Cadava (New York: Columbia University Press, 1986), p. 56.
86 ibid., pp. 58–9.
87 Stéphane Mallarmé, *Oeuvres Complètes* (Paris: Éditions Gallimard, 1945), p. 299.
88 ibid. Translation Barbara Johnson.
89 The Ghost of *Hamlet* indeed turns up in some unlikely places. For Marx, the Ghost is a figure for the revolution:

> But the revolution is thoroughgoing. It is still journeying through purgatory. It does its work methodically. By December 2, 1851, it had completed one half of its preparatory work; it is now completing the other half. First it perfected the parliamentary power, in order to be able to overthrow it. Now that it has attained this, it perfects the *executive power*, reduces it to its purest expression, isolates it, sets it up against itself as the sole target, in order to concentrate all its forces of destruction against it. And when it has done this second half of its preliminary work, Europe will leap from its seat and exultantly exclaim: Well grubbed, old mole!
> Karl Marx, *The Eighteenth Brumaire of Louis Bonaparte*, in Karl Marx and Friedrich Engels, *Selected Works* (New York: International Publishers, 1968), p. 170.

In Whitehead, it is a figure for mathematics:

> The study of mathematics is apt to commence in disappointment .... We are told that by its aid the stars are weighed and the billions of molecules in a drop of water are counted. Yet, like the

ghost of Hamlet's father, this great science eludes the efforts of our mental weapons to grasp it. – 'Tis here, 'tis here, 'tis gone' – and what we do see does not suggest the same excuse for illusiveness as sufficed the ghost, that it is too noble for our gross methods.

Alfred North Whitehead, *An Introduction to Mathematics* (New York: Henry Holt, 1911), p. 7.

90 See Goldberg, *Voice Terminal Echo*, p. 99.
91 J. Hillis Miller, *Fiction and Repetition: Seven English Novels* (Cambridge, Mass.: Harvard University Press, 1982), p. 6.
92 ibid., p. 9.
93 Walter Benjamin, "The Image of Proust," in *Illuminations*, trans. Harry Zohn (New York: Schocken Books, 1969), p. 202. De Man, too, turns to Proust as a test case for his two types of memory, pointing indirectly (via the *madeleine*) to the eating imagery behind the term *Erinnerung*: "Proust struggles with the distinction in his attempts to distinguish between *mémoire volontaire* – which is like *Gedächtnis* – and *mémoire involontaire*, which is rather like *Erinnerung*" ("Sign and Symbol in Hegel's *Aesthetics*," p. 772).
94 Friedrich Nietzsche, "The Use and Abuse of History," *Untimely Meditations*, trans. R.J. Hollingdale (Cambridge: Cambridge University Press, 1983), p. 62. Emphasis added.
95 ibid.
96 Jenkins, ed., p. 554.
97 See Marjorie Garber, " 'Remember Me': *Memento Mori* Figures in Shakespeare's Plays," *Renaissance Drama* 12 (1981): 15–17.
98 Nietzsche, p. 59. Emphasis added.
99 ibid.
100 ibid., p. 60.
101 ibid., p. 61. Emphasis added.
102 See Margaret W. Ferguson, "*Hamlet*: Letters and Spirits," in *Shakespeare and the Question of Theory*, ed. Patricia Parker and Geoffrey Hartman (New York: Methuen, 1985), p. 302.
103 Freud, *Interpretation of Dreams*, p. 143n.
104 ibid., p. 564.
105 Terry Eagleton, *William Shakespeare* (Oxford: Basil Blackwell, 1986), p. 72.
106 Goldberg, p. 99.
107 Sigmund Freud, "Further Recommendations in the Technique of Psychoanalysis: Recollection, Repetition and Working Through" (1914), in *Therapy and Technique*, ed. Philip Rieff (New York: Macmillan, 1963), p. 160–1.
108 ibid., p. 161.
109 ibid., p. 164.
110 ibid., p. 165.
111 Sigmund Freud, *Beyond the Pleasure Principle*, trans. James Strachey (New York: Bantam Books, 1959), p. 41.

112 ibid., p. 37.
113 ibid., p. 44.
114 ibid., p. 65.
115 ibid., p. 67.
116 Sigmund Freud, "Further Recommendations in the Technique of Psychoanalysis: Observations on Transference–Love" (1915), in *Therapy and Technique*, ed. Philip Rieff (New York: Macmillan, 1963), p. 172. Emphasis added.
117 Lacan, *The Four Fundamental Concepts*, p. 232.
118 ibid.
119 ibid.
120 ibid., 234.
121 Lacan, *Ecrits*, p. 199.
122 Georg Brandes, *William Shakespeare: A Critical Study* (New York: Macmillan, 1909).
123 Freud, *Interpretation of Dreams*, p. 299.
124 ibid., p. xxvi.
125 See, for example, the title and argument of Jeffrey Moussaieff Masson, *The Assault on Truth: Freud's Suppression of the Seduction Theory* (New York: Penguin, 1985).
126 Marianne Krüll, *Freud and His Father*, trans. Arnold J. Pomerans (New York: W.W. Norton, 1986), p. 63.
127 ibid., pp. 124–5; cf. Ernest Jones, *The Life and Work of Sigmund Freud* (New York: Basic Books, 1953), 1, pp. 10ff.
128 Krüll, p. 180.
129 John Gross, review of Krüll's *Freud and his Father*, in *The New York Times* (August 15, 1986): C25.
130 Masson, ed., 2 November 1896, p. 202; Freud, *Interpretation of Dreams*, pp. 352–3.
131 ibid., p. 353.
132 Krüll, p. 63.
133 Freud, *Interpretation of Dreams*, p. 352. Emphasis added.
134 Masson, ed., p. 202.
135 Sigmund Freud, *The Origins of Psychoanalysis. Letters to Wilhelm Fliess*, ed. Marie Bonaparte, Anna Freud, and Ernst Kris, trans. Eric Mosbacher and James Strachey (New York: Basic Books, 1954).
136 ibid., pp. xi–xii.
137 Freud, *Interpretation of Dreams*, p. 298.
138 ibid.
139 Freud, "Mourning and Melancholia," p. 169.
140 ibid.
141 ibid., p. 172.
142 ibid., p. 173. Emphasis added.
143 ibid., Emphasis added.
144 ibid., pp. 173–4.
145 ibid., p. 179.
146 ibid., pp. 167–8.
147 Shoshana Felman, "To Open the Question," in *Literature and*

Psychoanalysis, ed. Felman (Baltimore: Johns Hopkins University Press, 1982), p. 9.

148 Lacan, *The Four Fundamental Concepts*, pp. 149, 203.

149 Felman, p. 10.

150 Krüll, p. 208.

151 Sigmund Freud, letter to J. Thomas Looney, June 1938, in Looney, *Shakespeare Identified as Edward de Vere, the 17th Earl of Oxford*, 3rd edn, ed. and augmented by Ruth Loyd Miller (Port Washington, NY: Kennikat Press, 1975), 3, p. 273.

152 Letter 344 J, 6 January 1913, *The Freud/Jung Letters*, ed. William McGuire (Princeton, NJ: Princeton University Press, 1974), p. 540.

153 Shoshana Felman, *Writing and Madness* (Ithaca: Cornell University Press, 1985), p. 50.

154 Thomas Lodge, *Wit's Misery*, 1596, p. 56. Harold Jenkins notes that " 'Hamlet, revenge,' became a byword" citing Dekker, *Satiromastix*, 4.1.121; and Rowlands, *The Night-Raven*, 1620, sig. D2. See Jenkins, ed, p. 83.

155 See n 66.

156 Prosser, p. 246.

157 ibid., p. 247.

158 ibid.

159 ibid., p. 256.

160 ibid.

161 Prosser cites "a few ambiguous hints" in G. Wilson Knight's *The Wheel of Fire*, but more especially Harold Goddard, *The Meaning of Shakespeare* (Chicago, 1951); Roy Walker, *The Time is Out of Joint* (London, 1948); John Vyvyan, *The Shakespearean Ethic* (London, 1959); and L.C. Knights, *An Approach to "Hamlet"* (Stanford, Calif.: 1961). Since the publication of her book a number of other critics have argued this point as well.

162 *Alternative Shakespeares*, ed. John Drakakis (London: Methuen, 1985); *Political Shakespeare*, ed. Jonathan Dollimore and Alan Sinfield (Ithaca: Cornell University Press, 1985); *Shakespeare and the Question of Theory*, ed. Patricia Parker and Geoffrey Hartman (New York: Methuen, 1985).

163 J. Hillis Miller, "Ariachne's Broken Woof," *The Georgia Review* 31 (Spring 1977): 44–63.

164 Elaine Showalter, "Representing Ophelia: Women, Madness, and the Responsibilities of Feminist Criticism," in *Shakespeare and the Question of Theory*, ed. Patricia Parker and Geoffrey Hartman, pp. 77–94.

165 Paul de Man, "Literary History and Literary Modernity," in *Blindness and Insight* (Minneapolis: University of Minnesota Press, 1983), p. 157.

Index